ECONOMIC ANALYSIS OF ENVIRONMENTAL POLICY

T0314967

The tension between economic growth and environmental concerns has captured much public attention and poses serious challenges for policymakers around the world. *Economic Analysis of Environmental Policy*, a textbook for advanced undergraduate and graduate courses, provides a rigorous and thorough explanation of modern environmental economics within the context of contemporary issues and policy analysis.

The books opens with a discussion of contemporary pollution problems, institutional players, and the main policy instruments at our disposal. It then develops the core theories of environmental valuation and optimal control of pollution. Chapters that follow cover fundamental concepts such as tradable permits, regulatory standards, emission taxes, and polluter liability. Also addressed are advanced topics such as trade and the environment, sustainability, risk, inequality, and self-monitoring. Throughout the book the emphasis is on the use of clear, intuitive, and coherent analytical tools, so that students, academics, and practitioners can develop their skills at policy analysis while comprehending the debates and challenges within and surrounding this exciting and rapidly developing field.

ROSS R. McKITRICK is a professor in the Department of Economics at the University of Guelph.

ROSS R. McKITRICK

Economic Analysis of Environmental Policy

UNIVERSITY OF TORONTO PRESS
Toronto Buffalo London

© University of Toronto Press Incorporated 2011
Toronto Buffalo London
www.utppublishing.com
Printed in Canada

ISBN 978-1-4426-4226-3 (cloth)
ISBN 978-1-4426-1070-5 (paper)

Printed on acid-free, 100% post-consumer recycled paper with
vegetable based inks.

Library and Archives Canada Cataloguing in Publication

McKitrick, Ross, 1965–
Economic analysis of environmental policy / Ross McKitrick.

Includes bibliographical references and index.
ISBN 978-1-4426-1070-5 (pbk.).   ISBN 978-1-4426-4226-3 (bound)

1. Environmental economics.   I. Title.

HC79.E5M354 2010   333.7   C2010-905639-6

University of Toronto Press acknowledges the financial assistance to its
publishing program of the Canada Council for the Arts and the Ontario
Arts Council.

 Canada Council   Conseil des Arts    ONTARIO ARTS COUNCIL
for the Arts   du Canada   CONSEIL DES ARTS DE L'ONTARIO

University of Toronto Press acknowledges the financial support for its
publishing activities of the Government of Canada through the Canada
Book Fund.

To Renée, Madeleine, and Graham

Contents

List of Figures and Tables   xi

Preface: Why This Book?   xv

1 Issues, Instruments, Institutions, and Ideas   3
  1.1 Environmental Concerns: A Historical Survey   3
    1.1.1 *The Brundtland Report*   5
    1.1.2 *Warnings in the 1970s*   6
    1.1.3 *The Limits of the Earth, circa 1953*   7
    1.1.4 *The Imperative Duty of 1912*   8
    1.1.5 *Our Numbers Are Burdensome to the World*   10
  1.2 Environmental Issues   12
    1.2.1 *Conventional Air Pollution*   12
    1.2.2 *Global Environmental Problems: Ozone Depletion*   14
    1.2.3 *Global Environmental Problems: Global Warming*   17
    1.2.4 *Air Pollution and Economic Growth over Time*   24
    1.2.5 *Water Pollution*   30
  1.3 Policy Instruments: A Brief Introduction   31
    1.3.1 *Standards*   31
    1.3.2 *Emission Taxes*   34
    1.3.3 *Emission Permits*   34
    1.3.4 *Liability Law*   34
  1.4 Institutions and Rule-Makers   35
    1.4.1 *Federal Governments in the United States and Canada*   35
    1.4.2 *State and Provincial Governments*   36
    1.4.3 *Municipalities*   36
    1.4.4 *Courts*   36
  1.5 Growth and the Environment: The Tradeoff over Time   36

1.6 Does Growth Theory Predict the EKC?*   39
Review Questions   43
References and Extra Reading   44
Data Source Websites   44

2 **Valuation of the Environment**   49
2.1 Externalities   49
2.2 Some Results from Microeconomics and Welfare Economics   51
2.3 Pollution Damages in Utility Terms   56
2.4 Non-Market Valuation of Environmental Change   59
2.5 Aggregating Environmental Values   63
2.6 Discounting Environmental Damages over Time   64
   2.6.1 *Annuities*   64
   2.6.2 *Discount Rates**   66
2.7 Adding Up Benefits across People with Unequal Incomes   68
2.8 Uncertainty, Risk, and Risk-Aversion*   71
2.9 Non-linearity and Non-commutativity   74
Review Questions   76
References and Extra Reading   77

3 **The Value of Emissions and the Costs of Abatement**   79
3.1 The Optimal Output-Abatement Choice   79
3.2 The Marginal Abatement Cost Function   85
Review Questions   88

4 **Optimal Emissions: The Partial Equilibrium Case**   91
4.1 The Optimal Emissions Level   91
4.2 Static Short-Run Efficiency   95
4.3 Static Long-Run Efficiency*   101
4.4 The Balanced Budget Requirement   105
4.5 Non-Point Source Pollution*   106
4.6 Dynamic Efficiency and Technology Adoption Decisions   110
4.7 A Note about Terminology: 'Pollution' Taxes versus
     'Pigovian' Taxes   112
Review Questions   114
References and Extra Reading   119

5 **Information, Uncertainty, and Instrument Choice**   121
5.1 Incentives to Report Truthfully   121
   5.1.1 *Incentives to Under-report under an Emissions Tax*   122

*Sections indicated with an asterisk (*) contain more advanced material suitable primarily for graduate or fourth-year students.

5.1.2 *Many Small Firms*   124
5.2 Prices versus Quantities   125
    5.2.1 *Equivalence under Certainty*   125
    5.2.2 *Policy Choice When Damages Are Uncertain*   126
    5.2.3 *Policy Choice When the Marginal Abatement Cost
        Is Uncertain*   127
    5.2.4 *Instrument Choice under Uncertainty*   128
Review Questions   131
References and Extra Reading   132

6 **Pollution Standards, Monitoring, and Enforcement**   133
6.1 Standards versus Standards   133
    6.1.1 *Level Standard versus Emissions Intensity Rule*   136
6.2 Concentration Standards with Many Firms*   139
6.3 Monitoring and Enforcement   141
    6.3.1 *Standard Enforcement Model*   142
    6.3.2 *Regulation with Random Pollution and Uncertain
        Inspections*   144
Review Questions   150
References and Extra Reading   151

7 **Tradable Permits and Quotas**   153
7.1 The Competitive Case   153
    7.1.1 *The U.S. Sulfur Dioxide Market*   155
7.2 Market Power and Tradable Permits*   160
7.3 Auction versus Quotas   162
Review Questions   165
References and Extra Reading   167

8 **Emission Taxes and the General Equilibrium Model of
    Emission Pricing**   169
8.1 Review of Basic Concepts   169
8.2 Deadweight Loss   171
8.3 Revenue Recycling and Tax Interaction Effects   172
8.4 The Sandmo Model of Optimal Taxation in the Presence of
    Externalities*   179
    8.4.1 *First-Best Allocation*   180
    8.4.2 *Decentralized Competitive Outcome*   181
    8.4.3 *Optimal Second-Best Tax System*   183
    8.4.4 *Pollution Taxes and Deadweight Loss*   188
8.5 Subsidies   189
Review Questions   191

References and Extra Reading   192

9 Bargaining and Tort Law as Solutions to Externalities   193
9.1 Introduction   193
9.2 Multiple Victims and Joint Tortfeasors   197
    9.2.1 *Multiple Victims*   197
    9.2.2 *Joint Tortfeasors*   197
9.3 Contests over Damages*   204
9.4 Victim Overexposure   208
Review Questions   210
References and Extra Reading   212

10 International Trade and Pollution   214
10.1 Pollution Havens and Environmental Dumping   214
    10.1.1 *Trade Flows and Pollution*   215
    10.1.2 *Foreign Direct Investment and Pollution*   217
10.2 Trade Liberalization and the Environment   219
    10.2.1 *Model Set-up**   219
    10.2.2 *Welfare Analysis**   222
    10.2.3 *Environmental Effects of Trade Liberalization:*
           Pollution Haven Hypothesis versus Factor Endowment
           Hypothesis   224
Review Questions   227
References and Extra Reading   227

11 Sustainability and Optimal Growth   229
11.1 Introduction   229
11.2 Net National Product   231
11.3 Measuring Sustainability   236
    11.3.1 *Green Net National Product and Net Savings*   236
11.4 Hartwick's Rule on Sustainable Consumption Paths*   239
Review Questions   242
References and Extra Reading   242

12 Policy Debates, Practice Exam, and Supplementary Questions   244
12.1 Policy Debates   244
12.2 Practice Exam Questions   247
12.3 Further Study Questions   253

Index   255

Figures and Tables

Figures

1.1 Total % change (compared to 1964–1980 average) in global average stratospheric ozone density, 1965–2005   16

1.2 Global per capita CO2 emissions 1950–2007, expressed as metric tons of carbon equivalent   19

1.3 Top: global average temperature anomalies, 1901–2009. Bottom: Observed global average anomaly (denoted CRU) compared to climate model projections (GCMs)   20

1.4 Climate model simulations of late twentieth-century warming in the tropical mid-troposphere   22

1.5 Comparison of satellite-observed tropical average mid-troposphere temperature anomalies to lower and upper climate model-predicted rates (0.2–0.5°C/decade)   23

1.6 Hypothetical relationship between GDP and pollution   25

1.7 US real GDP and total particulate emissions   25

1.8 US real GDP and total carbon monoxide emissions   26

1.9 US emissions by type, 1945–1998   27

1.10 US air monitoring violations per station per year, CO and ozone   27

1.11 International income vs. TSP concentrations   29

1.12 International income vs. SO_2 concentrations   29

1.13 International income vs. NO_2 concentrations   30

1.14 International income vs. water pollution   31

1.15 Lake Ontario water pollution by year   32

1.16 Lake Erie water pollution by year   33

1.17 Production possibility boundaries between consumption and environmental quality 38

1.18 Indifference curves between consumption and environmental quality 39

1.19 Optimal path between consumption and environmental quality 40

1.20 Three PPB curves 43

2.1 Pareto-optimal and sub-optimal allocations in a two-person economy 55

2.2 Marginal damages 57

2.3 The expenditure function and the value of total damages (*TD*) 58

2.4 Risk aversion and the risk premium 73

3.1 Iso-emissions line, showing combinations of output y and abatement a that yield emissions e 80

3.2 Iso-profit lines, showing combinations of output y and abatement a that yield the same profit level 82

3.3 Iso-profit and iso-emission lines with optimal tangency path 83

3.4 The marginal abatement cost function (MAC) 85

3.5 Iso-emission lines 88

3.6 Output-abatement combinations 89

4.1 Marginal damages and marginal abatement costs 93

4.2 Relationship between iso-profits model and MAC model 94

4.3 Two firms subject to a uniform standard 97

4.4 Two firms subject to an emissions pricing rule 98

4.5 Two firms subject to an emissions tax set at the optimal level 100

4.6 Entry of a new polluting firm 104

4.7 Assessing the benefits of adopting a new technology 111

4.8 Pigovian tax in market for X 113

4.9 Optimal emissions level 114

5.1 Incentives to exaggerate costs under a standard 122

5.2 Incentives to report costs under an emissions tax 123

5.3 Equivalence of price and quantity instruments 125

5.4 Situation in which marginal damages are incorrectly estimated 127

5.5 Situation in which MAC is incorrectly estimated 128

5.6 Welfare analysis of making a mistake when the MAC is nearly flat 129

5.7 Welfare analysis of making a mistake when the MAC is steep 130

6.1 Comparison of a level standard and an intensity standard that achieves the same emissions level   137

6.2 Comparison of a level standard with a minimum abatement standard   138

6.3 The probability of having low emissions as a function of abatement effort   145

7.1 Sulfur dioxide permit prices in the United States, 2000–7   155

7.2 Estimated MAC for US sulfur emissions from plants covered by EPA SO_2 allowance market   157

7.3 Hybrid instrument   159

8.1 Emission taxes and payment thresholds   171

8.2 Deadweight loss in a standard demand-supply diagram   172

8.3 The revenue recycling effect   173

8.4 The tax interaction effect   175

8.5 Optimal emissions control taking policy costs into account   178

9.1 Bargaining directly over the level of an externality   195

9.2 Contest success function for defendant   207

9.3 Victim overexposure   209

10.1 Actual output and potential output of x 220

10.2 Opening trade between North and South   225

10.3 Elasticity of emissions with respect to trade liberalization, versus relative income, from Copeland and Taylor (2004)   226

12.1 Output-abatement combination   249

Tables

1.1 Mean atmospheric temperature trends in lower-troposphere, January 1979 to April 2009   24

1.2 Federal emissions control standards for all new cars and light trucks sold in the United States, indexed to 1966 = 100   28

2.1 Hypothetical net benefits from an environmental project   69

2.2 Hypothetical cost-benefit example   75

10.1 Changes in foreign investment and particulate pollution in three developing countries (Wheeler 2001)   218

Preface: Why This Book?

There are many introductory textbooks in environmental economics, and a few that are useful for intermediate teaching as well. But the gap between the level of theory that can be learned from the currently available textbooks and the level needed to read (or write) academic journal articles has become very wide, posing a challenge for those wanting to learn or teach environmental economics at the advanced level. The main purpose of this textbook is to fill that gap for students, instructors, researchers and practitioners in the field. My aim is to present the theoretical core of environmental economics and the issues surrounding environmental policy analysis in a coherent general equilibrium framework. Building a solid understanding of this theory is essential not only for navigating the path to the research frontier, but also for keeping environmental policy analysis on a rigorous footing, well-connected to the rest of economic theory.

The theory is built up in stages. To help motivate the subject I start with some historical perspective on environmental problems and a survey of contemporary issues, policy instruments and ideas about how economic growth affects the environment. I then begin with the theoretical and practical issues involved in valuing both environmental damages and the benefits of emissions (or costs of abatement). I then define the optimal level of polluting activity in partial equilibrium, and apply this concept to some comparative policy analysis. In Chapter 8, as part of the discussion of emission taxes, I present a multi-sector, general equilibrium treatment of optimal externality pricing, thus tying together the 'big picture' of the theory developed up to that point. Chapters 9 to 11 look at the additional topics of liability law and bargaining, international trade and sustainability. In Chapter 12 I pose some questions related to current environmental policies issues and discuss how economic tools can help frame the analysis.

There are a number of features of this book that I think instructors will find especially helpful.

- *Organization around theory rather than issues.* Many introductory textbooks in environmental economics are organized around current issues, an approach that I find makes for much repetition and a shallow exploration of the underlying theory. I have instead organized this text around the core theory and the related policy concepts. This permits a more rigorous derivation of key results and more detailed policy analysis.
- *Integration of policy material.* Despite the theoretical focus of this text, instructors wanting to cover contemporary policy topics will find that they are well-integrated into the text. For example, an instructor might want to cover the debates surrounding the 2006 Stern Review on the economics of climate change. The text provides extensive treatment of the underlying issues, including an introductory discussion of global warming and CO_2 emissions (Chapter 1), valuation of environmental change and the tools of cost-benefit analysis, including discounting and inequality measures, (Chapter 2), efficient policy design and the use of economic instruments (Chapters 3, 4, 7, 8), instrument choice under uncertainty (Chapter 5), and so forth. With these sections as a foundation, students will be well equipped to understand the subsequent debates involving writers like Nordhaus, Weitzman, Tol, Mendelsohn, Dasgupta, and others who have supported or disputed the Stern Review. As another example, the acid rain market in the United States is introduced in Chapter 1, the underlying theory is developed in Chapters 3 and 4, the issue of instrument choice is covered in Chapter 5, institutional details about the U.S. acid rain allowance market are covered in Chapter 7, which also explores the problem of market power in a tradable quota system, etc.
- *Accessibility of the material to students with varying levels of preparation.* The text is aimed at upper-year undergraduate and graduate students in environmental economics who have taken a course in advanced microeconomic theory and are familiar with calculus-based derivations of economic models. However, much of the analysis in the book uses graphical tools derived from the underlying theory, so a substantial amount of the material is accessible even to students

who lack a strong mathematical background. Sections indicated with an asterisk (*) contain more advanced material that will be primarily suitable for graduate students or fourth-year students with sufficient preparation. Note that the practice exam at the end contains some questions from starred sections.
- *Extensive practice material.* Each chapter includes practice questions, some of them with worked solutions, to help students solidify and deepen their understanding. The final chapter provides a list of discussion questions and a practice exam.

Much of the material in this textbook has been tested on fourth-year and graduate environmental economics students at the University of Guelph over the past 12 years. I have benefited from their feedback, comments, and input. I am especially grateful to two of my past students: Bin Hu, of the Central University of Finance and Economics in Beijing, and James Wishart of the College of the Rockies in Cranbrook, Northern British Columbia, for their discussions, input, and assistance over the past few years. Expert reviews were provided by a group of anonymous referees whose assistance is gratefully acknowledged. Of course all errors and omissions are my responsibility.

I would also like to thank Jennifer DiDomenico and the staff at University of Toronto Press for their encouragement and assistance throughout the publication process.

ECONOMIC ANALYSIS OF ENVIRONMENTAL POLICY

1 Issues, Instruments, Institutions, and Ideas

1.1 Environmental Concerns: A Historical Survey

Concern about the state of the environment and the depletion of natural resources is widespread. Examples in the media abound, such as the 3 April 2006 cover of *Time* magazine that showed a polar bear on a melting ice floe, beside the headline 'Be Worried. Be Very Worried.' Al Gore's *An Inconvenient Truth* and Leonardo DiCaprio's *The 11th Hour* are but two of the many recent movies and documentaries asserting an impending environmental crisis.

It will be clear from this book that economics has a lot to say about how to take care of the environment. The basic stance of this book is one of optimism regarding our success in dealing with environmental challenges up to now, and our likely ability to manage them in the future. This contrasts with some very prominent sources of pessimism in recent years. For instance in January 2000, the Sierra Club magazine introduced a symposium on the state of the environment with these thoughts:

> It's been a dismal thousand years, environmentally speaking. We cut down most of the earth's forests, drove most large carnivores to the brink of extinction, spread disruptive exotic species around the globe, manufactured poisons on a monumental scale, and set in motion a potentially catastrophic warming of the atmosphere. Now, with the blank slate of a new millennium before us, we have a chance to get it right. (*Sierra Magazine*, January 2000)

Carl Pope, the Club's executive director, began his comments in the same article by noting how attitudes towards the environment are beginning to change, albeit late in the day.

> We are headed off an environmental cliff, but governments and corporations continue to operate on short time horizons – resisting popular desire to minimize technological risk, for example, or exposure to toxic chemicals. Indeed, they may lag those they nominally serve by as much as a generation. So the question I would like to pose is this: How can our collective behavior catch up with our individual concerns? How, in the next century, can we translate public attitudes into real environmental progress?

These comments encapsulate three common views about the state of the environment. First, things have been getting worse lately because of modern economic growth; an earlier golden age has ended. Second, we face impending disaster, unnoticed by oblivious decision-makers in government and industry. Finally, we grasp these things now, but previous writers and thinkers failed to do so.

Here are some additional examples, all drawn from relatively recent publications:

> The gap between what we need to do to reverse the degradation of the planet and what we are doing widens with each passing year. How do we cross the threshold of political change that will shrink this gap, reversing the trends of environmental degradation that are undermining the economy? Most environment ministers understand that we are headed for economic decline, but there is not yet enough political support to overcome the vested interests that oppose changes. (Lester Brown and Jennifer Mitchell, *State of the World* 1998 [Worldwatch Institute, p. 183])

> The United States [is] approaching a turning point, leaving behind the false choices and short-sighted policies that for far too long guided American action, or more often, inaction. We were asked to choose between the economy and the environment, between jobs and the health of our communities. The goals of a prosperous economy and a clean environment are not mutually exclusive. We now recognize that economic growth demands environmental protection and that protecting the environment can create jobs. There are clear signs of America's renewed commitment to environmental sustainability. (Al Gore, former U.S. Vice-President, in *Environment Strategy Europe* 1993, 11)

Time is short for us to rectify the present unsustainable patterns of human development ... There is no turning back from realizing that we are heading towards a crisis of uncontrollable dimensions unless we change course. The North, as well as the rich in the South, will have to change their unsustainable consumption and production patterns. A global partnership must start with a commitment by industrialized countries to reduce sharply the burden they impose on the carrying capacity of the earth's ecosystems. (Gro Harlem Brundtland, Prime Minister of Norway and Chairman of the UN World Commission on Environment and Development, *Environment Strategy Europe* 1992, pp. 99–101)

Archaeological discoveries of recent decades suggest that even great civilizations, such as the Sumerians and the Mayans, met devastation at least in part by failing to live in harmony with the natural environment. We, too, have tempted fate for most of the past two hundred years, fuelled by breakthroughs in science and technology and the belief that natural limits to human well-being had been conquered. Climate change is a prime example of this. Today we know better, and have begun to transform our societies, albeit haltingly. So far, our scientific understanding continues to run ahead of our social and political response. With some honourable exceptions, our efforts to change course are too few and too little. (Former UN Secretary-General Kofi Annan, 'Towards a Sustainable Future,' Speech at the American Museum of Natural History, New York, May 2002)

We hear in these quotations the idea that economic growth is ruining the environment, disaster is imminent, and only now are we waking up to the problem. In the next few sections we will look at some important data on environmental conditions. Before doing that I'd like to examine whether public concern for resources and the environment is such a new idea.

1.1.1 The Brundtland Report

The same apocalyptic themes seen in the quotations above were raised in the 1987 Report of the UN World Commission on Environment and Development, better known as the Brundtland Commission (named after its chair, Gro Harlem Brundtland). The opening chapter, 'A Threatened Future,' describes how, in the past, societies wrestled with local resource and environmental challenges, but today the scale and severity of these challenges is increasing because of economic changes. 'Economics and ecology bind us in ever-tightening networks. Today, many regions face risks of irreversible damage to the human environment that threatens the basis for human progress' (p. 27). A long litany of growing environmental stresses was said to pose an imminent danger: 'Little time is available for corrective action. In some cases we may already be close to transgressing critical thresholds ... Failures to manage the environment and to sustain development threaten to overwhelm all countries' (pp. 35, 37).

Recognition of these concerns is presented as though it were novel. The Brundtland Commission quotes the late Charles Caccia, a former Canadian Member of Parliament (and Chair of the House of Commons Environment Committee):

> We are just now beginning to realize that we must find an alternative to our ingrained behaviour of burdening future generations resulting from our misplaced belief that there is a choice between economy and the environment. That choice, in the long term, turns out to be an illusion with awesome consequences for humanity. (p. 38)

1.1.2 Warnings in the 1970s

In 1972, a book called The Limits to Growth, published by a group called The Club of Rome, warned of imminent economic collapse due to heavy consumption of non-renewable minerals and fossil fuels. The same year, in a book entitled Population Resources Environment: Issues in Human Ecology, Stanford scientists Paul and Anne Ehrlich warned: 'Spaceship Earth is now filled to capacity or beyond and is in danger of running out of food. And yet the people traveling first class are, without thinking, demolishing the ship's already overstrained life-supporting systems' (p. 3). They went on to make some specific predictions about the coming 30 years. A now-famous chart on page 71 of their book predicted that by 2000 the world would have exhausted all supplies of natural gas, uranium, tungsten, copper, lead, zinc, tin, gold, silver, and platinum, and would have less than a 30-years supply of crude oil left. In their concluding chapter they warned that the planet was 'grossly overpopulated' and that

> [The] limits of human capacity to produce food by conventional means have very nearly been reached ... Attempts to increase food production

further will tend to accelerate the deterioration of our environment, which in turn will eventually *reduce* the capacity of the Earth to produce food. It is not clear whether environmental decay has now gone so far as to be essentially irreversible; it is possible the capacity of the planet to support human life has been permanently impaired. (pp. 441–2)

Ehrlich and Ehrlich also include a quotation from a valedictory address given at Mills College in 1969, poignantly expressing the pessimism of that age from a young woman's point of view: 'The future is a cruel hoax ... I am terribly saddened by the fact that the most humane thing for me to do is to have no children at all.'

This was written about 15 years before the Brundtland Report 'discovered' the environmental problem. But even this was not the beginning of such concerns. In 1963, Harold Barnett and Chandler Morse published a landmark study called *Scarcity and Growth: The Economics of Natural Resource Availability*. They set out to evaluate then-prevalent ideas about the growing scarcity of natural resources and the limits these would impose on economic growth. Based on their analysis of available data on prices, methods, and production trends, they came to reject the hypothesis of increasing scarcity, on the grounds that innovation had hitherto been sufficient to trigger discovery of new resources, replacements for scarce materials or new efficiencies.

> Few components of the Earth's crust, including farm land, are so specific as to defy economic replacement, or so resistant to technological advance as to be incapable of eventually yielding extractive products at constant or declining cost. (Barnett and Morse 1963, p. 10)

Their conclusion is telling, but so is the fact that as early as 1963 concerns about the limits to growth were so widespread as to necessitate their book.

1.1.3 The Limits of the Earth, circa 1953

Barnett and Morse provide a fascinating review of a series of books and papers published in the United States in the 1940s and 1950s raising concerns that would sound familiar in current environmental literature. Samuel Ordway's 1953 book *Resources and the American Dream* was written (they quote him saying) to present 'A Theory of the Limit of Growth' motivated by the fear that 'within foreseeable time increasing consumption of resources can produce scarcities serious enough to destroy our American Dream of an ever-higher level of living, and with it our present culture.' Henry Fairfield Osborne, president of the New York Zoological Society, wrote in his 1953 book *Limits of the Earth*, 'Now as we look, we can see the limits of the earth ... If we are blind to this law, or delude ourselves into minimizing its power, of one thing we can be assured – the human race will enter into days of increasing trouble, conflict and darkness' (quoted in Barnett and Morse 1963, p. 27). An earlier book by Osborne bore the title *Our Plundered Planet*. William Vogt's 1948 book *Road to Survival* asserted that strategies to prevent economic collapse were urgently needed, and 'unless population control and conservation are included, other means are certain to fail.'

In 1955 Dr Allan Gregg of the Rockefeller Foundation's Medical Division proposed that the presence of humans on Earth was analogous to a terminal disease. 'There is an alarming parallel between the growth of a cancer in the body of an organism and the growth of human populations in the earth's ecological community ... Humanity should now face the question of an optimum population' (quoted in Barnett and Morse 1963, p. 31). In 1950 economist W.C. Mitchell warned: 'The appalling wastes of natural resources that are going on seem due largely to the policy of handing over the nation's heritage to individuals to be exploited as they see fit ... what is rational on the basis of this short-run private view may be exceedingly unwise on the basis of long-run public interest' (Barnett and Morse 1963, p. 48).

The expressions of concern go back still further. In the 1930s and 1940s Presidents Roosevelt, Eisenhower, and Truman all expressed alarm about rapid depletion of resources, and established a series of commissions to advise the government on appropriate policy responses. President Roosevelt himself had expressed particular concern about the extensive changes in land cover during the settling of the American west, warning that 'the throwing out of balance of the resources of nature throws out of balance also the lives of men' (Barnett and Morse, p. 20).

1.1.4 The Imperative Duty of 1912

But even these writings are late compared to the voluminous work of the Conservation Movement in the United States at the turn of the twentieth century. This was an influential group led, in part, by President Theodore Roosevelt and his Chief Forester, Gifford Pinchot. In his 1910 book *The Fight for Conservation*, Pinchot warned:

> The five indispensably essential materials in our civilization are wood, water, coal, iron and agricultural products ... We have timber for less than thirty years at the present rate of cutting. The figures indicate that our demands upon the forest have increased twice as fast as our population. We have anthracite coal for but fifty years, and bituminous coal for less than 200. Our supplies of iron ore, mineral oil and natural gas are being rapidly depleted, and many of the great fields are already exhausted.

Three years later, William Temple Hornaday, director of the New York Zoological Park, published an impassioned book, *Our Vanishing Wildlife: Its Extermination and Preservation*, to accompany the founding of the Permanent Wildlife Protection Fund, devoted to campaigning for protection and preservation of wildlife. The preface was written by Henry Fairfield Osborne, mentioned above. Here, in a passage dated December 1912, Osborne sounds the same urgent alarm he would raise in his own book 40 years later:

> The preservation of animal and plant life, and of the general beauty of Nature, is one of the foremost duties of the men and women of today. It is an imperative duty, for it must be performed at once, for otherwise it will be too late ... Air and water are polluted, rivers and streams serve as sewers and dumping grounds, forests are swept away and fishes are driven from the streams. Many birds are becoming extinct and certain mammals are on the verge of extermination. Vulgar advertisements hide the landscape and in all that disfigures the wonderful heritage of the beauty of Nature today, we Americans are in the lead. (Henry Fairfield Osborne, 1912, from the Preface to *Our Vanishing Wildlife: Its Extermination and Preservation* by William Temple Hornaday)

The Conservation Movement, of which Hornaday's book was a part, is approximately dated from 1850 to 1920. It was influenced by the writing of Henry David Thoreau, public reaction against the intense deforestation that accompanied the settlement of the North American interior, and other intellectual currents, including the earlier writings of Thomas Malthus. Malthus, one of the better known catastrophists even today, warned in his *Essay on the Principle of Population* (1798) that population growth must inevitably outstrip the availability of natural resources (especially agriculture); the same idea can be found in Adam Smith before him.

Concern about resource depletion was not confined to the United States either. In 1865 the British economist Stanley Jevons published his book *The Coal Question*, warning that the United Kingdom was using up its coal too quickly and would thereby lose the resource upon which all its industry was based. In Canada, meanwhile, the deforestation wrought by agricultural settlers was decried by Prime Minister Sir John A. MacDonald, who in 1871 said: 'We are recklessly destroying the timber of Canada and there is scarcely the possibility of replacing it' (quoted in Elizabeth Brubaker, *Property Rights in The Defence of Nature*, p. 142). In June 1872 an article in the *Canadian Monthly* warned 'We are wasting our forests, habitually, wickedly, insanely, and at a rate which must soon bankrupt us in all that element of wealth' (quoted by Brubaker, p. 142). At the turn of the century the government of British Columbia was so concerned about the pace of deforestation that it convened the first Royal Commission (the Fulton Commission of 1905) into the state of the forests.

1.1.5 Our Numbers Are Burdensome to the World

We could go back further in history, and were the documents available, we would find in every age people warning about the depletion of resources and damage to the local environment. In 1844 Friedrich Engels described the Irk River near Manchester England as 'a narrow, coal black, foul-smelling stream full of debris and refuse ... from the depths of which bubbles of miasmatic gas constantly arise and give forth a stench unendurable even on the bridge forty or fifty feet above the surface of the stream' (quoted in Brubaker, p. 128). The British Parliament passed its first Smoke Abatement Act in 1853, a largely ineffective response to heavy smoke loads in urban air. The Parliamentary Committee examining the issue heard from boaters on the Thames complaining of smoke so thick there were stretches of zero visibility on calm days (see Brenner 1974). The British House of Lords convened a select committee into air pollution in 1862, and another one in 1878. The first inquiry heard of terrible destruction of woods, crops and pastures from the effects of burning sulfurous coal near St Helen's, while in Lancashire and Glamorganshire, airborne alkali, chlorine gas, and other emissions were implicated in increased rates of respiratory disease and death in factory towns. Life expectancy in London in 1841 was 37 years, whereas in heavily polluted Liverpool it was 26 and Manchester 24 (discussed in Brenner 1974, pp. 415–18).

All over sixteenth-century Europe the forests were disappearing. In 1548 the English government ordered an inquiry into the deteriorating state of its forests. Indeed resource scarcity was ubiquitous in Europe, and elsewhere, well before the twentieth century. Hence the need for gold, silver, and other metals was a driving force for exploration. In 1492 an Italian journalist named Matarazzo wrote that '[There is] a great shortage of timber ... people cut domestic trees ... as these do not suffice people have now begun to cut even olive trees and entire olive groves have been destroyed' (quoted in Cippola 1980, p. 246).

Our search doesn't end there. A famous quote from an even earlier writer shows just how much today's perceptions about the human 'footprint' on the Earth is was shared by much earlier generations.

Cultivated fields have subdued forests; flocks and herds have expelled wild beasts; sandy deserts are sown; rocks are planted; marshes are drained; and where once were hardly solitary cottages, there are now large cities. No longer are (savage) islands dreaded, nor their rocky shores feared; everywhere are houses, and inhabitants, and settled government, and civilized life. What most frequently meets our view (and occasions complaint), is our teeming population: our numbers are burdensome to the world, which can hardly supply us from its natural elements; our wants grow more and more keen, and our complaints more bitter in all mouths, whilst Nature fails in affording us her usual sustenance. In very deed, pestilence, and famine, and wars, and earthquakes have to be regarded as a remedy for nations, as the means of pruning the luxuriance of the human race.

The author was Tertullian, a theologian living in Carthage, circa AD 200. (*Treatise on the Soul*, Chapter 30). Tertullian was not writing an environmentalist tract, he was writing a philosophical critique of the Pythagorean doctrine of reincarnation. His argument was that if the Pythagoreans were correct, namely that the living arose from the dead and the dead proceed from the living, there would only ever be a fixed number of persons in the world, taking dead and living together. But even Tertullian and his contemporaries could observe that the world's population had grown over time, that some places had become decidedly overcrowded, and that the known world was everywhere affected by human settlements. Hence, there had to be new people added to the world over time.

Tertullian's tangential observations serve to remind us that concern about the natural environment is not new. Citing earlier writings on such concerns does not prove that they were misplaced, much less that contemporary concerns are, but it does remind us that human society has long grappled with the challenges of good resource management and care of the natural environment. Today, we face many new and more complex challenges, and it is hoped that the new and more complex tools of economics as outlined in this book will be sufficient to help us meet them.

1.2 Environmental Issues

The term 'environment' is so broad to be rather meaningless. Taken literally, it includes everything between you and outer space. To make the term useful we need to be specific wherever possible. Even terms like 'air pollution' can be too broad. For example, air pollution includes directly emitted gases and aerosols, as well as those that are formed from precursor emissions combined with natural atmospheric compounds. The difference is easily overlooked, but it matters for policy analysis because the same action, under different circumstances, can be good or bad for a specific air contaminant. For instance, reducing volatile organic compound levels in an urban atmosphere can increase ground-level ozone, depending on weather conditions and the amount of nitrogen dioxide in the air. On environmental issues, the devil is in the generalities: we should aim for proper specifics.

Regarding air quality, the six main contaminants are as follows, but there are hundreds of compounds that can potentially be of concern.

1.2.1 Conventional Air Pollution

PARTICULATE MATTER (PM)
These are small particles of smoke that get into the lungs and can cause disease or discomfort. The term 'PM$_{10}$' refers to particulate matter smaller than 10 microns; PM$_{2.5}$ refers to particulates under 2.5 microns diameter. The aggregate measure is sometimes abbreviated TSP, for Total Suspended Particulates.

OXIDES OF SULFUR (SOx)
Sulfur oxide (SO) and Sulfur dioxide (SO$_2$) are by-product of burning fossil fuels that contain sulfur. SO$_2$ is a precursor to acid rain.

Oxides of Nitrogen (NOx)

These gases are collectively referred to as 'NOx.' Nitrous oxide (N_2O) is also called 'laughing gas' and is used as a mild anesthetic. It breaks down in the atmosphere quickly so it is not counted in air quality statistics, but it does have infrared-absorptive properties so it is listed as a 'greenhouse' gas – see below. Nitrogen oxide (NO) and nitrogen dioxide (NO_2) are smog precursors. They contribute to the discolouring haze sometimes observed in urban air, and to the formation of ozone.

Volatile Organic Compounds (VOCs)

The term VOCs covers a large class of carbon-based compounds that can, depending on NOx levels, contribute to smog through catalytic formation of ozone. They are tied to fossil fuel use but there are also many natural sources, including trees.

Carbon Monoxide (CO)

CO (not to be confused with CO_2, or carbon dioxide) is a byproduct of incomplete combustion of fossil fuels. It interferes with the blood's absorption of oxygen. In high concentrations it is dangerous and even fatal.

Ground-Level Ozone (O_3)

Ozone is not emitted directly, it is formed in the air when NOx and VOCs mix under intense ultraviolet (UV) radiation.

The next section shows some time series and cross-sectional graphs of air quality in then United States, Canada, and around the world.

Water quality is more of a local issue than air quality, in the sense that water in one river doesn't typically affect quality of other river systems unless they are connected. But water pollution can accumulate when flows into lakes or into the ocean. Some issues of concern for water quality are as follows.

Drinking Water Quality

Cities usually draw water from lakes, rivers and/or underground aquifers, then filter and treat the water with chlorine or ultraviolet (UV) radiation to kill micro-organisms before piping it to homes. Dangerous contaminants may include fecal coliform bacteria, giardia, *E. coli*, and other germs. These must be killed by the treatment process, or public health will be placed at risk. The water may have a high mineral content ('hardness') and the usual remedy for this is to have individual homeowners to use a water softener.

General Water Quality

Some contaminants affect water other than that intended for drinking. Agricultural run-off, including nitrogen and phosphorous (from fertilizers) and inorganic pesticide residues, can enter river systems and accumulate where those rivers empty into lakes, affecting the appearance and suitability of water for recreation and aquatic life. The fertilizer residues (also called 'nutrients') stimulate growth of algae and underwater plants that deplete the water's oxygen levels, in turn making it hard for fish to survive. The algae can also make the water unsuitable for recreation since it can cause rashes and sometimes sickness for swimmers. Industrial effluent can include, depending on location, dioxins and furans from pulp mills and mercury from mines. These are toxic and need to be carefully controlled.

Other issues include land use and global environmental problems.

Land Use

While urban and suburban areas make up only a very small amount of land space (less than 3 per cent in North America) the conversion of forests and grassland to agriculture has had a large impact on our geography. It also affects habitat for wild species. Deforestation is also a concern in the tropics, especially the Amazon area of Brazil, and other places around the world including China and Africa. Large-scale hydroelectric projects, such as the James Bay dams in northern Quebec and the Three Gorges dam in China, flood large valleys and thereby change the regional geography.

1.2.2 Global Environmental Problems: Ozone Depletion

Use of Freons, or chlorofluorocarbons (CFCs) is believed to have led to a build-up of chlorine in the stratosphere (above 12 km), where it catalytically destroys ozone. While we consider O_3 a nuisance at the ground level, it is beneficial to us in the upper atmosphere since it filters ultraviolet-B (UV-B) radiation. Concern over stratospheric ozone loss led to an agreement called the Montreal Protocol, which banned CFC production and use around the world.

The atmosphere consists of several distinct layers: the boundary layer (up to about 1 km), the troposphere (1 to about 15 km), the stratosphere above that, the mesosphere, and beyond to outer space. The troposphere experiences continual turbulent mixing due to convection of warm air from the surface. The stratosphere is more stable, but undergoes continual changes in chemistry due to variations in the level of solar ultraviolet radiation with the seasons. UV-B acts on oxygen in the stratosphere to produce ozone (O_3), which then absorbs some of the UV-B that would otherwise reach the Earth's surface. Although ozone exists at all layers of the atmosphere it is much more abundant in the stratosphere. This is called the 'ozone layer,' although it is not at a single uniform level. We need protection from UV-B since it can cause damage to skin and eyes. At the Earth's surface the major variations in UV-B are experienced with changes in the seasons and North-South travel: UV-B flux peaks at the height of summer, and is much stronger at the equator than at the poles. But some variation is also experienced as a result of changes in the column density of ozone in the stratosphere, which is sometimes referred to euphemistically as the 'thickness of the ozone layer.'

Some variations in ozone density happen naturally, since ozone is an unstable, reactive molecule that is continually produced and depleted in the atmosphere. CFCs are believed to be having an effect on atmospheric ozone levels by depleting ozone in the stratosphere. It is not as simple as, say, cutting a hole in a roof, and the mechanism is still not fully understood (see Schiermeier 2007).

Figure 1.1 shows the percentage deviation in global stratospheric ozone density from the long-term average since 1965, based on data collected from satellites by the World Meteorological Organization (WMO 2006, Chapter 3). There were two large drops in ozone levels from 1976 to 1982, and from 1988 to 1993. The peak thinning reached about 6 per cent as of 1994, but ozone levels have since recovered since then to about 96 per cent of their original levels.

But looking at a global average only tells part of the story. The thinning is not evenly distributed in time and space. Very little thinning has occurred in the tropics, where UV-B levels at the surface are already far higher than in the mid-latitudes and polar regions due to the angle of solar incidence. In the northern mid-latitudes (30°N to 60°N, covering Europe and North America) the thinning occurred largely in the winter and springtime, peaked by 1994, and has recovered by half since then (WMO 2006, Chapter 3, p. 15). The thinning was insignificant in the summer and fall. This pattern is fortunate: in winter and early spring there is relatively little sun and people tend to be indoors or wearing long sleeves. During the months of most intense UV-B exposure (July

Figure 1.1 Total % change (compared to 1964–1980 average) in global average stratospheric ozone density, 1965–2005.

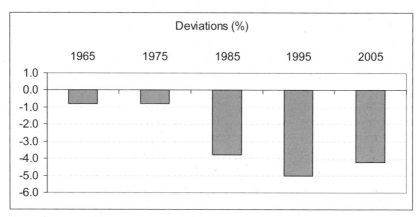

Source: WMO 2006.

and August) there was no significant ozone loss. The annual average declined until the early 1990s, and has since steadily recovered. In the Southern mid-latitudes the change in annual average ozone density was even across the seasons, declining by about 6 per cent by the mid-1980s and holding steady since then (WMO 2006, Chapter 3, p. 15).

The largest change occurred over the South Pole. Intense cold in the Antarctic stratosphere causes a unique chemical reaction in which nitric acid, water, and sulfuric acid condense to form what are called Polar Stratospheric Clouds. When chlorine contacts the molecules on these clouds it forms chlorine-oxygen pairs. In the presence of UV light these molecules react with ozone to break up the O_3 molecule, thus reducing the density of ozone in the stratosphere. That is why in the Antarctic spring (i.e., September and October), as the sun is rising over the South Pole, the polar stratospheric clouds disperse and the density of stratospheric ozone drops for a few months, then rebuilds as sunlight acts on the gases in the atmosphere to produce new ozone. This is an annual phenomenon unique to the South Pole, and only happens in the stratosphere.[1] The colder the polar winter, the more ozone loss in the polar springtime.

---

[1] See http://www.esrl.noaa.gov/csd/assessments/2006/chapters/Q10.pdf for a more detailed explanation.

Thinning ozone increases the amount of UV-B reaching the Earth's surface. You also experience more UV-B as you travel towards the equator. Since there is very little UV-B radiation reaching the surface in Antarctica, especially during its winter and early spring, it is worth noting that the largest thinning effect happens where it matters the least.

Concern about the effect of CFCs on the ozone layer led countries around the world to sign the Montreal Protocol, which bans production and use of these compounds. Since non-ozone-depleting substitutes were readily available, the treaty has been relatively successful in cutting global CFC use. The World Meteorological Organization forecasts that the ozone layer will have recovered to 100 per cent of its natural density within about 40 years.

1.2.3 Global Environmental Problems: Global Warming

Fossil fuel consumption releases carbon dioxide (CO_2) and N_2O, among other gases. Also, land-use changes can cause emissions of methane (CH_4). Each of these gases absorb infrared radiation (IR) in selected bands. There is a constant 'shine' of IR off the surface of the Earth, as part of the process by which solar energy absorbed by the Earth's surface is transported back to space, maintaining the balance of incoming and outgoing energy. Under fairly general conditions, increased IR absorption (by a solid or a gas) leads to an increase in temperature of the absorbing substance. Hence, accumulation of these gases in the atmosphere is expected to cause increased overall temperatures in the lower part of the atmosphere (below the stratosphere).

Water vapour is, by far, the strongest IR absorber, and it is abundant throughout the lower atmosphere. However, water vapour in the atmosphere is mainly governed by natural processes. Of the gases released by fuel consumption and other socioeconomic activity, CO_2 is not the strongest IR absorber but is released in the largest volume, making it the most important gas from the policy perspective. It is also a natural component of the atmosphere, with massive flows in and out of the atmosphere as a result of oceanic in- and out-gassing, plant growth and decay on land, and so on. It is not an air pollutant per se, since it is beneficial to plant life and not directly harmful to humans or animals (except at very high levels). However, CO_2 has become a focus of regulatory interest because of its IR spectrum and connection to global warming. The issues involved are much more complex than those associated with ordinary air pollution. IR emission in the atmosphere is only part of the energy transport mechanism by which incoming solar energy at the Earth's surface is balanced by outgoing energy. The other major mechanism is convection, or fluid dynamics, in which warm, moist air rises and is replaced by cool, dry air from aloft. The planetary-scale circulations and local turbulent mixing of air and water in the troposphere and boundary layer combine to give us our daily and seasonal weather patterns. Because of the complexity of the processes involved it is not possible to make straightforward predictions about how additional CO_2 and other IR-absorbing gases will affect long-term climatic patterns.

On its own, the addition of CO_2 to the air only enhances IR absorption by a small amount. If nothing else changes this would be expected to yield relatively little climatic change. But if a small amount of warming triggers an accumulation of water vapour in the atmosphere, the warming could be amplified around the world. The overall process is commonly referred to as the 'enhanced greenhouse effect,' although it is not the same as the mechanism by which a greenhouse warms up. A greenhouse warms up by blocking convection, whereas greenhouse gases act by slowing the flux of IR to the top of the atmosphere.

The core of the concern around CO_2 and other so-called greenhouse gases (GHGs) is that a large water vapour feedback might amplify the initial effects. GHG levels in the atmosphere should, other things being equal, increase temperatures at the surface and in the troposphere, while reducing temperatures in the stratosphere. But going into further detail requires modeling the fluid dynamics in the atmosphere, which involves non-linear and chaotic processes that are very difficult to forecast.

Global average emissions of carbon dioxide vary quite a bit across countries. Some poor sub-Saharan countries emit less than half a tonne of CO_2 per person annually, while the United States and Canada emit more than 5 tonnes per person annually. Annual per capita CO_2 emissions average out to about 1.2 tonnes per person globally, a rate that has been pretty constant since the early 1970s (see Figure 1.2). From 1960 to the present, the concentration of CO_2 in the atmosphere has risen from 316 parts per million to about 384 parts per million, as of 2007 (Keeling et al. 2008). If world population peaks at about 9 billion people in 2050, and per capita emissions stay in the range of 1.2 tonnes per capita, then total global emissions will peak at about 11 billion tonnes (gigatonnes) mid-century.

The Intergovernmental Panel on Climate Change (IPCC) produces Assessment Reports on the subject of global warming every 5 or 6 years

Figure 1.2 Global per capita CO2 emissions 1950–2007, expressed as metric tons of carbon equivalent.

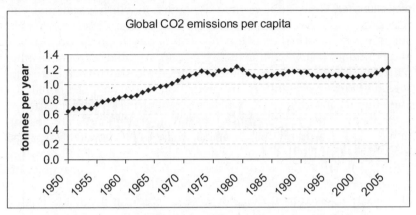

Source: Carbon Dioxide Information and Analysis Center http://cdiac.ornl.gov/ftp/ ndp030/global.1751_2006.ems as of December 18, 2008.

(available at www.ipcc.ch). For the past decade they have been forecasting global warming using a suite of emission scenarios that project emissions by 2050 of 8.5 to 27 gigatonnes, or 0.97 to 3.1 tonnes per person. Based on Figure 1.2 the upper end is probably unrealistic, unless the per capita series starts showing a rapid upward trend.

In its most recent report, the IPCC (2007) concluded that historical greenhouse gas emissions (chiefly CO_2) had caused most of the warming of the Earth in recent decades. Measuring exactly how much warming has occurred is not simple. There are many different methods in use for summarizing changes in the Earth's climate, but there is no theoretical basis for constructing an index of global warming (Essex et al. 2007). The most common approach is to calculate the global average of local deviations (or 'anomalies') from regional air temperature averages, as sampled at weather stations on land around the world, combined with local anomalies in sea surface temperature data collected by ships. This is referred to as the 'global average temperature anomaly.' Figure 1.3 (top panel) shows the monthly global average temperature anomalies as computed by the Climatic Research Unit (CRU) at the University of East Anglia in the United Kingdom (Brohan et al. 2006). The bottom panel shows the interval since 2001 and compares the CRU temperature series to the average prediction from 55 simulations from climate models (called General Circulation Models or GCMs) prepared for the

Figure 1.3 Top: global average temperature anomalies, 1901–2009. Bottom: Observed global average anomaly (denoted CRU) compared to climate model projections (GCMs).

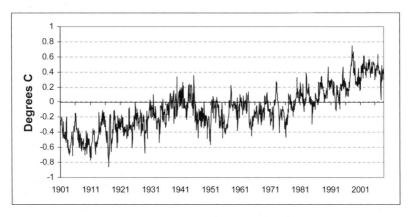

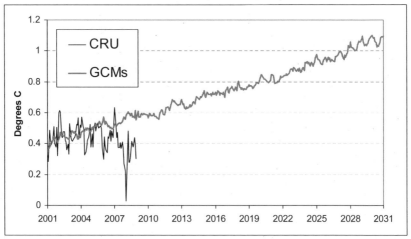

Source: Models http://climexp.knmi.nl. Observations from Climatic Research Unit http://www.cru.uea.ac.uk/cru/data/temperature/hadcrut3gl.txt.

most recent IPCC Report. The models have an upward trend of about 0.2°C per decade. For the past 10 years or so the observations have not exhibited this trend, but it may emerge in the future.

Most of the Earth's surface is covered with water, and data from the oceans have been sparse during much of the twentieth century. So the data shown in Figure 1.3 involve a lot of hidden assumptions, especially before 1940, and especially concerning how to merge oceanic temperatures collected using very different methods over time. Since 2003, oceanic temperature measurements have been collected on a consistent basis by a global system of 3,000 robotic buoys, called the Argo Network (see www.argo.net). As these data become available they will help refine the global average anomaly estimates. Over land, not all regions are equally sampled. Outside of the United States and Europe, coverage is very thin prior to the Second World War due to the lack of long-term temperature records in many low-income countries, and since 1990 there has been a large reduction (about 50% globally) in the number of active weather stations available for inclusion in the global sample (Peterson and Vose 1997). There has also been a longstanding concern that the data over land are affected by urbanization and equipment discontinuities, which have been shown to add a significant upward bias in measured warming trends since 1980 (McKitrick and Michaels 2004, 2007; deLaat and Maurellis 2004, 2006).

Other methods are available for measuring temperatures in the troposphere and stratosphere. Since 1958, temperature data has been collected on a global basis using instruments called radiosondes that are attached to weather balloons, and since 1979 temperature data has been collected by microwave sounding units (MSU) on weather satellites. MSUs measure microwave emissions from atmospheric oxygen, and scientists use these readings to infer temperatures throughout the major atmospheric layers (Spencer et al. 1990).

Satellites provide consistent measurement of temperatures in the troposphere and stratosphere. These regions are important because, according to the modeling work done for the IPCC, GHG-induced warming should be most apparent in the troposphere, especially over the tropics. The 2007 IPCC Report (and its predecessor, the 2001 IPCC Report) identified the mid-troposphere over the tropics as the region where much of the GHG-induced warming should have taken place in recent decades.[2] The tropical region, spanning 30°S to 30°N, accounts for half of the atmosphere and is hypothesized to be particularly susceptible to amplified warming due to a strong water vapour feedback; this is where warming is expected to be observed most rapidly in the future if greenhouse gases continue to build up in the atmosphere.

---

2 IPCC (2007), Figures 9.1 and 10.7; see also discussion in IPCC 2007, 764–5.

Figure 1.4 Climate model simulations of late twentieth century warming in the tropical mid-troposphere.

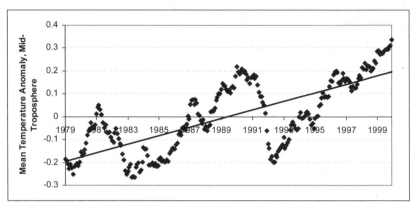

Note: The trend line shown is just under 0.2°C per decade.
Source: Data from Santer et al. (2008).

Because models have been used to simulate historical observations there is now a long-enough overlap period to compare their performance to observations. Figure 1.4 shows the average output from 49 climate models running a historical 'backcast,' that is, a simulation of the atmospheric changes expected under observed changes in greenhouse gas concentrations, solar variability, and so on, over the 1979–1999 interval. Models project a range of warming trend in the mid-troposphere of 0.1°C to 0.44°C per decade, with an average of 0.24°C per decade. The rate is forecast to increase in the early decades of the twenty-first century under the assumption that greenhouse gases continue to build up in the atmosphere (see IPCC 2007, Figure 10.7). Between 2000 and 2020 the warming rate in the tropical troposphere is expected to increase to between 0.25°C and 0.5°C per decade.

Satellite data for the mid-troposphere (about 5–16 km above the surface) are available from independent teams at the University of Alabama-Huntsville (Spencer et al 1990, denoted 'UAH') and Remote Sensing Systems in California (Mears et al. 2003, denoted 'RSS'). These data series start in 1979. The two are closely correlated. Figure 1.5 plots the average of these series over the tropics (sampled from 20°S to 20°N) and compares the data to trend lines running at 0.1°C per decade and 0.5°C per decade, representing the range of current warming rates implied in the IPCC climate modeling work. The trend in the tropical

Figure 1.5 Comparison of satellite-observed tropical average mid-troposphere temperature anomalies to lower and upper climate model-predicted rates (0.1–0.5°C/decade).

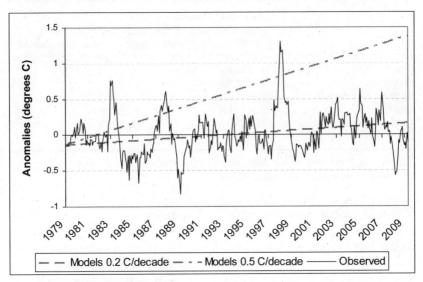

Source: UAH, RSS (see References).

troposphere data from January 1979 to April 2009 is only 0.06°C per decade and is statistically insignificant. Over this interval the atmospheric concentration of carbon dioxide went up by 14 per cent (Keeling et al. 2008). Because this temperature trend is below the low end of the warming rates expected by the IPCC for the region of the atmosphere hypothesized to be most sensitive to the effects of increased GHG's, this region has become an important area of focus for assessing how strong the overall effect of greenhouse gases is likely to be on the climate over the coming decades.

Table 1.1 shows regional trends in the lower troposphere (about 1 to 8 km above the surface) from the UAH satellite series. The global average is slightly higher in the lower troposphere than the mid-troposphere, and would work out to 1.2°C per century if it remains at its current rate. However, the only region showing a positive and significant trend is the Northern Hemisphere outside the tropics. The tropics themselves, the Southern Hemisphere and the South Pole have not exhibited the trend.

Table 1.1
Mean atmospheric temperature trends in lower-troposphere, January 1979 to April 2009.

	University of Alabama Temperature trend in °C/decade, 1979:1 to 2009:4 (t-statistic of Atmospheric Region trend in parentheses)
Globe	0.12 (2.94)
North Pole	0.44 (6.49)
Northern Hemisphere	0.19 (4.46)
Tropics	0.04 (0.63)
Southern Hemisphere	0.06 (1.60)
South Pole	−0.08 (1.29)

Source: http://vortex.nsstc.uah.edu/data/msu/t2lt/uahncdc.lt. Trend standard errors computed using arima (1,0,1) specification.

Should global warming on the scale predicted in model projections come to pass, the effects would likely be noticeable around the world in the form of longer summers, shorter winters, possible changes to precipitation (increases or decreases), and so forth. Major concerns are: if sections of Greenland or Antarctica were to melt and raise sea levels; if the Arctic permafrost were to melt and release methane; if warmer seas were to promote more frequent and/or intense hurricanes, etc. The data for recent years does not seem to support the more dramatic scenarios, but the scientific community continues to monitor these observational series to see if the trends change.

1.2.4 Air Pollution and Economic Growth over Time

We can now turn to some basic connections between the economy and the environment. There is a common perception that economic growth causes increased pollution. Many people would conjecture a relationship as in Fig. 1.6. Actual data show that the situation is more complicated. For instance, a scatterplot of U.S. per capita income and particulate emissions over the period 1945–1998 shows the relationship is actually downward-sloping (Fig. 1.7). On the other hand, American carbon monoxide (CO) emissions over the same interval show an upside-down-U shaped pattern (Fig.1.8).

A surprising feature of postwar U.S. economic growth is that by

Figure 1.6 Hypothetical relationship between GDP and pollution.

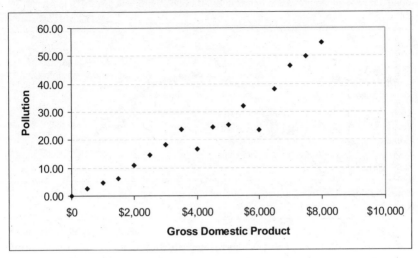

Figure 1.7 U.S. real GDP and total particulate emissions.

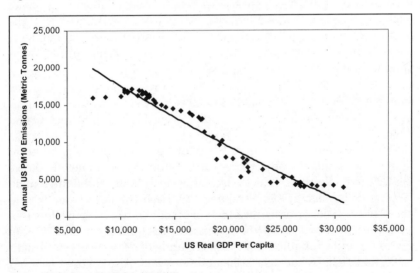

Source: Data from McKitrick (2006).

Figure 1.8 U.S. real GDP and total carbon monoxide emissions.

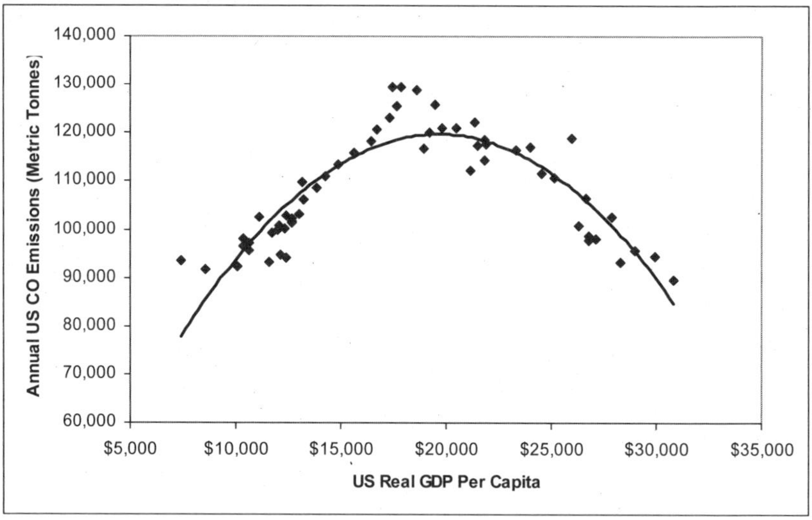

Source: Data from McKitrick (2006).

the end of the 1990s most air contaminant emissions were at or below where they were at the end of the Second World War (Fig. 1.9). The data in Figure 1.9 have all been scaled so the 1945 value equals 100. NOx grew until about 1975 and levelled off thereafter. After 1970 all other air pollution emissions fell, despite the overall economy growing about six-fold in size. Figure 1.10 confirms the improvement in air quality by showing the number of violations of air quality standards per monitoring station per year in the United States from 1975 to 2000, for CO and ozone.

The improvement in air quality can at least in part be attributed to tightening standards on factories and automobiles. Table 1.2 shows the U.S. federal motor vehicle standards since 1966 for the three main tailpipe emissions: VOCs, NOx, and CO. Each standard is indexed to equal 100 in 1966, prior to introduction of federal controls, to allow easier comparison over time (the estimated pre-control levels in 1966, in grams per mile, for autos were 10.6, 4.1, and 80, respectively; for trucks 8, 3.6, and 102). By the year 2005 all these standards had been reduced by approximately 95 to 99 per cent. New cars today emit about 4 per cent of the carbon monoxide (per mile) they were allowed to emit in the

Figure 1.9 U.S. emissions by type, 1945–1998.

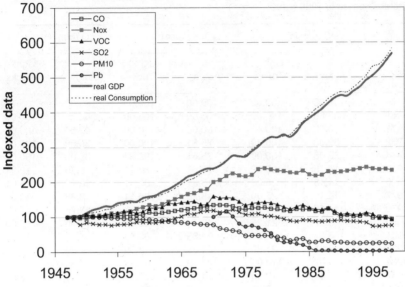

Source: Data from McKitrick (2006).

Figure 1.10 U.S. air monitoring violations per station per year, CO and ozone.

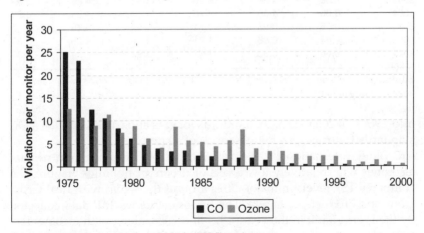

Source: http://www.fhwa.dot.gov/ohim/onh00/line1.htm.

TABLE 1.2

Federal emissions control standards for all new cars and light trucks sold in the United States, indexed to 1966 = 100.

Year	VOC (g/mile) Autos	VOC (g/mile) Light Trucks	NOx (g/mile) Autos	NOx (g/mile) Light Trucks	CO (g/mile) Autos	CO (g/mile) Light Trucks
1966	100.00	100.00	100.00	100.00	100.00	
1967	38.68	100.00	100.00	100.00	42.50	100.00
1971	38.68	100.00	100.00	100.00	42.50	100.00
1972	32.08	100.00	75.61	100.00	35.00	100.00
1974	32.08	100.00	75.61	100.00	35.00	100.00
1975	14.15	25.00	75.61	86.11	18.75	19.61
1976	14.15	25.00	75.61	86.11	18.75	19.61
1977	14.15	25.00	48.78	86.11	18.75	19.61
1979	14.15	21.25	48.78	63.89	18.75	17.65
1980	3.87	21.25	48.78	63.89	8.75	17.65
1981	3.87	21.25	24.39	63.89	4.25	17.65
1983	3.87	21.25	24.39	63.89	4.25	17.65
1984	3.87	10.00	24.39	63.89	4.25	9.80
1987	3.87	10.00	24.39	63.89	4.25	9.80
1988	3.87	10.00	24.39	33.33	4.25	9.80
1993	3.87	10.00	24.39	33.33	4.25	9.80
1994	2.36	4.00	9.76	33.33	4.25	3.33
1995	2.36	4.00	9.76	11.11	4.25	3.33
2001	2.36	4.00	9.76	11.11	4.25	3.33
2002	2.36	4.00	9.76	11.11	4.25	3.33
2003	2.36	4.00	9.76	11.11	4.25	3.33
2004	0.66	4.00	9.76	11.11	4.25	3.33
2005	0.66	0.88	1.71	1.94	4.25	3.33
2006	0.66	0.88	1.71	1.94	4.25	3.33
2007	0.66	0.88	1.71	1.94	4.25	3.33

Source: U.S. Federal Highway Administration. http://www.fhwa.dot.gov/environment/aqfactbk/page14.htm.

mid-1960s. In 2005 the NOx standards for cars and trucks, and the VOC standards for trucks, were tightened yet again.

Looking internationally, it turns out that high-income countries are also ones with relatively low levels of urban air pollution. Figure 1.11 compares TSP levels in major cities around the world with Real Gross Domestic Product per capita. The figure combines TSP data collected by the World Bank in the years 1994 and 2004, along with income data for the corresponding years in year 2000 U.S. dollars.

Figure 1.11 International income vs. TSP concentrations.

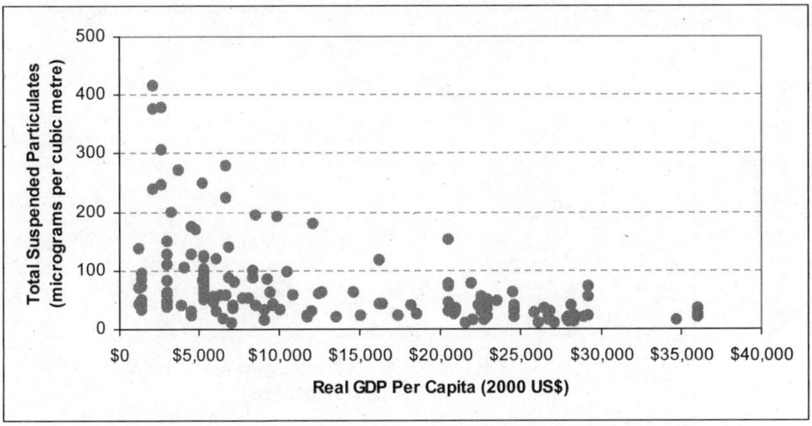

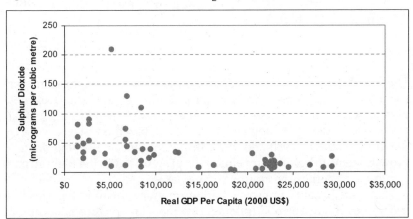

Sources: Income from Penn World Tables, pollution from World Bank (2008).

Figure 1.12 International income vs. SO$_2$ concentrations.

Sources: Income from Penn World Tables, Pollution from World Bank (1998).

Clearly the cluster of high-income countries enjoy better urban air quality than the group of low-income countries. A similar pattern is observed for SO$_2$. Figure 1.12 shows urban SO$_2$ levels versus income, from World Bank surveys over the interval 1995–2005.

For NO$_2$ (Figure 1.13) the pattern is less clear. For most countries

Figure 1.13 International income vs. NO$_2$ concentrations.

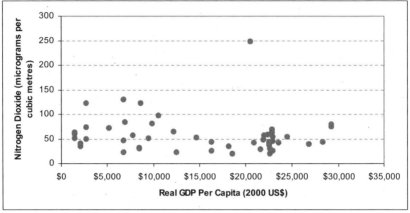

Source: Income from Penn World Tables, pollution from World Bank (1998).

there is a slight reduction as income grows, except for one outlier (Milan) which has high income and high NO$_2$.

1.2.5 Water Pollution

The upside-down-U shape seen in the plot of U.S. CO emissions ver-sus income is also observed in water pollution data. Figure 1.14 plots organic water pollution per worker, in Kg/day per worker, against na-tional real income per capita (in 1985 $U.S.), based on two surveys by the World Bank in 1980 and 1993. In the low-income setting, income growth seems to accompany emissions growth, but in the high-income group the pattern turns around somewhat.

That water quality improves with economic growth in high-income economies might seem surprising, but the same picture is borne out when looking at the Great Lakes. Figures 1.15 and 1.16 show the chang-es in concentrations of organic toxins in herring gull eggs from sites around Lake Ontario (1974–96) and Lake Erie (1974–99). All of the se-ries start at 1974 = 100, and by 1996 they have all fallen by 80 per cent or more. DDE is the compound that the pesticide DDT breaks down into once it is in the environment.

There is a lot more that could be said about environmental quality: air and water pollution, land use, and so on. This is just a smattering of

Figure 1.14 International income vs. water pollution.

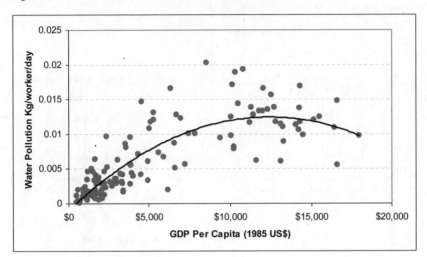

Source: McKitrick and Shufelt (2002).

the available evidence. But one pattern is clear. In high-growth economies there is no clear connection between economic growth and pollution; nor does pollution inexorably rise with time. The worst air and water quality problems are currently found in low-income countries. Hence, economic growth may actually help them clean up, under the right circumstances. The theoretical material we develop in the rest of this book will help to explain what those circumstances are.

1.3 Policy Instruments: A Brief Introduction

1.3.1 Standards

Standards can take many forms, but at heart each one is a 'command-and-control' mechanism to directly influence pollution levels. A *level* standard is a requirement that a source keep total emissions below a certain level. A *ratio* standard is a requirement to maintain emissions per unit of something to below a certain target. For instance, the standard may permit smoke from a chimney to contain no more than 100 parts per billion of benzene. If a standard is adjusted based on a firm's output it may, in effect, be a ratio standard. For instance if a firm is allowed to emit 10 tons of SO_2 for every 1000 tons of steel it produces, it faces a ra-

Figure 1.15 Lake Ontario water pollution by year.

Contaminant Levels in Herring Gull Eggs, Lake Ontario

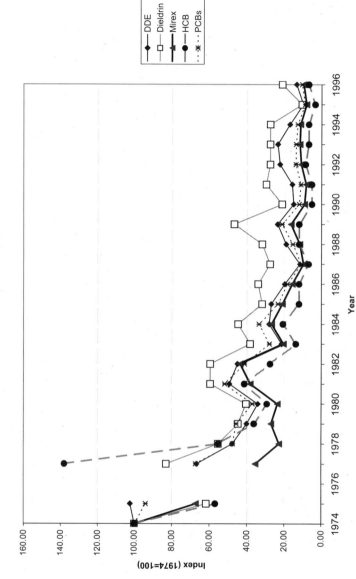

Source: Data from Canada Centre for Inland Waters.

Figure 1.16 Lake Erie water pollution by year.

Contaminant Levels in Herring Gull Eggs, Lake Erie

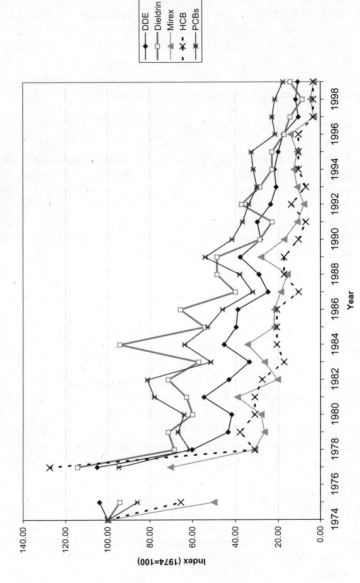

Source: Data from Canada Centre for Inland Waters.

tio standard of 0.01 units of SO_2 per unit output. A *process* or *technology* standard does not prescribe emissions; instead it requires installation of certain pollution control equipment. For example, cars must have catalytic converters, regardless of how much they are driven. Some process standards only stipulate that firms must use the 'Best Available Technology,' and regulators then decide what the standard means in light of currently available abatement equipment options.

1.3.2 Emission Taxes

An emissions tax is simply a charge per unit of emissions. The term 'Pigovian' tax originally referred to a charge on a commodity based on the externalized social cost associated with it. However, taxing the output of a firm only equates to a tax on its emissions in the special case where emissions and output vary linearly. Because this is not generally true in the models we examine herein, we will avoid using the term 'Pigovian' tax, and refer instead to *emissions* taxes. In Section 4.5 we will discuss the difference in greater detail.

1.3.3 Emission Permits

Another way of putting a price on emissions is to require firms to hold a permit for each unit of pollution they release, while allowing them to buy and sell the permits. This system is called *Tradable Emission Permits* or some similar term (e.g., tradable quotas, tradable credits, etc.) The best-known system of tradable permits is the U.S. SO_2 market. Large emitters of sulfur dioxide in the United States must buy permits to cover their emissions, and there is an active market in permits for both current and future emissions. You can see information about U.S. tradable permit programs at the website http://camddataandmaps.epa.gov/gdm/.

1.3.4 Liability Law

The use of courts to control pollution predates modern environmental laws. The British common law has long recognized the right of property owners to be protected against *torts*, or harms, that can take specific forms such as *nuisance* and *trespass*. A *nuisance* is an interfering action which prevents a person from using or enjoying his or her property. It can take the form of noise, smell, or other interference. A *trespass* is an invasion of one's property, including deposition of pollution, with damaging consequences. The law of torts prescribes remedies such as monetary damages and, usually, an injunction preventing further harm. French civil law contains an analogous concept called the law of *Delicts*. Delicts are not categorized by form, the way common law torts are, instead they are determined based on tests to establish whether blame can be assigned and damage occurred. Finally, where damage to waterways occurs, common-law courts have historically been asked to intervene based on the *riparian* rights of landowners adjacent to the waterway.

1.4 Institutions and Rule-Makers

1.4.1 Federal Governments in the United States and Canada

In the United States, the federal Environmental Protection Agency (EPA) sets national air quality standards and has the power to enforce stringent remedial measures on counties determined to be out of compliance. It established emission limits for SO_2 and NOx and runs a tradable permits system for these pollutants. It oversees the 'Superfund' program for cleaning up contaminated waste sites. Other U.S. federal agencies are also important, for instance the Department of the Interior, which controls habitat protection programs under the Endangered Species Act, and the Department of Transport, which sets motor vehicle emission standards and abatement technology requirements.

In Canada, the federal body primarily responsible for environmental regulation is Environment Canada. However, under the Canadian constitution, primary responsibility for air and water quality rests with the provincial governments. The federal government coordinates provincial action through the Canadian Council of Ministers of the Environment, including devising targets and sharing policy initiatives. The federal government exercises direct authority in some areas, however. First, it has sole jurisdiction for signing international treaties, such as the Canada-U.S. Acid Rain treaty and the Kyoto Protocol. Second, federal transport regulations establish standards for automobiles and trucks. Third, the federal government exercises control over some water quality issues because they have authority over fisheries and navigable waterways. Fourth, laws like the Species at Risk Act give the federal government some authority over habitat protection, and the Canadian Environmental Protection Act gives it authority over some pollutants, chiefly those designated as 'toxic.' Also the federal government has established legislation requiring environmental assessments for large projects.

1.4.2 State and Provincial Governments

U.S. states have some independence in air and water pollution regulation. They can propose more stringent rules than the EPA prescribes, but these must be approved by the federal government. If states are out of compliance with federal standards they can be compelled to implement federally mandated remedies. States have authority over mining but the federal government controls much public forestry that occurs on federal land. In Canada, provinces have constitutional authority over air and water regulation, as well as most resource management issues like forestry and mining.

1.4.3 Municipalities

In both Canada and the United States, municipal governments control issues like garbage and recycling facilities, land-use zoning, and some resource management issues, like groundwater use.

1.4.4 Courts

The jurisdiction of courts in English Canada and the United States has diminished over the postwar era as governments have introduced regulations and placed matters previously subject to the common law under direct government control. However, tort and property law continue to serve as instruments for individuals affected by pollution to press claims for compensation and to assert their rights not to suffer the damages due to pollution.

1.5 Growth and the Environment: The Tradeoff over Time

As noted in the Preface, many people worry about the earth's ability to bear up under the pressure of economic development. Will economic growth inevitably lead to more pollution? Many economists would point to two conflicting influences.

1. On the one hand, growth involves increased output, resource use,

pollution, garbage, etc. This is the 'substitution' effect: a society gives up some environmental assets to obtain more consumption goods.

2. On the other hand, growth means consumers have more money and more leisure time, which translates into demand for a cleaner environment and the resources to achieve it. This is the 'income' effect: since environmental quality is a normal good, as national income rises, people demand more of it and put resources into its production (or conservation as the case may be).

Which is the stronger of the two effects? There is good evidence that at low income levels the substitution effect dominates the income effect, and growth leads to worsening environmental quality. But as income continues to rise, a turn-around point is reached, after which the income effect dominates, and growth begins to support improved environmental conditions. This effect is called the 'Environmental Kuznets Curve,' or EKC, after the 'Kuznets' curve in the study of income distribution, where inequality is sometimes observed to increase then decrease during the growth process.

It is easy to illustrate a mechanism behind the EKC. Consider a simple economy with a fixed population producing consumption goods C from its environmental endowment E. At an early stage of development, the production frontier is linear, reflecting the fact that production primarily takes the form of extraction and consumption with little value-added through secondary production. As the economy's capital stock grows, the production possibility boundary pivots upwards along the C axis, since the maximum endowment of E, denoted E^M, remains more or less fixed. Also, since capital is used to add value to what is extracted from nature, the PPB displays more and more curvature, indicating the diminishing returns to scale inherent in secondary and tertiary processing. So the sequence of PPBs under technological advance looks like Figure 1.17. Social preferences are illustrated by indifference curves between E and C. They have the usual quasi-concave shape, although at very high levels of E they might begin to bend back upwards, since people don't necessarily like to rough it in the wilds all the time. So a group of indifference curves would look like Figure 1.18.

If we combine the two diagrams we can get Figure 1.19.

We assume that the economy chooses optimal pairs of E and C, denoted (E_i, C_i) $i = 1, 2, 3$. At low levels of development and consumption, the country is willing to trade off a lot of E to get relatively small

Figure 1.17 Production possibility boundaries between consumption and environmental quality.

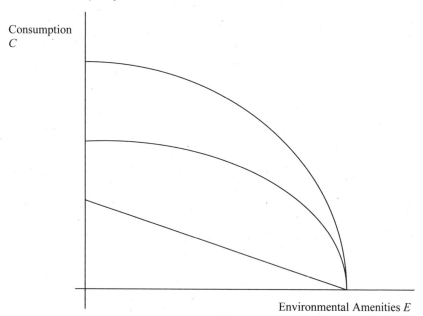

increments of C. Where simple survival is at issue, the loss of environmental amenities is clearly not going to stop people harvesting trees for fuel and shelter, or hunting and fishing endangered species. In addition, people will accept more pollution and ecological degradation in exchange for economic development and enhanced consumption possibilities. As development proceeds, society moves to higher PPBs and indifference curves. Then the relative cost of consumption (in terms of lost E) may go up if the PPB becomes relatively flatter in the interval we are examining, but eventually it will go down. As the real cost of E declines and income grows, resources can be put into both increased consumption and environmental preservation. So, from the first to second indifference curve we observe increased income and consumption paired with decreasing environmental quality, but from the second to third, and beyond, income growth supports increased environmental quality.

Figure 1.18 Indifference curves between consumption and environmental quality.

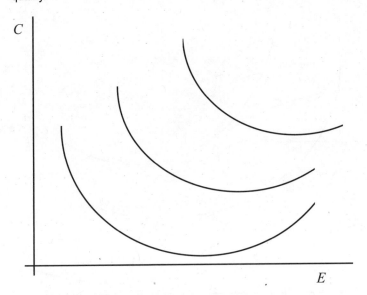

1.6 Does Growth Theory Predict the EKC?*

A long-standing literature uses neoclassical optimal growth models to examine the optimal allocation of income among consumption, investment, and pollution control, to maximize the discounted present value of utility over an infinite horizon. Forster (1973) solves a basic form of the optimal growth problem and finds that the steady-state values of capital (K) and consumption (C) with optimal pollution growth were strictly lower than the steady-state values of K and C without optimal pollution control. This is intuitively clear enough: if income is not devoted to environmental preservation, too much growth occurs and welfare falls. Forster treats pollution as a flow variable. By contrast, Keeler, Spence and Zeckhauser (1971) treat pollution as a cumulative stock variable. They find that two steady-states exist, one with no money spent on pollution control and one with money allocated to both consumption and pollution control. Utility is lower in the first steady state. Unfortunately, Keeler et al. did not analyse stability. Also, in both these papers pollution is treated as a fixed proportion of production or

Figure 1.19 Optimal path between consumption and environmental quality.

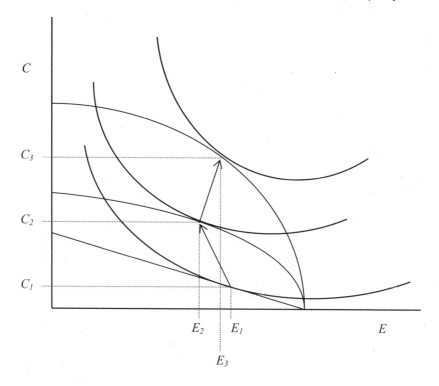

consumption. Other studies tend to do the same, and focus on proving the existence and stability of resulting equilibria. Brock (1977) examined growth and pollution and concluded that zero discounting is
a sufficient condition for the existence of a saddle point optimum.
Tahvonen and Kuuluvainen (1993) explored a model with stock pollution effects and renewable resources. They show that an optimal path
can be attained through the use of emission taxes.

These papers continue to examine existence and stability issues,
whereas the question we tend to be more interested in is: Will economic
growth inevitably lead to rising pollution levels? This question became
the focus of empirical work associated with the debate in the United
States about the possible environmental side effects of the North American Free Trade Agreement. Grossman and Kreuger (1995) obtained data

on air and water pollution levels for cities all over the world from 1972 onwards and then used a simple reduced-form regression to examine the link between total emissions and per-capita income. They found evidence of an inverted-U shaped function relating income to pollution for some kinds of air pollution (smoke, heavy particulates), organic water pollutants, and some heavy metal water contaminants. They found that the turn-around point occurs by about $6,000–8,000 U.S. per capita income for many pollutants. A similar study (Selden and Song 1994) found the turn-around point came somewhat later ($8,000–10,000 U.S.), but they were using indirectly estimated national air pollution emissions, rather than actual ambient concentrations.

While the empirical results are certainly suggestive, there are a number of problems with them. The curves which have been estimated appear to be very sensitive to model specification (Galeotti and Lanza 1998). Fitting a curve requires ad hoc decisions about the data (levels, logs, differences, etc.) and the number of terms in the polynomial equation to be estimated. Regardless of the actual pattern in the data, using a 2nd-degree polynomial forces it to 'reveal' either a U-shape or a ∩-shape, while a cubic polynomial forces a 'sideways-S' shape. Because the most interesting inferences from such models pertain to inflection points and limits, this sensitivity to modelling assumptions would warrant care in drawing conclusions. Hilton and Levinson (1998) estimate polynomials relating atmospheric lead levels to per capita GDP. They conclude that the relationship is inverted-U, but their parameter estimates yield a variety of patterns depending on the specification: U, ∩, ~, etc. (see their Figure 3).

The empirical results prompted renewed interest in theoretical models that could rationalize the EKC. But models which are rich enough to generate non-linear pollution dynamics appear to be able to rationalize *any* pollution path. Andreoni and Levinson (1998) show that, in a simple model with preferences over consumption and environmental quality, income effects (by which increases in environmental quality become marginally more valuable as income grows) can dominate substitution effects (the trading off of environmental quality to obtain more consumption and investment), if the pollution abatement technology exhibits increasing returns to scale. Under other plausible assumptions, the pollution-income path can be linear in income or U-shaped.

Beltratti (1996) develops a simple dynamic model as follows. Preferences between consumption C and environmental quality E are given by the simple Cobb-Douglas utility function

$$U = \frac{1}{1-\eta}(CE)^{1-\eta}.$$

Production is by a linear production function $y = \beta K$. Environmental quality evolves according to $\dot{E} = R(E) - yv(K)$ where R is the 'recovery' function and v is the function which relates the stock of capital to the factor by which output deteriorates environmental quality. Capital evolves according to the investment equation $\dot{K} = y - C$. The optimal path for the economy can be found using the Hamiltonian equation:

$$H = \frac{(CE)^{1-\eta}}{1-\eta} + \lambda_1(\beta K - C) + \lambda_2(R(E) - \beta K v(K)).$$

A simple version would use $v(K) = GK$ where G is a constant. However, this would not generate the kind of non-linearities we are looking for, so a more complex version must be used. Suppose that we define

$$v(K) = \frac{G}{K} + K^{\alpha-1}e^{-\gamma K}.$$

This specification allows for a variety of plausible non-linear relationships between $\dot{E}$ and K, depending on the parameter values, yet is tractable enough to solve. It has the attractive features that as $K \to 0$, $v(K) \to \infty$ and $v'(K) \to -\infty$, so output is extremely damaging at low capital levels, but as $K \to \infty$ both v and v' tend to zero, so output is asymptotically benign. This matches our intuition about the Kuznets curve dynamics. The model thus specified is as simple as one can get without assuming away the non-linear growth-pollution relationship.

It turns out (see Beltratti 1996, pp. 49–52) that this model exhibits quite unexpected dynamics. First, it has no steady state. Second, for a plausible set of parameters, the relationship between production y and the state of the environment, E, is U-shaped, with the *worst* environmental effects associated with the *highest* levels of output. This is not what intuition or data would have led us to expect.

The lesson here is that pure growth theory is unlikely to settle the deeper questions about the relationship between growth and the environment. While economists continue to explore dynamic models, the need at present is for a better link between empirical work and existing theory.

Figure 1.20 Three PPB curves

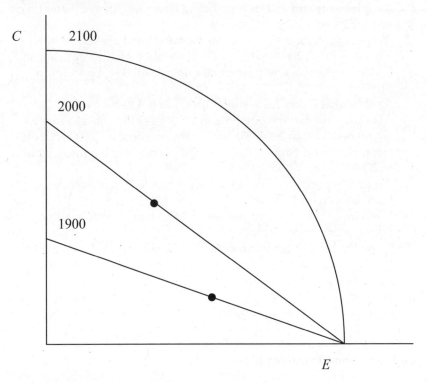

Review Questions

1. Is concern for the environment a new phenomenon? Why do you suppose so many recent writers present the issue as if ours is the first generation to be concerned about pollution control and re-source depletion?
2. Do any of the trends in environmental measures presented in this chapter surprise you? Why or why not?
3. Why is it important not to generalize about 'the environment'?

   The next questions refer to Figure 1.20, which shows possible PPBs for an economy during the years 1900, 2000, and 2100. The dots show the observed outcome. The indifference curves are not drawn, but you will need to draw them in to answer the questions. The outcome represented by a dot is not necessarily a tangency.

4. Suppose consumption C and environmental quality E are perfect complements and 1900 is an efficient outcome. Are we better off in 1900 or 2000?
5. Suppose preferences are not complements, and are such that we are better off in 2000 than in 1900. If we got better off by reducing E, does that mean environmental quality will be even lower in 2100?
6. Assume that C and E are substitutes, but not perfect substitutes. Also suppose that the outcome in 1900 was efficient, and that we are no better off in 2000. Show that the outcome in 2000 is not efficient. What will happen to C and E if we move to a tangency point in 2000?
7. Suppose we are at an efficient outcome in 2000. Are we better off than we were in 1900?
8. Is environmental quality costlier in 2000 than in 1900? (Define your cost measure carefully.)
9. Show the level of environmental quality which would have been attained in 2000 if there had been an income effect but no substitution effect over the previous 100 years.
10. What must the public's attitude towards consumption be if we are worse off in 2000 compared to 1900?

References and Extra Reading

Andreoni, J., and A. Levinson (1998). 'The Simple Analytics of the Environmental Kuznets Curve.' National Bureau of Economic Research Working Paper 6739.

Barnett, Harold, and Chandler Morse (1963). *Scarcity and Growth: The Economics of Natural Resource Availability*. Washington: Resources for the Future.

Beltratti, A. (1996). *Economic Growth with Environmental Assets*. Milan: FEEE.

Brenner, J.F. (1974). 'Nuisance Law and the Industrial Revolution.' *Journal of Legal Studies* 3(2): 403–33).

Brock, William (1977). 'A Polluted Golden Age.' In *Economics of Natural and Environmental Resources* (V.L. Smith, ed.), pp. 441–61. New York: Gordon and Breach.

Brohan, P., J.J. Kennedy, I. Harris, S.F.B. Tett, and P.D. Jones (2006). 'Uncertainty Estimates in Regional and Global Observed Temperature Changes: A New Dataset from 1850.' *Journal of Geophysical Research* 111, D12106, doi:10.1029/2005JD006548.

Brown, Lester, and Jennifer Mitchell (1998). *State of the World 1998.* Washington: Worldwatch Institute.

Brubaker, Elizabeth (1995). *Property Rights in Defence of Nature.* London: EarthScan.

Brundtland, Gro Harlem (ed.) (1987). *Our Common Future: Report of the UN World Commission on Environment and Development.* New York and Oxford: Oxford University Press.

Cipolla, Carlo M. (1980). *Before the Industrial Revolution,* 2nd edition. New York: Norton.

Dasgupta, Partha, and Geoffrey Heal (1979). *Economic Theory and Exhaustible Resources.* Cambridge: Cambridge University Press.

De Laat, A.T.J., and A.N. Maurellis (2004). 'Industrial CO_2 Emissions as a Proxy for Anthropogenic Influence on Lower Tropospheric Temperature Trends.' *Geophysical Research Letters* 31, L05204, doi:10.1029/2003GL019024.

De Laat, A.T.J., and A.N. Maurellis (2006). 'Evidence for Influence of Anthropogenic Surface Processes on Lower Tropospheric and Surface Temperature Trends.' *International Journal of Climatology* 26:897–913.

Ehrlich, Paul, and Anne Ehrlich (1972). *Population Resources Environment: Issues in Human Ecology.* San Francisco: Freeman.

Essex, Christopher, Andresen, Bjarne, and Ross McKitrick (2007). 'Does a Global Temperature Exist?' *Journal of Nonequilibrium Thermodynamics* 32(1) 1–28.

Forster, B (1973). 'Optimal Capital Accumulation in a Polluted Environment.' *Southern Economic Journal* 39: 544–7.

Galeotti, Marzio, and Alessandro Lanza (1998). 'Desperately Seeking (Environmental) Kuznets.' Fondazione Eni Enrico Mattei Working Paper, Venice.

Grossman, Gene, and Alan Krueger (1995). 'Economic Growth and the Environment.' *Quarterly Journal of Economics* 112: 353–77.

Heston, Alan, Robert Summers, and Bettina Aten (2006). 'Penn World Table Version 6.2.' Center for International Comparisons of Production, Income and Prices at the University of Pennsylvania, September.

Hilton, F.G., and A. Levinson (1998). 'Factoring the Environmental Kuznets Curve: Evidence from Automotive Lead Emissions.' *Journal of Environmental Economics and Management* 35: 126–41.

Holtz-Eakin, Douglas, and Thomas Selden (1995). 'Stoking the Fires? CO_2 Emissions and Economic Growth.' *Journal of Public Economics* 57: 85–101.

Intergovernmental Panel on Climate Change (IPCC) (2007). *Fourth Assessment Report Working Group I – the Scientific Basis.* Cambridge: Cambridge University Press.

Keeler, E., M. Spence, and R. Zeckhauser (1971). 'The Optimal Control of Pollution.' *Journal of Economic Theory* 4: 19–34.

Keeling, R.F., S.C. Piper, A.F. Bollenbacher, and J.S. Walker (2008). 'Atmospheric CO_2 Records from Sites in the SIO Air Sampling Network.' In *Trends: A Compendium of Data on Global Change*. Carbon Dioxide Information Analysis Center, Oak Ridge National Laboratory, U.S. Department of Energy, Oak Ridge, Tenn., online at http://cdiac.ornl.gov/trends/co2/sio-mlo.html.

Lomborg, Bjorn (2001). *The Skeptical Environmentalist: Measuring the Real State of the World*. Cambridge: Cambridge University Press.

Lucas, Robert (1976). 'Econometric Policy Evaluation: A Critique.' In *The Phillips Curve and Labour Markets* (K. Brunner and A.H. Meltzer, eds.), pp. 19–46. Amsterdam: North Holland.

McKitrick, Ross R. (2006) 'Why Did U.S. Air Pollution Decline after 1970?' *Empirical Economics* 33(3): 491–513, DOI:10.1007/s00181–006–0111–4.

McKitrick, R.R., and P.J. Michaels (2007). 'Quantifying the Influence of Anthropogenic Surface Processes and Inhomogeneities on Gridded Global Climate Data.' *Journal of Geophysical Research*, 112, D24S09, doi: 10.1029/2007JD008465.

McKitrick, R.R., and P. J. Michaels (2004). 'A Test of Corrections for Extraneous Signals in Gridded Surface Temperature Data.' *Climate Research* 26(2): 159–73; Erratum, *Climate Research* 27(3): 265–8.

McKitrick, Ross, and Timothy Shufelt (2002). 'Environmental Impacts of Enhanced Property Rights.' *Environment and Energy* 13(3): 367–82.

Meadows, Donella, et al. (1972). *The Limits to Growth: A Report for the Club of Rome's Project on the Predicament of Mankind*. New York: Universe Books.

Mears, Carl A., Matthias C. Schabel, and Frank J. Wentz. (2003). 'A Reanalysis of the MSU Channel 2 Tropospheric Temperature Record.' *Journal of Climate* 16(22) (November 1): 3650–64.

Peterson, Thomas C., and Russell S. Vose (1997). 'An Overview of the Global Historical Climatology Network Temperature Database.' *Bulletin of the American Meteorological Society* 78(12) (December 1): 2837–49.

Pinchot, Gifford (1910). *The Fight for Conservation*. New York: Doubleday.

Plourde, G. (1972). 'A Model of Waste Accumulation and Disposal.' *Canadian Journal of Economics* 5: 119–25.

Santer, B.D., P. W. Thorne, L. Haimberger, K.E. Taylor, T.M.L. Wigley, J.R. Lanzante, S. Solomon, M. Free, P.J. Gleckler, and P.D. Jones (2008). 'Consistency of Modelled and Observed Temperature Trends in the Tropical Troposphere.' *International Journal of Climatology*. DOI: 10.1002/joc.17.

Selden, T.M., and D. Song (1994). 'Environmental Quality and Development: Is There a Kuznets Curve for Air Pollution Emissions?' *Journal of Environmental Economics and Management* 27: 147–62.

Shafik, N., and S. Bandyopadhyay (1992). 'Economic Growth and Environmental Quality.' Background Paper for the World Development Report, World Bank, Washington D.C.

Shiermeier, Quirin (2007). 'Chemists Poke Holes in Ozone Theory.' *Nature* doi:10.1038/449382a 26 September 2007.

Tahvonen, O., and J. Kuuluvainen (1993). 'Economic Growth, Pollution and Renewable Resources.' *Journal of Environmental Economics and Management* 24: 101–18.

Spencer, Roy W., and John R. Christy (1990). 'Precise Monitoring of Global Temperature Trends from Satellites.' *Science* 247(4950) (March 30): 1558–62. doi:10.1126/science.247.4950.1558.

World Bank (2008). *World Development Indicators*. Washington: Author.

World Meteorological Organization (WMO) (2006). Ozone Assessment Report, 2006 http://www.wmo.ch/pages/prog/arep/gaw/ozone_2006/ozone_asst_report.html.

Data Source Websites

Global Warming-Related

Climate4you, A compendium of scientific data on climate: http://www.climate4you.com

Atmospheric carbon dioxide levels: http://cdiac.ornl.gov/trends/co2/sio-mlo.html

Climatic Research Unit, United Kingdom: http://www.cru.uea.ac.uk/cru/data

UAH satellite data: http://vortex.nsstc.uah.edu/data/msu

RSS satellite data: http://www.remss.com/msu/msu_data_description.html

Cryosphere Today (global sea ice): http://arctic.atmos.uiuc.edu/cryosphere/index.html

Carbon Dioxide Information and Analysis Centre (national and global CO_2 emissions): http://cdiac.ornl.gov/trends/emis/meth_reg.html

Climate Explorer, a collection of climate modeling output data: http://climexp.knmi.nl/

Ozone Layer-Related

Ozone layer assessments: http://www.esrl.noaa.gov/csd/assessments

Ozone hole over Antarctica: http://ozonewatch.gsfc.nasa.gov

World Ozone and Ultraviolet Radiation Data Centre: http://www.woudc.org/data_e.html

Air Pollution

U.S. Air quality trends: http://www.epa.gov/airtrends/aqtrends.html
U.S. Department of Transport Air Quality Factbook: http://www.fhwa.dot.
gov/environment/aqfactbk/index.htm
Environment Canada National Air Pollution Surveillance data: http://www.
etc-cte.ec.gc.ca/NAPSData/main.aspx

2 Valuation of the Environment

2.1 Externalities

We are concerned with situations in which one person's actions affect the welfare of another, such that 'external costs,' or 'externalities,' are imposed. There are several important aspects to an externality. We will use the following definition:

> *Externality:* When one agent's activities affect the utility or productivity of another agent or agents, without the former paying the price for the damages incurred by the latter, and without the latter having any control over the level of the activity.

There must be an imposition from one agent to another in which the former does not pay the cost and the latter does not have complete control over the magnitude. If a smelter emits a lot of smoke and fouls the air in a town, that would be an externality, unless the firm were paying the townspeople an agreed-upon sum of money for their suffering, in which case it is bearing the cost of its actions internally. If neighbour A's noise disturbs neighbour B, that too is an externality, unless B happens to be in A's house uninvited, in which case he has exposed himself to the nuisance.

The situations we have in mind can be described in economics terms with some examples. Consider first a firm-on-firm externality. Suppose there are 2 firms with production functions defined over labour L and capital K:

$$Q_1 = f^1(L_1, K_1)$$

$$Q_2 = f^2(L_2, K_2, Q_1)$$

In this case the productivity of the second firm is affected by the output of the first firm. The effect may be beneficial or harmful. Suppose it is beneficial (e.g., if the bees from the honey-producer help pollinate the orchard next door). In that case the owner of firm 1 is not receiving a payment to reflect his contribution to the operations of the orchard. This is not necessarily a boon for the orchard-grower, since he might be even better served if the beekeeper had twice as many bees, but the only way the beekeeper would do that would be if he were paid to do so.

The effect may also be harmful. If a smoky factory diminishes the quality of pies at the bakery next door, the factory is not paying the full costs of its production. Hence, it will tend to produce more than would be socially desirable.

Another example is that of a firm-on-consumer externality, for example:

$$Q_1 = f^1(L_1, K_1)$$

$$U = U(x_1, ..., x_n, Q_1)$$

Here the consumer's utility U is a function not only of the consumption of the n goods $x_1, ... x_n$, but also of the output level of firm 1. Firm 1 might, for example, emit some air pollution that is a nuisance, annoyance, or hazard for the person. In this case it is a negative externality.

Another distinction is between 'public' and 'private' externalities. A public externality is not depleted when one person suffers its effects. For instance, the noise pollution endured by a group is not diminished if another person moves within hearing range. By contrast, if a truck spills oil on one person's property, that oil cannot also then be spilled out of the truck again, elsewhere. So it is a 'private' externality. Another term for a private externality is a 'depletable' externality, since the more is inflicted upon one recipient, the less there is to inflict on other recipients. In this book we will primarily be concerned with public, firm-on-consumer externalities.

Pollution concerns us both as a stock and as a flow. The stock of pollution is the level of contamination in the environment. The flow of pollution is the level of new emissions. Suppose the stock of pollution at time t is Z_t, and the emissions level at time t is e_t. The simplest type of pollution is one for which

$$Z_t = e_t$$

That is, there is no accumulation of the pollutant over time: it disperses instantly. An example of this is noise pollution.

If the pollution does accumulate, but breaks down at a percentage rate δ each period, the relation between the stock and flow is

$$Z_t = Z_{t-1}(1-\delta) + e_t.$$

An example of this type is smoke, which builds up as emissions are added, but disperses and breaks down over time. A more complex dynamic case is one in which the dispersion rate δ is a function of the stock of pollution:

$$Z_t = Z_{t-1}(1-\delta(Z_{t-1})) + e_t$$

such as when the build-up of pollution in a lake detracts from the lake's ability to naturally regenerate itself. In this case δ gets smaller as Z gets larger.

For the most part we will confine our attention to the simplest case. This reflects the fact that while we are affected by the pollution stock, policy can only affect the flow. So, for practical reasons, most of the environmental economics literature assumes that pollution is a pure flow variable. But some of the more interesting and pressing problems of our time involve pollution stocks.

2.2 Some Results from Microeconomics and Welfare Economics

We need to review some basic ideas that will be essential for supporting the normative conclusions to follow. These ideas should be familiar from intermediate and advanced microeconomics textbooks. The most important idea that comes out of this discussion is that *prices have meaning* in a market economy. Relative prices tell us something about how things are valued by consumers in a society. The prices that firms face for labour, capital, materials, and energy tell us something about how we value the inputs that get used up in the production process. Profits tell us something about how we value the outputs of a firm relative to its inputs. Because environmental policy will tend to change prices and profits, we need to be able to interpret those price changes in terms of the utility, or welfare, effects, to understand the costs of a policy, and to compare these costs to the extra utility gained by the environmental improvement.

1. Firms maximize profits.

This is a standard behavioural assumption about firms, and it generates a number of helpful corollaries. Suppose output y is a function of labour L and capital K, and sells for price p. The wage rate on labour is w and the rental rate on capital is r. Then profits are:

$$\pi(w,r,p) = \arg\max\{pF(L,K) - wL - rK\}$$

where the term 'arg max' means the value of the expression in braces when L and K are chosen optimally. The first-order conditions from the firm's optimization problem yield the familiar rule that the firm chooses labour and capital such that the value-marginal product of each equals its variable cost:

$$pF_L = w$$

$$pF_K = r.$$

Thus we have

1a: Factors are hired until their respective value marginal products just equal the variable costs.

An alternate way of expressing the firm's problem is to maximize the difference between total revenue py and the production costs, as defined by a cost function $c(w,r,y)$. That is,

$$\pi(w,r,p) = \arg\max\{py - c(w,r,y)\}$$

Here the firm chooses the optimum output level by setting price equal to marginal cost:

$$p = c_y$$

Thus we have

1b: Output is produced up to the point where marginal cost just equals price.

Economic profits, or rents, include a charge for the opportunity cost of capital. If, after making such an adjustment, the firm is still earning profits, this will attract entry by other firms into that market, driving down the price and raising input costs until the economic profits have gone to zero. Alternatively, if economic losses are incurred, firms will exit until the output price rises and input costs fall sufficiently to bring economic profits to zero. Thus:

2. *In a competitive equilibrium, economic profits are zero.*

This always holds true if firms have a constant returns to scale technology. It is not true if technology is everywhere decreasing returns or increasing returns. But if it has a region of initially increasing returns which gives way to a region of decreasing returns, an intermediate point will exhibit locally constant returns, which will coincide with the minimum average costs; and at that point the firm will have zero economic profits in the long run.

3. *Consumers maximize utility.*

This behavioural assumption yields a number of important points regarding the social value of consumption and the meaning of prices. If utility is described by a function $U(x_1, ..., x_n)$ defined over n goods, each with a price p_i, and if consumer income is M, the consumer maximizes utility subject to his or her budget constraint, which is written:

$$\max_{\mathbf{x}} U(x_1, ..., x_n) \text{ subject to } \mathbf{p} \cdot \mathbf{x} \le M$$

where characters in bold face are vectors. This yields the familiar first-order conditions:

$$\frac{\partial U}{\partial x_i} = \lambda p_i \tag{2.1}$$

where λ is a Lagrange multiplier. (2.1) can be re-written:

$$\frac{\partial U}{\partial x_i} \bigg/ p_i = \lambda$$

which implies

> 3a: *The marginal utility of the last dollar spent on each good is equal across all goods.*

Alternatively we can write (2.1) as

$$\frac{\partial U}{\partial x_i} \bigg/ \frac{\partial U}{\partial x_j} = p_i / p_j$$

which implies

> 3b: *Price ratios indicate ratios of marginal values of consumption to consumers.*

Economic theory tells us that we can normalize one price. That is, we can set it equal to 1 by making it the 'currency' or numeraire good. We can also normalize the marginal utility of that good to equal 1. That lets us assert:

> 3c: *The price of a good in a competitive market indicates the marginal social benefit of consumption of that good relative to the numeraire.*

Therefore

> 3d: *A rise in price (in numeraire units) indicates a rise in the marginal social value of that good, and vice versa.*

And

> 3e: *When a firm earns economic profits, the marginal social value of the production of the good exceeds the marginal social value of the resources and inputs used in its production.*

From 3e, an increase in economic profits in one sector indicates that increased production of that good would be socially beneficial at the margin, and vice versa. When all firms earn zero economic profits, the market price of each good is that which equates the marginal social value of consumption to the marginal cost of production. Thus we have

> 4. *In a competitive market, the socially optimal amount of each good is produced, and the socially optimal amount of each factor is employed.*

Figure 2.1 Pareto-optimal and sub-optimal allocations in a two-person economy.

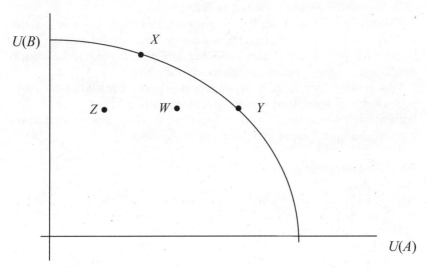

This leads directly to the First Theorem of Welfare Economics:

5. A competitive equilibrium is Pareto optimal.

In other words, starting from a competitive equilibrium, we cannot make any one person better off without making at least one other person worse off. Equivalent terminology is: no 'Pareto improvement' is possible. Furthermore:

6. A competitive equilibrium is efficient.

In other words, output of one good cannot be increased without decreasing the production of another good.

We can illustrate these postulates through the use of a utility possibility frontier, as shown in Figure 2.1. It shows the possible distributions of utility between persons in a two-person competitive economy.
Start at point Z. This is neither Pareto optimal nor efficient. The move from Z to W makes person A better off and person B no worse off. A move from Z to X makes both better off. So both of these moves are Pareto improving, that is, at least one person is made better off and

no one is made worse off. At point W, a Pareto improvement is still possible by (say) moving to Y. The move from W to X is not a Pareto improvement, because person A is made worse off.

Points X and Y are both Pareto optimal. The move from either one to the other improves welfare for one but reduces it for the other. From point X it is impossible to move in either direction without reducing the welfare of another person, and similarly for point Y.

This analysis says nothing about whether point X would be 'socially' preferred to point Y. If person B is averse to inequality it is possible that both may prefer outcome Y to X. Later in this chapter we will discuss the weighting of inequality when ranking policies.

2.3 Pollution Damages in Utility Terms

At this point we make an important assumption: *The damages due to pollution can be measured in monetary terms.* There are some respects in which this statement is not controversial. Contaminated land must be cleaned up, which is costly. Air and water pollution may necessitate expenditures on averting damages (e.g., by buying bottled water and using ventilation equipment) or avoiding damages, by moving away from a polluted area. But we are actually making a stronger point here, by arguing that people place a specific dollar value on changes to environmental quality. Some people place a large intangible value on the idea of unspoiled nature, and they might view pollution of the natural environment as intrinsically, or morally, wrong. Placing a dollar value on some aspect of the environment assumes that people would accept the money in lieu of the lost environmental quality. This does not sit easily with some students of environmental policy.

On the other hand, if the damages really matter, they must matter to people, and if something really matters to people, that means they will be willing, in principle, to pay for it (i.e., in this case, to prevent the environmental damage).

So we will make use of the convention that all costs and benefits can be translated into commensurable monetary terms. We will also assume that the damage from each additional unit of pollution emissions is either constant or rising. Figure 2.2 illustrates this using a marginal damages (MD) curve. As we increase emissions along the e axis, each unit of new pollution does more and more additional harm.

While much of the analysis in environmental economics can be followed based on the simple intuition of an upward-sloping MD curve,

Figure 2.2 Marginal damages.

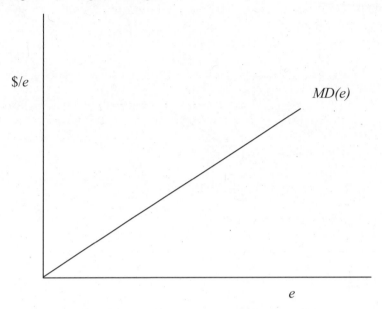

some important extensions to the theory require understanding exactly how pollution enters into the model of household welfare. To derive this will require some mathematics. Represent the (aggregate) consumer's preferences by a utility function $U(x,e)$ where x is a vector of consumption goods and e is the level of emissions. This is just like the usual consumer utility function except for the term e, which the consumer has to take as given, since it is an externality. The consumer faces a price vector p for consumption good vector x, and has income m. Solving the utility maximization problem yields continuous demand functions $x^*(p,e,m)$, which are defined implicitly by

$$U_x(x^*,e) - \lambda p = 0 \qquad\qquad (2.2)$$

where λ is the Lagrange multiplier. Note that pollution level e is an argument in the demand functions x^*.

The optimal consumption bundle can also be represented using the expenditure function. In this case we ask how much a consumer must spend in order to achieve utility level u when prices are at the level p. Intuitively we understand that consumers must spend more when

Figure 2.3 The expenditure function and the value of total damages (TD).

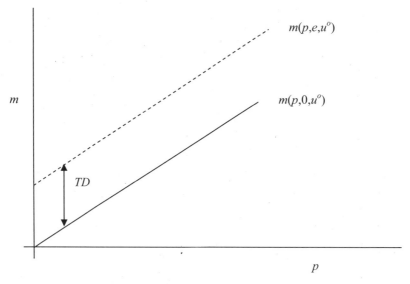

prices are higher, if they are going to get the same utility level as before. The idea is summarized as an expenditure function

$$m(p,e,u) = h$$

which says that the household must spend h dollars to get utility level u when prices are at level p and pollution is at level e. Figure 2.3 shows two linear expenditure functions (one with and one without an externality term) increasing in prices p.

Denote by u^o the household's optimized utility in the absence of any pollution, that is, when $e = 0$. Denote the household's expenditure function as $m(p,e,u^o) = h$, showing the minimum amount h the household must spend to achieve utility u^o, given prices p and pollution level e. The Total Damages function TD is defined by:

$$m(p,e,u^o) = m(p,0,u^o) + TD(p,e). \qquad (2.3)$$

This shows the amount the household would need to receive to be as well off in the presence of pollution e (assuming optimal choices on x)

as it would have been in the absence of pollution (at $e = 0$). Note that we are defining total damages as a function of e.

Rearrange (2.3) to get

$$TD(p,e,u^o) = m(p,e,u^o) - m_o \tag{2.4}$$

where $m_o \equiv m(p,0,u^o)$, which is a constant. The difference in required spending caused by the presence of emissions is illustrated in Figure 2.3. This is what we mean by total damages. Marginal damages MD are defined as the derivative of total emissions (suppressing unnecessary arguments):

$$MD(p,e,u^o) = \frac{\partial TD}{\partial e} = m_e. \tag{2.5}$$

MD is continuous with respect to e, by construction. Because MD is the first derivative of TD, TD is the integral of MD, which means that total damages can be represented as the area under the MD curve in Figure 2.2.

Suppose we compare two emission levels $e_2 > e_1$. Since emissions are a 'bad' as opposed to a 'good,' it must be the case that

$$m(p,e_2,u^o) \geq m(p,e_1,u^o).$$

Then if we express the differences using Δ,

$$MD = \frac{\Delta m}{\Delta e} \geq 0;$$

that is, marginal damages are positive or flat. Only in unusual cases could they be downward-sloping. We will usually draw them as upward-sloping, as in Figure 2.2.

2.4 Non-Market Valuation of Environmental Change

Equation (2.4) defines what we are trying to measure when we talk about the damages resulting from pollution. But how do we actually measure it in practice? The problem for empirical work is that while people may subjectively value environmental improvement, there is at best an incomplete market for it, so prices are not revealed anywhere. People can take care of their own property, or take measures they deem privately desirable (such as walking rather than driving), to show their preferences. But at the larger scale, air quality is a collective, or public, good, as are species conservation, water quality, and so forth. With no market for provision of these things, observable prices do not emerge. This creates a problem for comparing costs and benefits, because the expenditures needed for environmental protection measures can be observed and measured, but (most of) the benefits cannot.

To solve this problem, economists have explored ways of either inferring environmental values through market data or creating artificial markets through survey methods. Using market data to value changes related to local environments is called *hedonic* valuation. Using surveys to create artificial markets is called *contingent* valuation. The U.S. Department of Agriculture has an on-line resource at http://www.ecosystemvaluation.org that explains both hedonic valuation and contingent valuation methods. Hedonic valuation considers how the value of a marketed good changes as a result of a change in a non-marketed, complementary local attribute. This type of valuation is appropriate for measuring changes in environmental quality for amenities that people use or experience regularly. For instance, if the air quality in a city or neighbourhood improves, this will make the area a more attractive place to live, and will raise local property values. Property values can rise or fall for many reasons, including changes in crime rates, local economic conditions, and local environmental quality.

Contingent valuation (CV) at its simplest involves surveying people about how much they would be willing to pay in exchange for a specified improvement to air quality, land preservation, water quality, and so forth. A CV survey might ask homeowners how much they would pay to ensure an ecologically sensitive tract of wilderness in Alaska is preserved. The average might turn out to be something like $9.71. Multiplied by the U.S. population this would be about 3 billion dollars. But it might only make sense to multiply by the adult population, or by the number of households, depending on how the survey is defined.

The question of how many people to multiply the mean by is only one of the uncertainties. Another one concerns how to frame the bidding. Respondents might be presented with an escalating list of dollar values and asked to indicate what they would be willing to accept in compensation for the loss of the amenity, or they might be presented with a declining list of numbers and asked what is the most they would be willing to pay to preserve the amenity. These questions will not necessarily yield the same result. Or respondents might be presented with a single value and asked to indicate whether they would be willing to support a referendum that added this amount to their tax bill. By presenting different amounts to different people the CV survey could trace out a demand curve.

Another uncertainty concerns how to get access to respondents. One technique involves face-to-face interviews, but it is expensive. Telephone interviews are cheaper, but do not allow the interviewer to present much information about the issue before soliciting bids. Another inexpensive method is to intercept people 'on the street' or at a shopping mall. But this so-called convenience sampling makes it difficult to design a survey that is representative of the larger society.

The idea of CV surveys goes back to the 1940s, but became a topic of significant professional interest following the wreck of the *Exxon Valdez* in Prince William Sound, Alaska, in 1989. The *Valdez* spilled 11 million gallons of crude oil into the ocean and onto the shores. The U.S. and Alaska governments took Exxon to court, arguing that the dollar value of the damages included not only the cleanup costs, but also the lost *existence* value. The term 'existence value' refers to the fact that people may be willing to pay to protect an area of wilderness even if they never plan to visit or use it: they value its existence, either for its own sake or to preserve the option for future generations to use it. There is no market for existence values, and therefore they need to be estimated. Exxon vigorously opposed the use of CV surveys, arguing that the resulting numbers were meaningless because the underlying technique was not capable of accuracy. One of their arguments concerned the phenomenon of 'scoping' bias. A survey to find out how much people would pay to preserve a single lake will sometimes yield an estimate almost equal to what they would pay to preserve ten lakes. This indicates that the respondent is not really bidding on that particular lake, but on the general idea of conservation. As a result, CV surveys as a group might be overestimating public willingness to pay for environmental protection because if the results were added up there would be a lot of double counting.

Eventually the court upheld assessing awards based on existence values. In the aftermath of the *Exxon Valdez* spill, the U.S. National Oceanic and Atmospheric Administration (NOAA) was directed to write a set of guidelines for damage assessment. NOAA soon found itself flooded with strong opinions on the merits or flaws of CV surveying, and convened a panel of economists, led by Nobel prize-winners Kenneth Arrow and Robert Solow, to advise them on whether CV surveys were reliable enough to yield meaningful existence value esti-mates.

The NOAA panel largely concurred with the critics, arguing that CV survey accuracy was easily undermined by poor research design. How-ever, they did argue that under some specific circumstances, CV esti-mates could be considered reliable enough for assessing award values. Among other recommendations, they stated that respondents should be interviewed face-to-face, given detailed information about the pro-posed change as well as substitutes that may be available, and they should vote in a Yes/No referendum-style format, rather than picking a number from a list. The panel also recommended that CV surveys be used to elicit information about willingness to pay for potential future changes, not willingness to accept compensation for changes that have already taken place, and respondents should be reminded that such payments would reduce the amount available to spend elsewhere. The panel made specific recommendations about survey design to include questions that would check for scoping bias errors.

The release of the NOAA Expert Panel report helped diminish some of the controversies. However, some practitioners have argued that to follow the panel guidelines every time would be prohibitively ex-pensive, while some critics have expressed concern that the procedure would still be meaningless even if it followed the NOAA guidelines.

A symposium in the *Journal of Economic Perspectives* in the Fall 1994 is-sue spelled out the conflicting arguments. Hanemann (1994) presented the case for proceeding with carefully designed CV surveys, while Dia-mond and Hausman (1994) presented the case against any use of CV methods. Portney (1994), who was one of the NOAA Panel members, wrote a survey of the issue up to that time and provided some thoughts on the continuing debate.

Portney makes an interesting additional observation about existence values. Some supporters of strong action on the environment have em-braced the idea of existence values with the view that it might help inflate the benefits associated with environmental policies. But Port-ney points out that the concept could just as easily be employed on the other side. Although it is easy to suppose that someone might be will-ing to pay to preserve a forest in another area of the country even if he never plans to visit it, he might also be willing to pay to help keep a sawmill open in a town he never plans to visit, so its employees could keep their jobs. We can imagine a survey asking about peoples' willing-ness to pay to ensure the survival of a small town in an area dependent on the forest sector. While such a survey has not been undertaken, the theory justifying adding CV-estimated existence values to the estimated benefits of conservation would equally justify adding CV-estimated existence values to the estimated costs of conservation.

In the time since the release of the NOAA panel report there have been ongoing efforts to improve CV methods. One issue concerns the best way to elicit bids from respondents. Because people are conjecturing hypothetical valuations for amenities that they do not know much about (or care much about), there is a concern that the value elicited will depend to some extent on the way the question is asked, and that the valuations may be very uncertain even in the minds of the respondents. Surveys in which respondents are asked a sequence of valuation questions may help them 'discover' their own preferences better. Different referendum formats have been proposed, such as asking respondents whether their bid falls within a range, rather than exceeding a specific level, and asking people to indicate how certain they are of their bids (see Batemen et al. 2008). MacMillan and Hanley (2003) review some concerns about standard CV interview methods and propose a method akin to focus groups, in which much smaller samples of respondents (6–10) undergo two lengthy interviews a week apart. This proposal reflects the fact that although brief interviews can be conducted with large samples, they may yield unreliable results. Long, repeated interviews can yield more reliable valuations, but the cost per respondent is much larger, so samples must be small.

2.5 Aggregating Environmental Values

Once we have obtained estimates of the marginal damages of pollution we need to compare them to the costs of reducing pollution. Starting in the next chapter we will derive the appropriate definition of the marginal costs of reducing pollution. But before that we should look at an aspect of environmental valuation that can be as important as defining and measuring marginal damages: aggregation of measures into a single number.

The benefits of reducing pollution might not appear all at once: they may be spread out over time, and therefore we need to discount the future ones and add them up. In addition, these benefits accrue to people who are separated by income and other socioeconomic stratifications, and these socioeconomic difference must be taken into account when adding up marginal benefits. Finally, future outcomes are inherently uncertain, and the element of risk needs to be considered. In the next few sections we will explore some aggregation concepts from cost-benefit analysis that deal with these challenges.

2.6 Discounting Environmental Damages over Time

Suppose a project costs $9.00 and yields a stream of benefits equal to $1 per year for 10 years. Is it a good investment?
  A naive answer would be:

Benefit = 1+1+ --- +1 = 10.

  Cost = 9.00.

Because the benefit exceeds the cost, the project is therefore a good investment.
  But this ignores the opportunity cost of money over time. Denote the current interest rate as i. Suppose it is 10 per cent per annum. The $9 could buy an annuity which pays some amount Z each year for 10 years. If Z exceeds $1, then the proposed project would no longer be favoured. How do we calculate Z?

2.6.1 Annuities

Consider an annuity with a present value of A, which pays $1 for each of n years. The current interest rate is i. Denote $V = 1/(1+i)$, that is, the value of $1 discounted one year. Then V^2 is the value of $1 discounted 2 years, V^3 is the value of $1 discounted 3 years, etc. Note also that

$$1 - V = i/(1+i) = iV. \tag{2.6}$$

By definition,

$$A = V + V^2 + \cdots + V^n$$

and also

$$AV = V^2 + V^3 + \cdots + V^{n+1}..$$

Therefore

$A - AV = V - V^{n+1}$.

Using (2.6) this rearranges to

$$A = \frac{1-(1+i)^{-n}}{i}.$$ (2.7)

This defines the present discounted value (PDV) of an annuity paying $1 per year for n years at interest rate i per year. Suppose the annuity pays $2 per year: this is the same as two annuities paying $1 each, so its value is 2A. If an annuity pays Z per year, its present value is ZA.

What is the DPV of an annuity paying $1 per annum (pa) for 10 years at $i = 0.1$? Equation (2.7) implies that $A = \$6.14$. Thus, we would be willing to pay $6.14 for such an annuity, *not* $9, once we take account of discounting. Or, alternatively, what would an annuity have to pay each year for 10 years to make its present value worth $9? In this case

$$9 = ZA = Z\frac{1-(1+0.1)^{-10}}{0.1} = 6.14Z$$

and thus $Z = 1.47$. The annuity would have to pay $1.47 per year to have a DPV of $9.00.

What if the interest rate rises to 11 per cent? It is easy to check that A would fall to $5.89. As the interest rate rises, we are willing to pay even less today for the same stream of future payoffs. Note what has happened: *the stream of payoffs is the same, but it is less valuable to us at the present*. Consequently, the choice of discount rate is of fundamental importance in establishing the present value of a stream of benefits. Whenever we are considering a project which requires a payment *now*, and yields a stream of benefits *later*, the choice of discount rate may mean the difference between deciding whether the project is worthwhile or not. The higher the discount rate, the less it is worth investing now to secure future benefits.

This consideration is especially important when the planning horizon is longer. For instance, an array of policies to reduce greenhouse gas emissions will involve considerable costs in the short term, and a stream of (possible) benefits over a period as long as several centuries. If we discount the future at 2 per cent per year, we might be willing to approve spending many billions of dollars today to reduce greenhouse gases. But if we discount the future at 7 per cent, the amount we could justify spending today would be substantially lower. A benefit of 1 billion dollars realized 200 years hence, discounted at 7 per cent, has a present value of only $1,328!

In fall 2006, the U.K. Treasury released a review of the economics of climate change by Sir Nicolas Stern and his team (Stern et al. 2006). This report came to the dramatic conclusion that the costs of global warming, discounted to the present, could reach as high as 20 per cent of world GDP. However, many critics noted that, in addition to using very speculative concepts of the potential costs of global warming 200 years and more into the future, Stern applied a very low sequence of discount rates. Byatt et al. (2006) ascertained that the discount rates used in Stern (which were not stated in the report itself) were 2.1 per cent for 100 years, 1.9 per cent for the next 100 years, and 1.4 per cent thereafter. By contrast, the standard discount rate used by the U.K. government for project evaluation is 3.5 per cent. A Technical Annex to the Stern Review, released after the original review's publication, showed that applying a 3.5 per cent discount rate would cause the estimated present value of damages to fall by nearly three-quarters (Byatt et. al 2008).

2.6.2 Discount Rates*

The question of the appropriate discount rate can be contentious. We will begin by deriving the standard formula, which turns out to be rather ambiguous in practice.

The standard model derives a discount rate that corresponds to the opportunity cost of investment. The opportunity cost of investment in a project is equal to the marginal cost of capital, which we take to be the return associated with the alternative use to which funds could be put.

A basic continuous time optimal growth model involves maximizing the integral of the sequence of future utility levels subject to a constraint on savings and consumption:

$$\max_{\{C_t\}} \quad W_0 = \int_0^\infty e^{-\delta t} U(C_t) dt \text{ subject to } \dot{K}_t = f(K_t) - C_t$$

where W_0 is present discounted welfare at time 0, δ is the pure rate of time preference, K_t is the stock of productive capital at time t, C_t is the consumption level at time t, f is the production function, and a dotted variable denotes its derivative with respect to time. Form the Hamiltonian function

$$H = e^{-\delta t} U(C_t) + \lambda(f(K_t) - C_t)$$

and convert to current-value form by multiplying through the inverse of the discount factor:

$$H = e^{\delta t} H = U(C_t) + \lambda(t)(f(K_t) - C_t)$$

where $\lambda(t) = \lambda e^{\delta t}$. From control theory we know that the solution must satisfy the following first-order conditions:

$$H_C = 0 \Rightarrow U' = \lambda(t) \tag{2.8a}$$

$$H_\lambda = \dot{K}_t \Rightarrow \dot{K}_t = f(K_t) - C_t \tag{2.8b}$$

$$-H_K = \dot{\lambda}(t) - \delta\lambda(t) \Rightarrow \dot{\lambda}(t) = \delta\lambda(t) - \lambda(t)f_K \tag{2.8c}$$

From (2.8a),

$$\dot{\lambda}(t) = U'' \dot{C}_t \tag{2.9}$$

where $U'' = dU'/dC_t$. Combine (2.8a,b) and (2.9) to get

$$U'' \dot{C}_t = \delta U' - U' r_t$$

where $r_t = f_K$, i.e. the marginal product of capital. This rearranges to

$$r_t = \delta + \eta \frac{\dot{C}_t}{C_t} \tag{2.10}$$

where $\eta = -\frac{dU'}{dC_t} \frac{C_t}{U'}$, that is, the elasticity of marginal utility, or the percentage change in marginal utility given a percentage change in consumption.

Equation (2.10) says that a discount rate consistent with an optimal growth path should consist of three components: the pure rate of time preference (δ) plus the product of the rate of growth in consumption and the decreasing utility of that consumption. If a utility function is chosen such that η is constant (for example, $U = \ln(C)$ or $U = C^\alpha$ where $0 < \alpha < 1$) then as long as consumption is growing, a positive discount rate is still appropriate even if the pure rate of time preference is zero.

There is a tradition in some strands of public economics, tracing back to the work of Frank Ramsay in the 1920s, that the pure rate of time preference should be assumed to be zero. In Ramsay's famous words, a positive discount rate arises merely from a 'defect of the imagination' and is morally indefensible. Even with a zero value for δ the discount rate would be positive because of the other terms. But it is not so easy to justify a zero discount rate. This would imply, among other things, that when he was writing in the 1920s, Ramsay himself was just as concerned about our present generation as he was about himself and his own generation. It is unrealistic to suppose that he was or should have been.

The main reason we assume a positive rate of time preference is that people are impatient over their own lifetimes, and one's interest in future generations inevitably declines, if for no other reason than that one's descendants are genetically less and less one's own kin. Impatience and empathetic decay lead us to prefer jam today to jam tomorrow. Suppose that the rate of time preference is 2 per cent. If utility is logarithmic ($U = \ln(C)$) then $\eta = 1$. If consumption is expected to grow by 2 per cent per year, (2.10) implies that the discount rate for project evaluation should be 4 per cent. Different values of these parameters can be tried out, leading to a range of possible discount rates. As explained above, a change in the discount rate can reverse the decision about investing in a project with a long payoff horizon, and we therefore need to acknowledge an unavoidable uncertainty associated with intertemporal policy evaluation. This was an important aspect to the debates that arose over the Stern Review (Stern et al. 2006). A number of authors (e.g., Nordhaus 2006, Byatt et al. 2006, and Weyant 2008) argued that Stern's support for aggressive emission control policies depended on the use of unusually low discount rates, as well as implausibly low estimates of the mitigation costs.

2.7 Adding Up Benefits across People with Unequal Incomes

Benefits accrue not only across time, but also across individuals within time. Consider Table 2.1, which shows hypothetical outcomes for two persons, X and Y, faced with a choice between two projects.

Note that each project is a Pareto improvement, because at least one person is better off, and no one is worse off. But which project is the better? Answering this question requires us to aggregate the benefits into a single measure. When we looked for an appropriate discount rate

Table 2.1
Hypothetical net benefits from
an environmental project.

	Net Benefits	
	X	Y
Project 1:	2	12
Project 2:	5	5

we could make use of an optimization that emerged from the efficient savings behaviour of a hypothetical, infinitely lived agent over time. But we have no such solution concept available when dealing with inequality among people. Instead we have to consider various ad hoc approaches.

We could simply take the arithmetic mean. Under this rule, a project is preferred if the average benefit is greater than the alternative. This is referred to as the 'utilitarian' rule. Because the average net benefit is higher for Project 1, this rule would identify it as the better of the two. But the utilitarian rule has the disadvantage that it is indifferent to the distribution, and it is easy to construct examples where it would rank one outcome above another, even though an observer would think the ranking is wrong on grounds of inequality.

There are many ways to add up net benefits across people. Using the utilitarian rule, for a projects whose net benefit vector is $\mathbf{b} = (b_1, b_2, ..., b_n)$, the aggregate net benefit B^U is defined as the simple mean:

$$B^U = \frac{1}{n}\sum b_i \tag{2.11}$$

and similarly for a project with net benefit vector $\mathbf{c}$. For two projects with net benefit vectors $\mathbf{c}$ and $\mathbf{b}$, the ranking rule is simply that $\mathbf{c}$ is preferred to $\mathbf{b}$ if its mean is higher. Using this approach, the first row of Table 2.1 is preferred.

The utilitarian rule can be extended in a number of useful ways, such as by adding weights to (2.11), to give more consideration to, say, low-income people. The simple utilitarian rule is indifferent to inequality: it would rank (5, 5), (10, 0), and (−100, 110) the same, and each would be preferred to, say, (5, 4).

An alternative ranking rule that places maximum weight on achieving equality is the 'Rawlsian' criterion. For a vector of net benefits **b** the Rawlsian aggregate B^R is defined as the smallest element in the vector **b**:

$$B^R = \min(\mathbf{b}).$$

The Rawlsian criterion is sometimes called a max-min criterion, because it tells us to pick the project that maximizes the gain of the one who gains the least. It is maximally averse to inequality, since if almost everyone gains from a project, but one person gets nothing, the Rawlsian rule would say that the project itself has no value. The Rawlsian rule would reverse the ranking in Table 2.1, preferring the second project, since $5 > 2$. Only if all parties are made better off does a project get a positive score. The Rawlsian rule would rank $(5, 5)$, $(10,0)$, and $(-100, 110)$ in that order, whereas the utilitarian rule is indifferent among them.

An intermediate approach is to use the Cobb-Douglas aggregator B^C:

$$B^C = \left(b_1 b_2 \cdots b_n\right)^{1/n}$$

which is the geometric mean. The Cobb-Douglas rule is somewhat averse to inequality: it will allow some people to become worse off as long as enough others get sufficiently better off. In Table 2.1, the aggregator takes the values $24^{.5}$ and $25^{.5}$, so Project 2 is preferred. However, this rule cannot rank projects where net benefits are negative.

If we add to the utilitarian criterion the extra proviso that we do not want anyone to be made worse off, we arrive at what is called the Pareto rule. Under the Pareto rule we would accept a policy that made someone worse off, as long as those who gain from the policy give up some of their gains to compensate the loser. The potential Pareto criterion states that a policy change is a gain to society if the winners can, in principle, compensate the losers and still be made better off, whether or not such compensation actually occurs.

A general form for social welfare aggregators is the 'Mean of Order r Function':

$$B^M = \left[\frac{1}{n}\left(b_1^r + b_2^r + \cdots + b_n^r\right)\right]^{1/r} \tag{2.12}$$

where in this case r denotes the power mean parameter, not the discount rate as in the last section.

If $r = 1$, (2.12) reduces to B^U. If r goes to minus infinity, (2.12) reduces to B^R, and if r goes to zero, (2.12) reduces to B^C. We refer to r as the 'inequality aversion parameter' because the lower it goes, the more averse to inequality we are.

We can now ask the analogous question to our earlier one about discounting: What value of r should we choose? As mentioned above, we have no equilibrium conditions here to provide normative guidance. In fact the situation is even worse than that. Arrow's Theorem, the foundational result in the field of social choice, states that no one rule can aggregate a vector of social preferences into a single ranking that preserves the coherence of the underlying individual preferences. (More precise definitions can be obtained in advanced microeconomics textbooks, such as Kreps 1990.) Add to that the observation that there is no one rule for adjusting for inequality, because we do not know how much 'adjustment' is required. It is intuitively plausible that we might accept a lower average net benefit in exchange for a reduced dispersion, but there are no hard and fast rules for weighing these considerations. Equity and efficiency may not coincide in any one project.

One option would be to see what range of values of r would support a certain ranking. We might find that a ranking is unchanged from $r = 1$ all the way to $r = -1000$, in which case the choice has a certain robustness to it, even though the ranking might change as the magnitude of r becomes very large.

2.8 Uncertainty, Risk, and Risk-Aversion*

Benefits and costs accrue over time, over persons, and over *states of the world*. That is, the benefits and costs may be uncertain, and may depend on characteristics of the future of which we only have probabilistic information today. For example, suppose we choose to defer logging a forest in order to enjoy its scenic value for a while longer. There is a risk that the forest will burn down, in which case we would only be able to undertake limited salvage logging, which would yield less than the cost of the land. Suppose the net benefit from current enjoyment of the scenery and future timber sales is 100, as long as the forest does not burn down; whereas the net benefit from logging if the forest does burn down is −50. In that case, to assess the expected value we need to weigh the outcomes according to their respective probabilities. If the probability that the forest will burn down is 1 per cent, or 0.01, the net expected benefit from deferred logging is $0.99 \times 100 - 0.01 \times 50 = 98.5$.

The use of expected value – that is, the weighted average using probabilities for weights – is appropriate for aggregating across uncertain states of the world as long as we have a neutral view about risk. If the payoff is random, the expected value is the central tendency of the payoffs we would expect to receive over repeated instances of the project. Risk, however, refers to the range of final outcomes that cannot be offset by subsequent repetitions of the game. If the probability of each of two states is identical, the expected value of the state-contingent payoffs $V = (-50, 150)$ and $W = (50, 50)$ is the same, but the first project is riskier because we might experience an unrecoverable loss of 50. If we are nevertheless indifferent between the two games we are said to be *risk neutral*. If we prefer W to V we are said to be risk averse.

Risk aversion can be characterized as follows. Suppose utility is defined over the payoffs by the function U. We have a project that yields a payoff x with some probability p, and a payoff y with probability $(1 - p)$. Risk aversion means that we strictly prefer the expected outcome, delivered with certainty, to the possibility of the lower and higher outcomes:

$$U(px + (1-p)y) > pU(x) + (1-p)U(y). \tag{2.13}$$

(2.13) is the definition of a concave function. So, if the utility function for the net benefits of a project is concave over the range of the distribution of benefits, it implies risk-averse valuation.

Risk aversion means that a simple expected value does not adequately measure the welfare associated with a risky project. For proper cost-benefit analysis we need to deduct the *risk premium*. The simplest idea of a risk premium is the amount we would be willing to pay to guarantee a payoff with equivalent expected utility to the original project. Define an amount z such that

$$U(z) = pU(x) + (1-p)U(y). \tag{2.14}$$

Then the risk premium R is defined by

$$R = px + (1-p)y - z$$

Figure 2.4 Risk aversion and the risk premium.

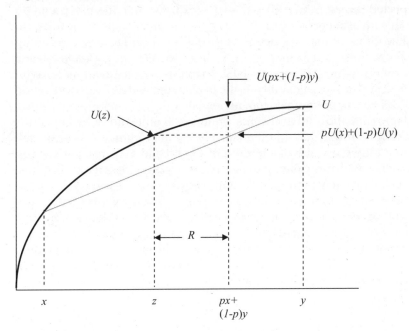

This is illustrated diagrammatically in Figure 2.4. The risk inherent in the situation is that payoff x might occur with probability p, or payoff y with probability $(1 - p)$. The expected payoff is $px+(1-p)y$. But the utility of that amount, $U(px+(1-p)y)$, would overstate the value of the project, because we do not get to run many repetitions of it. The expected utility of the payoffs is $pU(x)+(1-p)U(y)$, which equals $U(z)$ by definition. This is less than the utility of the expected payoff, $U(px+(1-p)y)$. In other words, the utility of having the expected payoff, with certainty, is greater than the expected utility of the uncertain payoffs. Consequently we would be willing to pay an amount up to R for a guarantee of the outcome z, rather than the chance of x or y. R – the risk premium – represents the value of certainty, which takes the form of a willingness to give up the possibility of greater gains at outcome y in exchange for the guarantee of not facing the lower outcome at x. Failure to deduct the risk premium in this case would cause us to overstate the value of the set of state-contingent outcomes.

We can illustrate this with a numerical outcome as follows. Suppose the utility function is $U(x) = \sqrt{x}$. An investment has a 30 per cent chance of paying of paying $10 and a 70 per cent chance of paying $100. The expected payoff is $0.3 \times 10 + 0.7 \times 100 = \$73$. What is the risk premium on this investment?

The utility of the expected payoff is $\sqrt{73} = 8.54$. The expected utility of the payoffs is $0.3 \times \sqrt{10} + 0.7 \times \sqrt{100} = 7.95$. We can compute z using $\sqrt{z} = 7.95$, which gives us $z = 63.2$. So in this case, a guaranteed payoff of 63.2 yields the same utility as the investment with its expected payoff of 73. The risk premium is just under $10.

Figure 2.4 shows that the risk premium R will tend to be larger, the more curvature U has. Mathematically, the curvature of U is measured as the absolute value of the ratio of the second and first derivatives: $-U'' / U'$, which is called the measure of absolute risk aversion. When investments carry random risks with known variance we can characterize the risk premium as follows. Suppose w is a risky asset with mean payoff of zero and a payoff variance of σ^2. We have a choice between a project with payoff x and another project with payoff $x + w$. If the utility function is U, what is the risk premium for the latter project that would give it an expected utility value equivalent to $U(x)$? The answer is given by the Arrow-Pratt risk premium equation:

$$\pi = -\frac{U''}{U'}\frac{\sigma^2}{2}.$$

Then $E[U(x + w + \pi)] \approx U(x)$.

There are advanced tools of financial calculus available to compute risk premiums for more complex payoff and uncertainty structures.

2.9 Non-linearity and Non-commutativity

We have discussed three axes along which benefits need to be aggregated: time (discounting), income groups (inequality), and uncertain states of the world (risk). The methods presented allow us to take a group of numbers and replace them with a single number. Now we can ask in what order the aggregations should occur. The answer is that there is no prescribed order. For instance, it is mathematically feasible to compute the discounted values of utilities, or the utility of discounted values. But because the operations may be non-linear, the order in which they are done may make a difference to the results.

Table 2.2 presents some benefit and cost information for a hypothetical project. There are two income classes: rich and poor. There are also two possible states of the world over time: the up state and the down

Table 2.2

Hypothetical cost-benefit example.

COSTS	Rich		Poor	
Year	up	down	up	down
2011	5	120	8	75
2020	3	140	6	77
2030	12	350	4	90
2040	15	500	3	93
BENEFITS	Rich		Poor	
Year	up	down	up	down
2011	5	33	1	180
2020	7	45	2	250
2030	11	120	20	270
2040	14	360	20	290

state. There are 4 time periods of interest: 2010, 2020, 2030, and 2040. We assume an interest rate of 4 per cent and an inequality aversion parameter for equation (12.7) of -10. We assume that the probability of the up state is 0.9. The utility function is $U = \ln(x)$. Given all this information, are the net benefits of the project positive or negative?

In order to answer the question we need to reduce the contents of Table 2.2 to a single benefits measure and a single costs measure. We will look at three different answers.

Discounting first: If we discount over time, then aggregate over income classes, and then compute the risk-adjusted expected utility value of costs and benefits, the net gain is 0.18 units.

Averaging over income groups first: If we aggregate over income classes first, then aggregate over states of the world and then discount over time we get a net loss of 0.84 units.

Adjust for risk first: Finally, if we compute the risk-adjusted utility, then discount over time, then aggregate over income groups, we get a net loss of 0.86 units.

Which of these is the correct answer? Does the project have a positive net value? Unfortunately the answer is that they are all equally correct, so we cannot say if the project has a positive net value. There is no rule that says we have to discount over time before doing the other calculations. Because the inequality and risk-adjustment operations are non-linear, the order in which they are done matters.

Review Questions

1. One way of measuring the damages resulting from, say, air pollution, is to calculate the total dollar amount that needs to be spent on cleanup in order to restore the victim's property to the condition it was in prior to the emissions. Explain why this would not be a suitable measure of the welfare cost of emissions.

2. Suppose a utility function is $U(x_1, x_2, e) = x_1^\alpha x_2^\beta - e^2$, where x_1, x_2 are consumer goods with corresponding prices p_1, p_2, $\alpha + \beta = 1$ and e is pollution emissions. Total income is denoted M. Derive the Total and Marginal Damage functions.

Answer

Because the utility function is Cobb-Douglas, the demand curves are of the form

$$x_1 = \alpha M / p_1; \ x_2 = \beta M / p_2.$$

Substituting these into the utility function yields the indirect utility function

$$V(p, M) = \frac{\theta M}{p_1^\alpha p_2^\beta} - e^2$$

where $\theta \equiv \alpha^\alpha \beta^\beta$. Solve this for income to get the expenditure function (changing U for V):

$$M(p, e, U) = (U + e^2) \frac{p_1^\alpha p_2^\beta}{\theta}.$$

Equation (2.4) implies

$$TD(e) = \frac{p_1^\alpha p_2^\beta}{\theta} e^2$$

and

$$MD(e) = \frac{2p_1^{\alpha} p_2^{\beta}}{\theta} e.$$

3. If the pure rate of time preference is zero, does that imply that the discount rate for project evaluation should also be zero?
4. What is the present value of a stream of payments of $100 per year for 15 years, if the interest rate is 4 per cent over the 15-year span?
5. Why is the elasticity of marginal utility in the equation for the discount rate (12.5)? Explain the role that it plays in revaluing money over time.
6. Consider two simple utility functions: $U = \ln(x)$ and $U = \sqrt{x}$. For a given value of x, which one embodies a higher rate of risk aversion? What does that imply about the different risk premiums associated with each one?
7. Give an example of conditions under which the three aggregations involved in benefit-cost analysis would yield identical results regardless of the order in which they are performed.
8. If we use a 4 per cent discount rate, we can only consider a million dollars' worth of damages 100 years from now as being worth $19,800 to us at present. Does this mean we are discriminating against future generations when we use discounting? Or would we be giving future generations an unfair advantage if we do not discount? Explain your reasoning.
9. Explain what is meant by the 'maximin' criterion for deciding among alternative social outcomes.
10. Looking at the example in Section 2.9, do you think one of the orders of operations makes more sense than others?

References and Extra Reading

Bateman, Ian J., Diane Burgess, W. George Hutchinson, and David I. Matthews (2008). 'Learning Design Contingent Valuation (LDCV): NOAA guidelines, preference learning and coherent arbitrariness' *Journal of Environmental Economics and Management* 55(2): 127–141.

Berck, Peter, and Knut Sydsaeter (1993). *Economists' Mathematical Manual.* 2nd ed. Berlin: Springer-Verlag.

Byatt, Ian Ian Castles, Indur M. Goklany, David Henderson, Nigel Lawson, Ross McKitrick, Julian Morris, Alan Peacock, Colin Robinson, and Robert

Skidelsky (2006). 'The Stern Review: A Dual Critique.' *World Economics* 7(4): 1–68.

Cornes, Richard (1992). *Duality and Modern Economics*. Cambridge: Cambridge University Press.

Deaton, Angus, and John Muellbauer (1980). *Economics and Consumer Behaviour* Cambridge: Cambridge University Press.

Diamond, Peter A., and Jerry A. Hausman (1994). 'Contingent Valuation: Is Some Number Better Than No Number?' *Journal of Economic Perspectives* 8(4): 45–64.

Hanemann, W. Michael (1994). 'Valuing the Environment Through Contingent Valuation.' *Journal of Economic Perspectives* 8(4): 19–43.

Kreps, David M. (1990). *A Course in Microeconomic Theory* Princeton: Princeton University Press.

Macmillan, Douglas, and Nick Hanley (2003). 'New Approaches to Data Collection in Contingent Valuation.' *AERE Newsletter* 23(12): 23–6.

Nordhaus, William D. (2006). 'The Stern Review on the Economics of Climate Change.' NBER Discussion paper W12741, December.

Portney, Paul R. (1994). 'The Contingent Valuation Debate: Why Economists Should Care.' *Journal of Economic Perspectives* 8(4): 3–17.

Stern, N., S. Peters, V. Bakhshi, A. Bowen, C. Cameron, S. Catovsky, D. Crane, S. Cruickshank, S. Dietz, N. Edmonson, S.-L. Garbett, L. Hamid, G. Hoffman, D. Ingram, B. Jones, N. Patmore, H. Radcliffe, R. Sathiyarajah, M. Stock, C. Taylor, T. Vernon, H. Wanjie, and D. Zenghelis (2006). *Stern Review: The Economics of Climate Change*, HM Treasury, London.

Weyant, John P. (2008). 'A Critique of the *Stern Review*'s Mitigation Cost Analyses and Integrated Assessment.' *Review of Environmental Economics and Policy* 2(1): 77–93.

3 The Value of Emissions and the Costs of Abatement

3.1 The Optimal Output-Abatement Choice

In order to develop the tools for policy analysis we need to develop a model of why firms generate pollution and how they would respond to emission rules. In this section we will develop a simple but powerful model that will be the basis for subsequent analysis throughout the book. Much of our use of the model will be graphical, but the derivation will also be presented mathematically, to explain why the graphs take the shape they do.

Suppose that a firm or industry produces output y using inputs that cost w, and it engages in non-negative levels of pollution abatement a. Output sells for p per unit. Emissions e are generated based on the level of output and abatement. Thus, profits can be written

$$\pi(p, y, w, a) = py - c(w, y, a) \tag{3.1}$$

and emissions can be expressed as a function

$$e = e(y, a). \tag{3.2}$$

Here 'profits' denote value added by the firm, or the excess of the value of what is produced over the cost of its production after inputs, energy, and variable factors have been paid their opportunity costs. As such it indicates the social value of the use of capital for the productive activity yielding the emissions.

We will assume that emissions are increasing in output at an increasing rate, and emissions are decreasing in abatement activity at a dimin-

Figure 3.1 Iso-emissions line, showing combinations of output y and abatement a that yield emissions e.

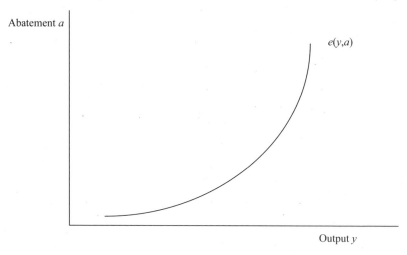

Abatement a

$e(y,a)$

Output y

ishing rate. In mathematical terms we write this as: $e_y > 0, e_{yy} > 0, e_a < 0,$ and $e_{aa} > 0$. Graphically, we can represent this using an iso-emissions line which shows the combinations of output and abatement that yield a constant emissions level. Figure 3.1 shows an example. You should be able to figure what would happen to emissions if you move up and to the left of the line, as opposed to down and to the right.

An iso-emissions line provides a graphical representation of an emissions constraint. Suppose the firm faces an emissions control policy which takes the form of an upper limit on emissions:

$$e(y,a) \le e_1 \tag{3.3}$$

Because the policy reduces pollution below what was observed in the unregulated case, we can treat the constraint as binding, that is, write (3.3) as an equality. To analyse the shape of (3.3) we take its total differential:

$$e_y dy + e_a da = de_1.$$

For a fixed target (i.e., $de_1 = 0$) this can be rearranged to yield the iso-emission line in (y, a) space with the (positive) slope

$$\frac{\partial a}{\partial y} = \frac{-e_y}{e_a} > 0 \tag{3.4}$$

That is, the locus of combinations of output and abatement which yield the same emissions level is an upward sloping line when abatement is graphed against output, as in Figure 3.1. If we assume that

$$e_{ay} > e_a e_{yy} / e_y ,$$

then

$$\frac{\partial^2 a}{\partial y^2} = \frac{-e_a e_{yy} + e_y e_{ay}}{e_a^2} > 0.$$

So the line is convex upwards, that is, increasing at an increasing rate. For a given level of output, emissions rise as abatement falls, and for a given level of abatement, emissions rise as output rises, so movement to points below and to the right of the line indicates higher emissions.

On the cost side, assume that costs are rising in output at an increasing rate and costs are increasing in abatement activity, which we write as: $c_y > 0$, $c_{yy} > 0$ and $c_a \geq 0$. We will also impose a boundary condition that states that, at zero abatement, the first unit of abatement has zero marginal cost. This is not strictly necessary, but it will ensure interior solutions:

$$c_a(w, y, 0) = 0 \tag{3.5}$$

The firm will choose the pair (y, a) that maximizes profits. If there are no emission controls then the solution obeys $p = c_y$ and $c_a = 0$. Together these define the privately optimal combination of output and abatement in the absence of pollution regulation, which we denote $(y^*, 0)$. These yield the unregulated emissions level, which we denote as $\bar{e}$.

We can put the firm's profit function on the same axes we used in Figure 3.1, by drawing iso-profit lines. The shapes turn out to be semi-circles, as shown in Figure 3.2.

To work out the shape analytically, totally differentiate (3.1) and set $d\pi = 0$, which yields

$$d\pi(p, y, w, a) = p\partial y - c_y\partial y - c_a\partial a = 0$$

Figure 3.2 Iso-profit lines, showing combinations of output *y* and abatement *a* that yield the same profit level.

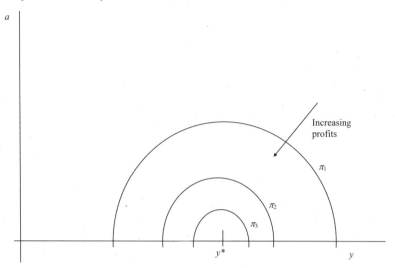

which can be rearranged to yield an expression for the slope at every point:

$$\frac{\partial a}{\partial y} = \frac{p - c_y}{c_a} \tag{3.6}$$

We are interested in graphing the lines that show constant profits ($d\pi = 0$) in the (y, a) axes. We can use (3.6) to figure out the slope along each line as follows.

For positive levels of abatement, that is, $a > 0$, note the following:

$y < y^* \Rightarrow \partial a / \partial y > 0$ (the line is upward sloping to the left of y^*);

$y = y^* \Rightarrow \partial a / \partial y = 0$ (the line is horizontal at y^*);

and $y > y^* \Rightarrow \partial a / \partial y < 0$ (the line is downward sloping to the right of y^*).

At $a = 0$,

$y <> y^* \Rightarrow \partial a / \partial y = \infty$ (the line is vertical)

Figure 3.3 Iso-profit and iso-emission lines with optimal tangency path.

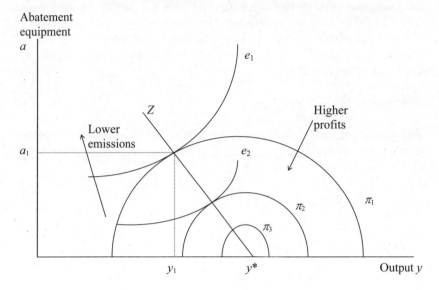

and $y = y^* \Rightarrow \partial a / \partial y = 0/0$ (we have converged to a point).

Thus, the iso-profit lines are semi-circles which cut the y-axis vertically and which converge concentrically to a single point at $(y^*, 0)$. A set of iso-profit lines is shown in Figure 3.2 (labelled π_1, π_2, and π_3). Because for a given output level increases in a decrease profits, the direction of increasing profits must be towards the centre, as shown.

Now we want to find the output-abatement pair that maximizes profits subject to the emission constraint (3.3). The firm will try to get to the best possible profit level subject to the constraint that it remains on the iso-emissions line. This will yield a tangency point between the two lines, and a tangency path if the emission constraint moves, as shown in Figure 3.3.

The firm wants to move onto the lowest possible iso-profit line, subject to the restriction that it must still be touching (or above) the required iso-emissions line. In Figure 3.3 the tangency is drawn for e_1 such that it occurs on π_1 and for e_2 such that it occurs on π_2. The corresponding optimal output and abatement levels are indicated for the e_1 case. Looking at the e_2 case, note that the higher iso-profit line π_1 satisfies the emissions constraint but does not maximize profits. The lower iso-profit line π_3 gives higher profits but does not satisfy the emissions constraint. The tangency point is the unique solution.

For some of the policy analysis to follow we need to work out an analytical representation of this constrained optimization. We set up the Lagrangian function

$$L = py - c(w, y, a) - \lambda \big(e(y, a) - e_1 \big)$$

and maximize with respect to y and a. The first-order conditions for the firm's problem are

$$p - c_y = \lambda e_y$$

and

$$-c_a = \lambda e_a.$$

Dividing the first by the second yields

$$\frac{p - c_y}{-c_a} = \frac{e_y}{e_a}. \tag{3.7}$$

Compare (3.7) with (3.4) and (3.6): the slope of the iso-profit line equals the slope of the iso-emissions line whenever firms are maximizing profits under the emissions constraint. If we shift the emissions constraint line back, equation (3.7) will define a locus of tangencies drawn as the line Zy^* in Figure 3.3.

Confronted with emissions constraint e_1, the firm responds not simply by installing abatement equipment, but by combining use of abatement equipment (a_1) with a reduction in output to level y_1. In trying to estimate the 'cost' to the firm of meeting the emission constraint it would be incorrect to simply add up the cost of the abatement equipment. The firm also bears a cost by changing its output level. The *actual* cost to the firm of meeting the emissions constraint is the loss in profits between π^* and π_2.

The importance of assumption (3.5) is that it ensures that the iso-profit lines cross the y-axis vertically, and therefore an upward-sloping emissions constraint will always be tangent to an iso-profit line at interior points in the (y, a) space, ruling out corner solutions. That is,

Figure 3.4 The marginal abatement cost function (MAC).

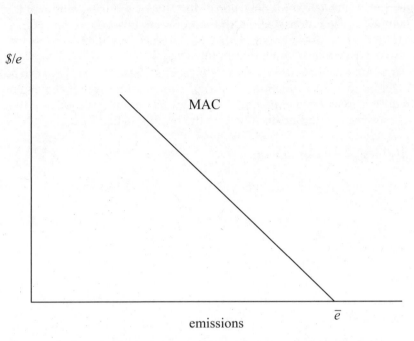

(3.7) can only be satisfied when $a > 0$: the firm will use combinations of output reduction and abatement equipment, rather than abatement equipment alone or output reductions alone, to respond to even very low levels of required emissions reductions. If $c_a > 0$ at $a = 0$, then (3.7) might not hold near the a axis. The firm might use output reductions alone to control emissions at first, and only use abatement equipment to handle large emission reductions.

3.2 The Marginal Abatement Cost Function

We can now derive the marginal abatement cost (MAC) function, a key tool in environmental economics. The intuition behind the MAC is straightforward. Figure 3.4 shows an example. The vertical axis shows dollars per unit of emissions and the horizontal axis shows emissions. The MAC equals zero at the unregulated emissions level ($\bar{e}$), indicating that the first unit of abatement costs nothing. (The reason is that when the firm is maximizing profits in the absence of pollution regulation, marginal profits from the last unit of output are zero, and the firm could achieve some emission reductions by reducing output at the margin). As emissions decline, the cost of each subsequent unit of emission reduction rises along the MAC line. Hence, the line is downward-sloping when read from left to right.

The formal derivation goes as follows. First, assume that $e(y, a)$ can be inverted to yield a function $a = a(y,e)$, showing the level of abatement required to achieve emissions e for a given output level y. Note that $a_y > 0$ and $a_e < 0$. Substituting into the profit function for a gives

$$\pi(p,y,w,a) = py - c(w,y,a(y,e))$$

and taking partial derivatives yields

$$\pi_y = p - c_y - c_a \frac{\partial a}{\partial y}$$

and

$$\pi_e = -c_a \frac{\partial a}{\partial e}.$$

The second equation is the partial derivative of profits with respect to emissions. The total derivative of π is $d\pi = \pi_y dy + \pi_e de$. This can be re-arranged to yield

$$\frac{d\pi}{de} = \pi_y \frac{dy}{de} - \pi_e.$$

Then substitute in the partial derivatives to get

$$\frac{d\pi}{de} = \left(p - c_y - c_a \frac{\partial a}{\partial y} \right) \frac{dy}{de} - c_a \frac{\partial a}{\partial e}.$$

Along the tangency locus (3.7) we have $(p - c_y) = -c_a e_y / e_a$. This plus (3.6) implies that the term in the brackets is zero. Thus, when the firm is optimally adjusting output in response to changes in emissions:

$$\frac{d\pi}{de} = -c_a \frac{\partial a}{\partial e}. \tag{3.8}$$

Equation 3.8 defines the marginal abatement cost curve corresponding to the locus of optimal output-abatement pairs in (3.7). This is the line shown in Figure 3.4. It shows the marginal cost, that is, the change in profits, resulting from to a policy-driven change in e, with y adjusted optimally in the background.

Intuitively we would suppose that (3.8) is positive, because the constraint reduced the firm's emissions below the level they would have been in the absence of regulations, implying positive costs, or equally that an increase in allowable emissions should lead to higher profits. Since $a_e < 0$ and $c_a > 0$ we can confirm that the function is positive whenever $a > 0$. At $a = 0$, that is, when the firm engages in no abatement, assumption (3.5) implies that the MAC curve must be also be zero, that is, it hits the horizontal axis.

The slope of the MAC curve can be characterized by differentiating (3.8) with respect to e, yielding:

$$\frac{d^2\pi}{de^2} = -\left(a_e c_{ae} + c_a a_{ee}\right).$$

Because marginal costs of abatement are lower at higher emission levels, $c_{ae} < 0$. Also, because abatement activity has diminishing effectiveness, $a_{ee} > 0$. Thus $\frac{d^2\pi}{de^2} < 0$; that is, the MAC curve is downward sloping.

A few important points of interpretation should be noted.

- The MAC can be interpreted as the marginal cost of reducing emissions by one more unit, or the marginal profit of increasing emissions one more unit. The latter interpretation suggests an analogy with factor demand curves, and indeed we will view the MAC as the 'demand curve' for emissions.
- The MAC is defined *with respect to a policy structure*. The target in this derivation was the level standard (3.3). Had the constraint been some other kind of standard (e.g., a ratio standard or technology standard) the MAC would differ. We will see how this happens in Chapter 6, when we look at alternative forms of regulation, such as intensity standards. This point is often overlooked in introductory environmental policy analysis. An estimate of the optimal emission reduction target based on the MAC associated with one type of policy may be inappropriate if the type of emissions control policy changes.

Figure 3.5 Iso-emission lines.

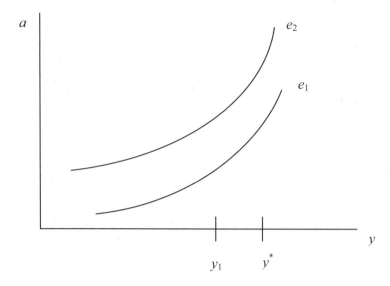

- As long as we are interested in emissions themselves (not emissions per unit of output or some other target), the MAC as derived in this section represents the minimum cost of reaching a target. Hence, the MAC defined for an intensity standard would be higher than the MAC for a level standard when graphed along the emissions axis.

Review question 7 asks you to show, in effect, that the MAC in the case of an emissions tax is the same as that for an emissions standard (for a single firm).

Review Questions

1. Use the iso-profits/iso-emissions diagram to illustrate the firm's optimal output-abatement combinations when emissions are strictly a function of output, and abatement effort has no effect.
2. In Figure 3.5, illustrate the cost to the firm if it reduced emissions from e_1 to e_2 but it was also required to keep output at level y_1. Show the cost to the firm of the output constraint.
3. Suppose the firm is told that it must reduce emissions from e_1 to

Figure 3.6 Output-abatement combinations.

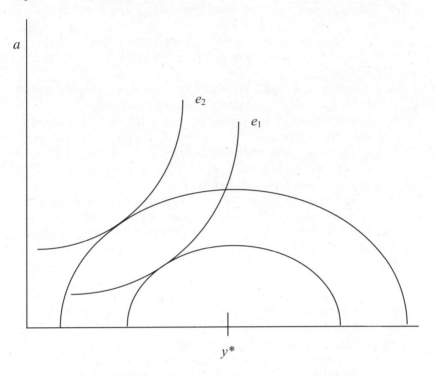

e₂, but the regulator will now subsidize all its abatement costs. What, if anything, will happen to the firm's output level?

4. Compare the amount of pollution abatement equipment (a) the firm will purchase under this arrangement to the amount it would buy if it had to pay for its own equipment.

5 Suppose the regulator has constrained a firm to some emissions level e_1. If the standard is reduced further, to e_2, show on a single diagram the difference between: (1) the cost of the abatement equipment required if the firm does not adjust output; (2) the cost of the abatement equipment if the firm optimally adjusts output; and (3) the firm's actual abatement cost (i.e., the area under the MAC).

6. Put the letters on Figure 3.6 in the correct location.
   a The unregulated output level
   b The output level under emission standard e_2

    c The abatement level under emission standard e_2

    d The value to the firm of being allowed to increase emissions from e_2 to e_1

    f The change in abatement if emissions increase from e_2 to e_1

    g The abatement used if emissions fall from e_1 to e_2 but y stays constant

    h The abatement used if emissions fall from e_1 to e_2 but the regulator subsidizes all abatement costs (y can adjust)

    i The output level if emissions fall from e_1 to e_2 but the regulator used a tax to control emissions

    j The abatement level if emissions fall to e_2 but the regulator used a tax to control emissions

    k The unregulated abatement level

7. A firm has a cost function $c(w,y,a)$ where w is the wage rate, y is the output level and a is abatement effort. Output sells at price p. The firm's profits are $\pi = py - c(w,y,a)$. Emissions are given by the function $e(y,a)$. Prove that the firm will choose the same combination of output and abatement under the following two policy scenarios:

(a) An emissions constraint of the form $e(y,a) \le \hat{e}$.

(b) A tax τ on emissions set at a level high enough that total emissions fall to $\hat{e}$.

Hint: under an emissions constraint the firm maximizes a Lagrangian function yielding first-order conditions that take the form of equation (3.7). Under an emissions tax the firm maximizes $py - c(w,y,a) - \tau e(y,a)$. Derive the first-order conditions when maximizing this with respect to y and a and see if they can be rearranged into a form equivalent to (3.7).

8. What conditions would need to hold for the iso-emissions line to be concave? Is this likely to be observed?

9. As emission limits are tightened, will it always be the case that the optimal level of abatement equipment rises? Draw an example where abatement effort would decline while emissions go down.

10. Explain why the marginal abatement cost curve is a 'demand curve' for emissions.

4 Optimal Emissions: The Partial Equilibrium Case

4.1 The Optimal Emissions Level

In 1990, the U.S. Congress passed the Clean Air Act Amendments which, among other things, mandated a 40 per cent reduction in sulfur dioxide emissions, from about 15 million tons to about 9 million tons annually. Three years earlier, nations around the world had agreed to the Montreal Protocol, which mandated a 100 per cent reduction in ozone-depleting chemicals like chlorofluorocarbons. Two years later, nations gathered in Rio de Janeiro to sign the UN Framework Convention on Climate Change, and adopted the so-called Rio target, which called for a 10 per cent reduction in greenhouse gas emissions by the year 2000. However, none of the signatories actually complied with the Rio target (intentionally, at least) and greenhouse gas emissions in industrialized countries continued to rise over the next decade.

Across three different issues, we observed three different emission reduction targets: 40 per cent, 100 per cent, and 10 per cent (or, in practice, zero). Why did the targets differ? Should they differ? More generally, how should we decide what targets to aim at? The first part of this chapter will answer these questions by developing the concept known as the optimal emissions level. In the second part of the chapter we will introduce the concept of the optimal distribution of emitting activities across multiple polluters, and thereby complete the derivation of efficient pollution levels in a first-best, decentralized economy.

The analysis begins by looking at the incentives facing a polluting firm. Suppose a competitive firm's production process generates emissions e, which can be offset with abatement activity a. Because units of abatement are, by assumption, costly but otherwise unproductive, the firm would ordinarily set a equal to zero, unless compelled to reduce emissions. Reducing emissions means reduced profits. The loss of profits at the margin, as a function of the level of emissions, is shown by the marginal abatement cost (MAC) function. If the firm can increase emissions slightly, the benefit to the firm is the amount of profit it did not have to forgo by holding emissions down.

Note that the firm's profits reflect the total value (from society's point of view) of the production activity generating the pollution, in the sense that when a firm is earning positive profits, the marginal value to consumers of what is produced exceeds the marginal value of the resources and factors used in its production. So by illustrating the reduction in profits resulting from an emissions cut, the MAC captures the marginal social costs of reducing emissions (when read from right to left); and because it shows the marginal increase in profits if emissions increase slightly, the MAC shows the gross marginal social benefit of emissions (when read from left to right).

The marginal damages curve captures the benefits to society of reducing pollution. Consequently, the point where it intersects the MAC is an optimum for society, while the polluting firm's private optimum is where marginal benefits are zero, that is, where the MAC reaches the horizontal axis.

We can illustrate the social gain to pollution control using a graphical treatment as shown in Figure 4.1. If emissions are initially at $\bar{e}$, the total social damage equals the area under the MD curve, which is $a + b + c$. If emissions are reduced to e^*, the cost of doing so is represented by the area under the MAC function between $\bar{e}$ and e^*, which is b. The reduction in damages is equal to the area $b + c$. Consequently, the net gain of reducing emissions is area c. If emissions were reduced further, the marginal cost of doing so (shown along the MAC curve) would exceed the marginal reduction in damages (shown along the MD curve), so such a move would be welfare-reducing. And if emissions were not reduced as far as e^*, the foregone benefits of emission reduction would exceed the cost savings. Consequently, the optimal emissions level e^* occurs where MD = MAC, and at this point the net social gain (area c) of pollution reduction is maximized.

The vertical axis in Figure 4.1 shows dollars per unit of emissions. At the optimal emissions level e^*, there is a corresponding dollar value which we denote P^*, to highlight the fact that when the optimal emissions *level* is defined, the optimal *price* is also defined. While people are accustomed to thinking about pollution in terms of quantities or levels,

Figure 4.1 Marginal damages and marginal abatement costs.

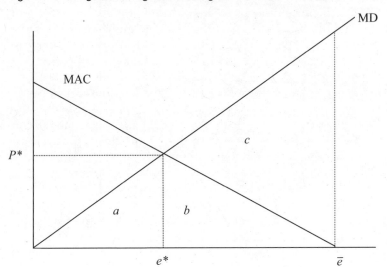

the pollution price is the more important variable from the economic point of view. However, it is usually defined only implicitly in a regulatory outcome. For every emissions level there are associated MD and MAC levels. The optimal emissions price is the value where those two curves cross.

Figure 4.1 resembles a simple demand-supply model from an introductory economics text. This is more than coincidental. The MAC line is like a demand curve, and the MD line is like a supply curve. But unlike a demand-supply model, decentralized markets in emissions do not tend towards the optimal outcome where demand equals supply. Instead they tend towards the unregulated emissions level. To get to the optimal emissions level usually requires some form of intervention.

The relationship between Figures 4.1 and 3.3 is shown in Figure 4.2. In the diagram on the left, suppose the emissions constraint is reduced from e_1 to e_2. As a result the firm drops to a lower iso-profits line. The change in profits is $\Delta\pi$. This quantity corresponds to the area under the marginal abatement cost curve in the diagram on the right. The amount $\Delta\hat{a}$ shows how much extra abatement effort would be required to reduce emissions if output were held constant. The cost of this change is unobserved and does not appear in the diagram on the right. Nor does the cost of the actual change in a, denoted Δa. The cost

Figure 4.2 Relationship between iso-profits model and MAC model.

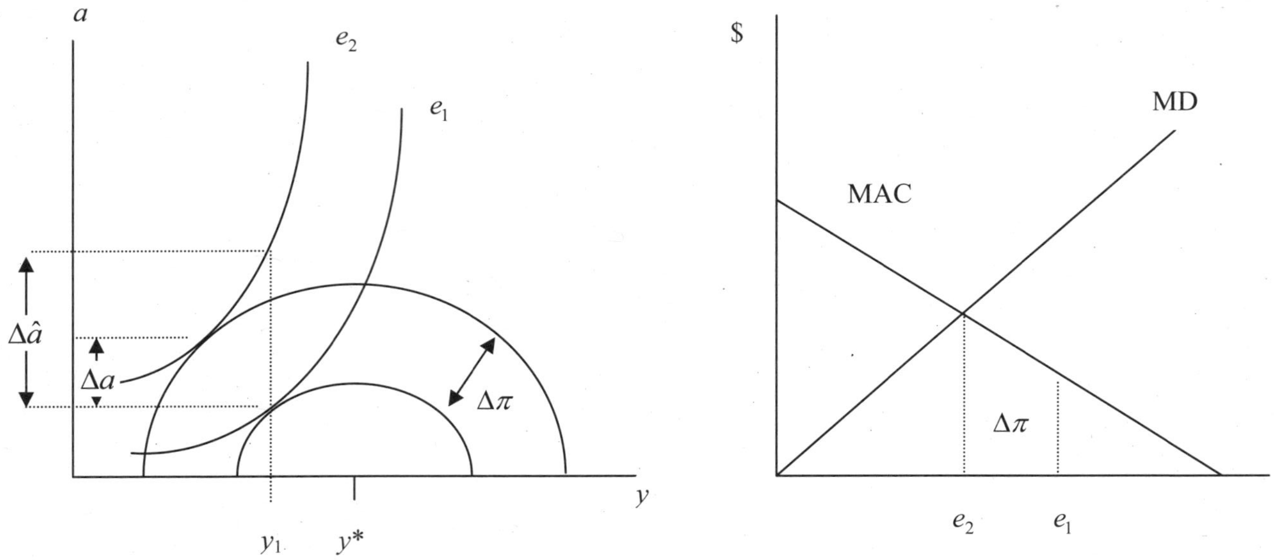

of Δa (which equals $\partial c/\partial a$) is not the same as the marginal abatement cost since

$$-c_a \neq \frac{d\pi}{de}.$$

As mentioned previously, the MAC on the right is defined for a particular policy situation. In this case we are assuming firms are able to meet an emissions constraint without any restriction on how they do so. If the move from e_1 to e_2 also involved output constraints, or if the regulator promised to cover some or all of the abatement costs, then the MAC would change shape.

4.2 Static Short-Run Efficiency

We have already considered the notion of optimality in setting a maximum level of pollution. The optimal, or *efficient* level is one at which the marginal damages just equals the marginal benefit of pollution, where the marginal benefit is (by definition) equivalent to the marginal abatement cost. In this section we consider a related concept in policy design, that of cost-effectiveness. A policy which is cost-effective in a static sense is one that, for a given total emissions level, minimizes the cost of abatement, or equivalently, maximizes the net benefits of the pollution. Cost-effectiveness (which is also called cost-efficiency) is a necessary, but not sufficient, condition for optimality. It is possible that a cost-effective policy still achieves an overall emissions level that exceeds the socially optimal level. However, a policy which is optimal cannot simultaneously be cost-inefficient. This will be made clear in the discussion below.

The key to cost-efficient pollution policy is that marginal abatement costs across all polluters must be equal. This is called the 'equimarginal' principle. Suppose that, as a result of a pollution control policy, two firms (A and B) are told to reduce their emissions by prescribed amounts. Suppose the last unit of emissions reduction cost firm A \$1200, and the last unit of emission reduction cost firm B \$200. If A had been allowed to pay B, say, \$300, in exchange for having B cut its emissions by one more unit, and then A were allowed to increase its emissions by one more unit, A would save $(1200 - 300) = \$900$, while B would earn \$300 for an action that cost it \$200, for a net gain of \$100. Consequently, while the overall emissions would have been identical, both firms would have been better off. As long as MACs differ at current emission levels, the possibility for a mutually advantageous rearrangement of abatement activity exists. Cost-efficiency is a necessary condition for optimality, since if the MACs differ at the margin, they cannot all have abated to the point where marginal damages equal marginal abatement costs, which defines the optimal level of emissions for each source.

We can formalize the notion of cost-efficiency in a simple way by using the profit function presented in the previous chapter. Note that we are assuming that emissions mix uniformly in the environment, so all polluters face a common MD curve. Each polluter i gets decreasing marginal benefits from generating emissions e_i so its profits can be written as a function of emissions: $\pi^i(e_i)$, and its marginal benefits of emissions, also known as its marginal abatement cost curve, can be written

$$\frac{\partial \pi^i}{\partial e_i}.$$

The regulator wants to achieve some overall emissions level $E = \sum_i e_i$. The policy challenge is to do this in such a way as to minimize the economic costs, or equivalently, to maximize the economic benefits from the allowed emission levels. We write this as a constrained optimization:

$$\max w.r.t.\{e_i\} \quad \sum_i \pi^i(e_i) \text{ subject to } \sum_i e_i = E.$$

The Lagrangian function for this problem is:

$$L = \sum_i \pi^i(e_i) - \lambda \left[\sum_i e_i - E \right]. \tag{4.1}$$

The first-order conditions, with respect to the e_i's are each written

$$\frac{\partial L}{\partial e_i} = \frac{\partial \pi^i(e_i)}{\partial e_i} - \lambda = 0 \tag{4.2}$$

and since the λ's are constant this implies

$$\frac{\partial \pi^i(e_i)}{\partial e_i} = \frac{\partial \pi^j(e_j)}{\partial e_j} \tag{4.3}$$

for any pair of polluters i,j. In other words, the MACs across all pollution sources must be equal.

Figure 4.3 Two firms subject to a uniform standard.

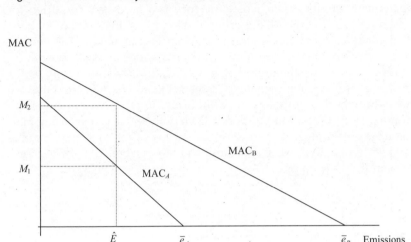

The main policy instruments at the disposal of a pollution regulator are standards (e.g., ambient, emission, or process standards), pricing instruments (emission taxes, tradable permits) and legal liability. It turns out that only some of the instruments are inherently cost-effective, namely taxes and tradable permits. Because of this, they are referred to as 'economic instruments.' Standards by contrast are referred to as 'command and control' instruments. Liability laws are potentially optimal in cases where a single polluter and a single victim can negotiate, but when there are multiple parties the outcome is unlikely to be cost-efficient, as we shall see in Chapter 9.

The challenge of achieving cost-effective outcomes under command-and-control is illustrated in Figure 4.3. Consider a pollution standard imposed on the two firms, A and B, whose marginal abatement costs are as shown.

Firms A and B start at differing pollution levels prior to regulation, namely at $\bar{e}_A$ and $\bar{e}_B$, respectively. Suppose the regulation requires both firms to cut back emissions to $\hat{E}$. Clearly, at this level, the marginal abatement costs are different between the firms: M_1 for firm A and M_2 for firm B. Consequently this cannot be a cost-effective way to achieve the total emissions level $2\hat{E}$.

Economic instruments achieve cost-efficiency by confronting firms with a common price for pollution activity, rather than a common

Figure 4.4 Two firms subject to an emissions pricing rule.

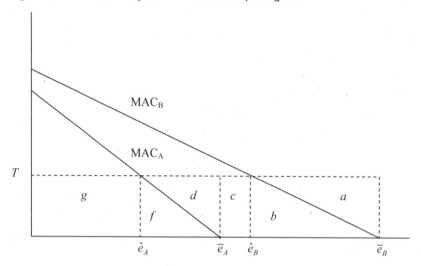

quantity target. This is illustrated in Figure 4.4, using an emissions tax T.

Firms A and B initially pollute at $\bar{e}_A$ and $\bar{e}_B$ respectively, where their MACs are zero. Now suppose the government imposes a tax T on each unit of emissions. Consider firm A first. If it continues to pollute as before, it will pay $g + d + f$ in taxes. By reducing emissions one unit, its tax burden falls by T, but its abatement costs are nearly zero. So it is in the firm's interest to reduce emissions. It continues to be in the firm's interest to reduce emissions until the cost of one more unit of emissions reduction has risen to equal the tax rate, which occurs at $\hat{e}_A$. The firm's tax bill falls by $d + f$, but it only incurs abatement costs f, for a net savings of d. Similarly, firm B finds it worthwhile to reduce emissions to $\hat{e}_B$. At this point it saves $a + b$ on its tax bill, while incurring costs b in abatement, for a net savings of a.

At the resulting emissions level, both firms are polluting at a level where their respective MACs equal the tax rate T. We can easily reiterate mathematically the point made diagrammatically. Each firm's net profit (after paying the emissions fee) is

$$\pi^i(e_i) - Te_i.$$

If these are maximized,

$$\frac{\partial(\pi^i(e_i) - Te_i)}{\partial e_i} = 0 \Rightarrow MAC^i = T$$

for all i. Because the tax rate is the same for all firms, this policy leads to an outcome consistent with the equimarginal principle.

If, instead of a tax, the government pays each firm a subsidy T for each unit by which it reduces emissions below its initial level, the same outcome is attained. In Figure 4.4, firm A finds it advantageous to reduce its emissions one unit, which earns it T in subsidy but costs it nearly zero in abatement costs. This same reasoning applies up to the point where the marginal abatement cost equals the subsidy rate. Consequently firm A reduces pollution to (again) $\hat{e}_A$, earning $d + f$ in subsidies, spending f in abatement costs, and pocketing d, the difference. Similarly firm B earns $a + b$ in subsidies, and its net gain is a. The result in this case is the same as under the tax, but there are important long-run differences in outcomes between taxes and subsidies, because the subsidy creates a different incentive to enter this industry than does the tax. We will consider this contrast in a later section.

The use of tradable permits can also be illustrated in Figure 4.4. Suppose a market for such permits exists and the going price is T. We are assuming for simplicity that firms do not have market power in the permits market, which not always a realistic assumption, but which will suffice for the moment. Firm A finds it worthwhile to buy its first permit, because the cost is T but the benefit of the first unit of pollution is where MAC_A intersects the vertical axis. Similarly the firm finds it worthwhile to buy more and more permits, until the point $\hat{e}_A$, where MAC_A dips below the price T. Beyond this, the marginal benefit of polluting falls lower than the marginal cost of buying permits. Similarly, firm B wishes to buy $\hat{e}_B$ permits, at the market price T. Notice that the MAC defines the quantity of permits a firm wishes to buy at each price, and hence we can also use the MAC as the firm's demand curve for permits in a tradable pollution permits market. (We can also use the MD curve as society's 'supply' function for pollution). Because both firms face a common price, they will choose to pollute at levels which satisfy the equimarginal criterion.

It is not always the case that firms have to buy all their permits. In some cases the government distributes a number of permits freely, then allows firms to trade them. If, in this case, the regulator distributed $\hat{E} = \hat{e}_A + \hat{e}_B$ permits we would expect the same outcome to prevail. In the example given after deriving the equimarginal criterion, it was clear

Figure 4.5 Two firms subject to an emissions tax set at the optimal level.

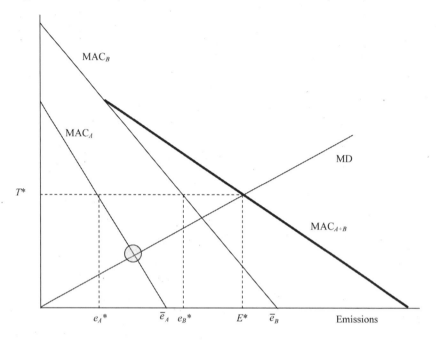

that as long as MACs differ between firms, they have an incentive to reallocate abatement activity between themselves. The tradable permit system allows them to do this, and the outcome is the equality of their MACs at a price where their total emissions equal the aggregate set by the regulator.

Continuing with our two-firm example, we can now illustrate the relationship between a policy which is cost-effective and one which is optimal.

In Figure 4.5 the heavy black line is the aggregate MAC curve, defined as the horizontal summation of the two firms' own MAC curves, and denoted MAC_{A+B}. This crosses the MD curve at a price level T^*. This defines the optimal total emissions level E^* as well as the tax rate T^*. Facing the tax rate T^*, the firms choose emission levels e_A^* and e_B^*, which sum to E^*, and at which their MACs are equal. Consequently this policy is both *cost-efficient* and *optimal*. Had the tax rate been set at a different level, the resulting total emissions level would be different, so the policy would not be *optimal*, even though it would still be *cost-efficient* because the tax yields identical MACs. By similar reasoning a subsidy or tradable permit policy could achieve either cost-efficiency alone or both cost-efficiency and optimality. The latter case would correspond with the outcome if the regulator auctioned off a total of E^* permits and the firms each paid the same price T^*. But a system of standards could not achieve cost-efficiency or optimality, except in the lucky case where the standards for the firms are set exactly at the outcome generated under the optimal tax policy.

To test whether you understand the concepts in Figure 4.5, note the grey shaded circle. You should be able to explain why that intersection point plays no role in explaining the outcome under the emissions price T^*. Although it is clear in the diagram that it plays no role, when students work through algebraic examples of the multi-firm optimum they can easily get caught solving for that point, rather than for the actual optimum.

Efficiency is not the only criterion we need to be concerned about when examining pollution policy. Other important issues include administrative ease, monitoring and enforcement costs, and the dynamic incentives created by the policy. With respect to the first, some of the economic instruments may be at a disadvantage. It is sometimes easier to impose a technology standard than to administer a new tax or establish a permits system. However, administrative expedience should not be an over-riding concern if there are large economic costs resulting from an inefficient policy. Efficiency losses not only mean wastage of resources, but also mean that less pollution control is ultimately achieved than would have been possible under an efficient policy. The issues of monitoring and enforcement are closely related, and are pertinent to all policies which attempt to control the volume of emissions directly. We will look at those issues in Chapter 6. The question of dynamic incentives is also important, because the polluters themselves are often in the best position to develop innovative and cost-saving methods to reduce pollution. We will look at this in Section 4.6.

4.3 Static Long-Run Efficiency*

Most studies of pollution policy assume that the number of regulated firms is fixed. However, policies change firms' profits, and we might therefore expect some firms to enter or exit a regulated industry. This can be a very important consideration for policymakers if they are concerned about firms shutting down in response to new pollution regulations. We can show that under some circumstances, some firms should exit an industry in response to optimal policy.

We need to expand the notation of our model somewhat in order to define the optimal number of firms, as well as the optimal output and abatement levels of each firm. Consider an economy in which a group of firms indexed by $i=1, \ldots, n$ emit a homogeneous pollutant denoted e_i, with total emissions denoted $E = \sum_{i=1}^{n} e_i$. We will assume that each firm sells its output y_i into a perfectly competitive market at price p.

Each firm's cost function is of the form $c^i(y_i, e_i)$. Costs rise as output goes up, that is, $c_y^i > 0$ and $c_{yy}^i > 0$. Because emissions control is costly, costs go down (at a decreasing rate) as emissions rise: $c_e^i < 0$ and $c_{ee}^i > 0$. We also assume $c^i(0,0) = c_e^i(y_i, 0) = 0$. Denote $E_{-i} \equiv e_1 + \cdots + e_{i-1} + e_{i+1} + \cdots + e_n$ and thus $E = E_{-i} + e_i$. The social planner's objective function is

$$W = \sum_{i=1}^{n} [py_i - c^i(y_i, e_i)] - D(E) \tag{4.4}$$

where D is a convex aggregate damage function, with $D' > 0$ and $D'' > 0$. The planner optimizes (4.4) by choosing outputs and emissions to solve the first-order conditions:

$$\frac{\partial W}{\partial y_i} = p - \frac{\partial c_i}{\partial y_i} = 0 \tag{4.5}$$

and

$$\frac{\partial W}{\partial e_i} = -\frac{\partial c_i}{\partial e_i} - D'(E) \frac{\partial E}{\partial e_i} = 0. \tag{4.6}$$

Assume that $\partial E / \partial e_i = 1$ (i.e., that each firm decides its emissions independently of the others). Firms draw from a common local factor market, and with increasing costs there is an endogenous market size at which the last firm to enter earns zero profits. From the planner's perspective, the producer surplus of the last firm to enter should just offset the pollution damages. We will assume an integer value of the optimal n exists which is defined by:

$$W(n) - W(n-1) = 0 \text{ and } W(n+1) - W(n) < 0$$

or

$$py_n - c^n(y_n, e_n) - (D(E) - D(E_{-n})) = 0. \tag{4.7}$$

Equations (4.5) to (4.7) define the social planner's optimum, which we will denote $(\{\hat{y}_i, \hat{e}_i\}, \hat{n})$.

Suppose the regulator imposes a pollution tax equal to marginal social damages at the optimal emissions level,

$$t = D'(\hat{E}). \tag{4.8}$$

In response to (4.8), firm i solves

max (w.r.t. y_i, e_i) $\pi_i = py_i - c_i(y_i, e_i) - D'(\hat{E})e_i$.

The resulting privately optimal output level y_i^* and emissions level e_i^* solve

$$p - c_y^i(y_i^*, e_i^*) = 0 \tag{4.9}$$

and

$$c_e^i(y_i^*, e_i^*) - D'(\hat{E}) = 0. \tag{4.10}$$

Assume that the last firm to enter this economy will earn exactly zero profits, so n^* occurs where

$$py_n^* - c^i(y_n^*, e_n^*) - D(\hat{E})e_n^* = 0. \tag{4.11}$$

It is clear that the tax rule (4.8) causes (4.5) and (4.6) to correspond with (4.9) and (4.10). Equation (4.7) will match (4.11) only if

$$D'(\hat{E})e_n = D(\hat{E}) - D(\hat{E}_{-n}). \tag{4.12}$$

Equation (4.12) will hold if D is linear. It also holds if there are many small firms such that $e_n \to 0$, since a derivative is defined by Newton's quotient as

$$D'(\hat{E}) = \lim_{e_n \to 0} \frac{D(\hat{E}) - D(\hat{E}_{-n})}{e_n} \Rightarrow \lim_{e_n \to 0} D(\hat{E}) - D(\hat{E}_{-n}) = D'(\hat{E})e_n.$$

Consider the following diagram (Fig. 4.6) showing D'. Area $a =$

Figure 4.6 Entry of a new polluting firm.

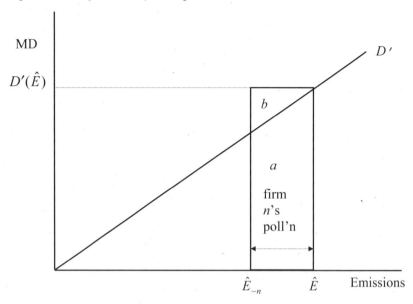

$D(\hat{E}) - D(\hat{E}_{-n})$. Area $a + b = D'(\hat{E})e_n$. Thus, area $b = D'(\hat{E})e_n - (D(\hat{E}) - D(\hat{E}_{-n}))$. This is sometimes referred to as a quasi-rent or inframarginal rent on the environmental good. The socially optimal entry condition (4.7) requires that the firm pay a for its emissions. The optimizing firm confronting the tax (4.8) pays $a + b$. Thus, unless each firm makes a negligible contribution to marginal damages, or the total damage function is linear, the pollution tax (4.8) will cause excessive exit of firms from the market. This can be remedied if each firm receives a lump-sum payment equal to b, but it will be more or less impossible to calculate such an amount. Alternative mechanisms which charge firms only a include the rental emission permits system suggested in Collinge and Oates (1982) and the differential damages tax (McKitrick 1999).

In sum, policies which yield short-run optimality must give each firm the correct marginal incentives. That is, they must price emissions at the rate of aggregate marginal damages evaluated at the optimal emissions level. Long-run optimality requires that firms pay the value of incremental damages, that is, that the marginal firm earns profits just equal to its marginal contribution to social damages. For further on this topic, see McKitrick and Collinge (2000).

4.4 The Balanced Budget Requirement

The topic of long-run efficiency is closely related to the issue of whether the total payments by firms under an emissions charge are commensurate with the total social damages done by the emissions. If the optimal emissions level is E^* and firms pay a tax per unit of emissions equal to marginal damages, that is,

$$\tau = D'(E^*)$$

then the total fees paid by the firm will equal $D'(E^*) \times E^*$, whereas the total damages will equal $D(E^*)$. These will only be equal if

$$D' = D / E$$

That is, if marginal damages equal average damages, which is only the case if the total damages function is a straight line out of the origin. If the TD line is convex, then $D' > D / E$, and if the optimal tax is used this implies

$$\tau E^* > D(E^*),$$

in other words that the firms subject to an emissions tax pay more in fees than the value of the damages they cause. This observation initially led some authors to conclude that emission taxes are inherently unfair, and would cause excessive exit from a polluting industry. But this is not so. In any competitive market with an upward-sloping supply curve the buyers pay price times quantity, whereas the total supply cost is the area under the supply curve. The difference is simply producer surplus. The existence of producer surplus does not destroy the efficiency of the competitive market outcome, because it is a form of market rent. In the same way, the amount $\tau E^* - D(E^*)$ is a form of 'pollution victim surplus' and is simply the analogue to producer surplus in the shadow market for emissions.

   The 'balanced budget' requirement, namely that the total fees paid by polluters should not exceed either total damages or $D'(E^*) \times E^*$, becomes especially important in cases where the emission charge is based on some condition other than marginal damages. The next section gives an example.

4.5 Non-Point Source Pollution*

Thus far we have been assuming that pollution emissions are observable on a source-by-source basis. Discrete, observable pollution sources are referred to as 'point' sources. 'Non-point' sources are unobservable, either because emissions are pooled at the point of entry into the environment, or because the individual sources are unobservable for practical or technical reasons. Devising policies for non-point sources continues to be an interesting and active area of research (see Shortle and Horan 2001).

The classic example of non-point source (NPS) pollution is agricultural runoff into a river. In a watershed there may be several hundred farms leaching fertilizer or other contaminants into a waterway. The flux of contaminants by each source may be unobservable if it happens through groundwater mixing, and if it depends on runoff-control activities (such as timing of application and implementation of control methods) known only to the farmer. In such cases it would be impractical to apply either emission standards or pricing mechanisms.

A simple model of NPS pollution was introduced by Segerson (1988). Suppose that the regulator cannot observe individual emissions e_i, but can observe the ambient concentration Z in the air or watershed. The simplest model treats Z as a function only of total emissions $\Sigma_i e_i(y_i, a_i)$, that is,

$$Z = Z(\Sigma_i e_i(y_i, a_i)). \tag{4.13}$$

More complex models introduce random environmental effects, different transport coefficients connecting the emissions from firm i to level of impingement on Z, et cetera. We will proceed with the simplest model for now. Damages D are a function, not of total emissions, but of Z. Then the social welfare function is the sum of profits less the value of damages:

$$W = \Sigma_i \pi_i - D(Z) \tag{4.14}$$

where $\pi_i(p, y_i, w, a_i) = py_i - c^i(w, y_i, a_i)$ and Z is as defined in (4.13). This is maximized with respect to output and abatement.

The first-order conditions (assuming a fixed number of firms) are

$$p - c_y^i - D'Z'e_{y(i)} = 0, \ i = 1, \ldots, n \tag{4.15}$$

and

$$-c_a^i - D'Z'e_{a(i)} = 0, \ i = 1, \ldots, n. \tag{4.16}$$

where $Z' = \frac{\partial Z}{\partial E}$, $e_{a(i)} \equiv \frac{\partial e_i}{\partial a_i}$ and $e_{y(i)} \equiv \frac{\partial e_i}{\partial y_i}$. Although these appear to be different than the usual conditions, we can rearrange them into a form identical to equation (3.7), noting $\partial e_i / \partial y_i \equiv e_y^i$, et cetera:

$$-\frac{p - c_y^i}{c_a^i} = \frac{e_{y(i)}}{e_{a(i)}} \tag{4.17}$$

which is identical to the tangency condition derived previously. In other words, despite restating the problem in NPS terms we are still seeking an outcome which involves the optimal mix of output and abatement for each firm. This, in turn, defines the lowest-cost MAC for each polluter i. Because the solution to a maximization of (4.14) involves a maximization of the sum of profits across firms, marginal profits (with respect to emissions) must be equal, otherwise it would be possible to increase W by reallocating emissions across firms. Hence the usual equi-marginal condition holds.

So, the NPS problem has the same solution as a standard optimal emissions control problem. The challenge is that we cannot implement such a solution using either an emissions standard or an emissions charge, because the emissions cannot be observed. We will assume that only Z can be observed. Hence, we need to define an instrument for the firm that depends on Z rather than e_i. One candidate might be a linear tax t on the ambient concentration. Then the firm's profits are

$$\pi_i \left(p, y_i, w, a_i \right) = p y_i - c^i \left(w, y_i, a_i \right) - tZ(\Sigma_i e_i(y_i, a_i)). \tag{4.18}$$

For a profit-maximizing firm, the first-order conditions are

$$p - c_y^i - tZ' e_{y(i)} = 0, \ i = 1, \ldots, n \tag{4.19}$$

and

$$-c_a^i - tZ' e_{a(i)} = 0, \ i = 1, \ldots, n. \tag{4.20}$$

We assume that each firm can correctly observe the effect of its own emissions on the ambient concentration level, i.e. Z'. If we set

$$t = D'(Z^*) \tag{4.21}$$

where Z^* denotes the optimal ambient concentration, then the firm's first-order conditions will correspond to those of the social planner, and we obtain the correct outcome.

This appears to be a rather neat solution, but there is a catch. We have defined damages over Z. The total value of damages (including the 'seller's surplus' discussed in the previous section) is ZD'. But we collect this amount from each firm, making the total tax collection nZD'. This breaks the budget-balancing condition by imposing too high a cost on the firms. Segerson (1988) suggests instead that we impose the charge

$$T_i = D'(Z - \bar{Z}) \tag{4.22}$$

and define $\bar{Z} = Z_{a=0}$, that is, the ambient concentration if no firms engage in abatement. Because $Z < \bar{Z}$ T_i is negative, so (4.22) is now a subsidy. This is preferable from the firms' point of view, but still doesn't balance the budget.

If the regulator knows the optimal ambient concentration Z^*, then another option is

$$\bar{Z} = \frac{n-1}{n} Z^*. \tag{4.23}$$

Because this is an exogenous amount, the first-order conditions for the firm will be changed. Using (4.22) and (4.23) the optimal ambient level would result, and the total tax collection will be

$$nD'\left(Z^* - \frac{n-1}{n} Z^*\right) = D'Z^*$$

which is the correct outcome.

Segerson (1988) introduced uncertainty in a simple way. Suppose that emissions are only a function of abatement a, but not output y. Then assume that the ambient concentration Z depends on e_i based on some random term θ, which is the same for all emitters. Then

$$Z = Z(\Sigma_i e_i(a_i, \theta))$$

and the probability function for Z is $F(\bar{Z}, \mathbf{a})$, denoting the probability that $Z \leq \bar{Z}$ given abatement **a**, which denotes the vector $(a_1, \ldots, a_n)$ of abatement levels.

The social welfare function (4.14) now becomes

$$W = \Sigma_i \pi_i - E\left[D\left(Z(\Sigma_i e_i(a_i, \theta)) \right) \right] \tag{4.24}$$

where E denotes the expectation operator.

The first-order conditions for a social optimum now become

$$p - c_y^i = 0, \; i = 1, \ldots, n \cdot \tag{4.25}$$

and

$$-c_a^i - E\left[D'Z'e_{a(i)} \right] = 0, \; i = 1, \ldots, n. \tag{4.26}$$

If we confront each polluter with a charge based on the expected ambient concentration:

$$t \cdot E\left[Z(\Sigma_i e_i(a_i, \theta)) \right]$$

then the firm's private first-order conditions will be

$$p - c_y^i = 0, \; i = 1, \ldots, n \tag{4.27}$$

and

$$-c_a^i - t \cdot E\left[Z'e_{a(i)} \right] = 0, \; i = 1, \ldots, n. \tag{4.28}$$

(4.25) and (4.27) are equal because we have made the output decision irrelevant, by assumption. In order to equate (4.26) and (4.28) we set

$$t = \frac{E\left[D'Z'e_{a(i)} \right]}{E\left[Z'e_{a(i)} \right]}. \tag{4.29}$$

If the damage function is linear then (4.29) reduces to (4.21). That is, it yields the same solution as before. The problem of over-collection then arises, and is addressed, in an identical way.

Cabe and Herriges (1992) introduced an interesting wrinkle by supposing that the regulator and polluters have different views about the marginal effect of emissions on Z. Then the expectation terms must distinguish between the regulator's expectation E_R and the firm's expectation E_F. Equation (4.29) then becomes

$$\tilde{t} = \frac{E_R\left[D'Z'e_{a(i)}\right]}{E_F\left[Z'e_{a(i)}\right]}. \tag{4.30}$$

Suppose that polluters believe that their own emissions have a smaller effect than the regulator believes. Then the denominator in (4.30) will be smaller than the numerator, all else remaining equal, which implies that the tax $\tilde{t}$ would have to be higher than before. In an extreme case, if the firm believes it has *no* effect on Z, then the denominator in (4.30) goes to zero and the system breaks down. From (4.28) the firm would set $a = 0$ and the regulator would have no control over emissions except by setting $\tilde{t}$ so high as to drive some firms out of business altogether. There is no interior solution in this problem: instead the regulator must change the firm's beliefs regarding Z' (assuming that the regulator is correct and the firm wrong).

4.6 Dynamic Efficiency and Technology Adoption Decisions

Firms which generate pollution need incentives not only to use existing abatement technology, but also to help improve it and to adopt better versions as they become available. If a policy provides the correct incentives for firms to innovate and adopt new technologies, it is said to achieve *dynamic* efficiency. In general, we do not *always* want firms to invest in pollution control technology, or to adopt new pollution control devices; it depends on the costs. If the costs of the new technology exceed the payoff in terms of reduced pollution damages then we are better off not undertaking the investment. Figure 4.7 shows a situation in which a firm can choose between two abatement technology options, x and y, which imply two different MACs.

The firm currently employs technology x, represented by the higher MAC line. It can innovate by switching to technology y at a resource cost of 25 dollars. The innovation allows for emission control at a lower cost to the firm and hence to society. Using technology x, the firm would face the optimal standard e_{x}, which is at 50 units. Using technology y the standard would be set at 40 units, reflecting the lower optimal emissions level. If instead the regulator uses taxes to control emissions, the tax rate would be 10 under technology x and 8 under technology y.

Figure 4.7 Assessing the benefits of adopting a new technology.

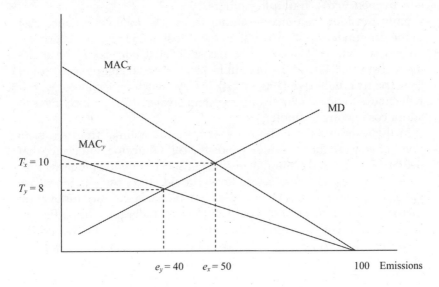

We want to know under what circumstances the firm *would* switch from x to y, and when it *should* switch.

The answer to the first question depends on the policy. Consider the situation under emission standards. When technology x is used, the firm incurs abatement costs equal to the area under the MAC_x curve, which equals 250. When technology y is used, the abatement costs are 240. The firm would not pay 25 to adopt the innovation because it only saves 10. But from society's point of view this is not necessarily the desirable outcome. The switch from technology x to y means that emissions 50 through 100 are now abated more cheaply, which is a resource savings. The reduction in emissions is also a net welfare gain. The resource savings is the area under MAC_x minus the area under MAC_y between 50 and 100, which in this case equals $83\frac{1}{3}$ (you should be able to verify this). The reduction in emissions from 50 to 40 yields a reduction in total damages net of the additional abatement cost (under MAC_y) of $16\frac{2}{3}$. So, the social welfare gain of the technology change is 95 in total, less a resource cost of 25, for a net value of 70. Therefore, society would have preferred the firm to adopt the new technology. Clearly, emission standards do not provide adequate dynamic incentives in this case. This inefficiency is not related to the lack of cost-effectiveness across multiple emitters.

Now consider the outcome under taxes. The total compliance cost to the firm under tax T_x is the abatement cost of 250 plus the tax of 500 on emissions for a total compliance cost of 750. Under tax T_y the abatement costs are 240 and the tax bill is 320, for a total compliance cost of 560. The firm will save (190 – 25 =) 165 by switching technology, so it will choose to do so. Clearly a tax system creates stronger incentives to adopt cost-saving technologies.

In this example the technology adoption is optimal from society's point of view, so the tax policy yields the right outcome. But notice that neither policy exactly internalizes the net social benefit. Standards provide too weak an incentive, and taxes provide too strong an incentive. We can therefore construct examples in which taxes induce innovation that should not occur and would not occur under standards. For instance, if the cost of adopting the innovation was 125, this would exceed the net social benefits. The tax policy would still induce adoption of the innovation but the standards policy would not.

What can we say about the propensity of economic instruments and regulations to generate correct incentives for dynamic efficiency? Milliman and Prince (1989) were the first to show that neither standards nor emission taxes consistently generate the correct incentives for innovation. Not much progress has been made since then in designing instruments which do provide proper incentives. It is an important area of research which would benefit from more attention.

4.7   A Note about Terminology: 'Pollution' Taxes versus 'Pigovian' Taxes

Many introductory economics textbooks call emission taxes 'Pigovian' taxes, and explain them using a diagram like Figure 4.8. This shows a market for commodity X. The line labeled S = MPC is the supply curve (S) corresponding to the marginal private cost (MPC) of production. The line labeled MEC shows the 'marginal external cost' of production, that is, the costs externalized by the firm onto society. The line MSC shows MPC + MEC, the marginal social cost of production. Where it intercepts the demand curve D the optimal production level X^* is defined. But actual production occurs where D intercepts the MPC line, at X_1. Because the firm ignores the external costs MEC, the result is too much production and a market price P_1 below the optimal price

Figure 4.8 Pigovian tax in market for X.

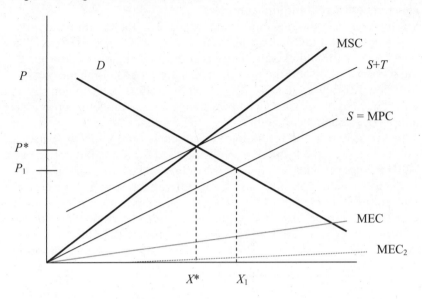

P^*. The Pigovian solution is a tax $T = MEC(X^*)$ equal to the marginal external cost evaluated at the optimal production level X^*. This raises the supply curve to $S + T$, leading to the correct output and (consumer) price level.

One of the problems of this approach is that it requires the regulator to estimate X^* in every market where the externality is observed. A key reason for using economic instruments is to gain efficiency when there are many firms all emitting the same pollutant. If n firms are all selling different products in different markets, the regulator has to compute n Pigovian taxes and implement them in separate markets, substantially increasing the administrative burden and the inefficiency of the system.

The other, and more serious problem, is that the analysis assumes there is no role for abatement. Emissions are treated as a fixed fraction of output. Suppose that by purchasing some abatement equipment a, the relationship between emissions and output can change so the marginal eternal costs are now along the MEC_2 line. In this case the optimal output level will be very close to X_1, the optimal price will be very close to P_1, and T will now be the wrong tax rate. From both the firm's and society's point of view it might be preferable for the firm to install

Figure 4.9. Optimal emissions level.

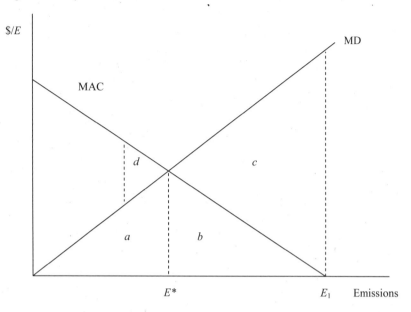

the abatement equipment *a* and produce X_1, rather than ignoring abatement and producing at X^*. But the Pigovian tax provides no incentive for the firm to seek this outcome, and the government will not have the computational ability to identify it either. As we saw in Chapter 3, a tax on emissions rather than output induces the firm to choose the optimal combination of output and abatement rather than adjusting output alone, so it is a superior approach compared to the old-fashioned Pigovian tax.

Review Questions

1. What is the definition of the optimal level of pollution?
2. What two things are measured by the area under the marginal abatement cost curve (MAC)?
3. What is measured by the area under the marginal damages curve (MD)?
4. Referring to Figure 4.9, suppose emissions are unregulated. Why does the firm emit at E_1?

5. What is the magnitude of the benefit to society of reducing emissions to E^*?
6. What is the cost to society of the same reduction?
7. What is the net benefit?
8. What is the meaning attached to area d?
9. Suppose that instead of imposing an emissions constraint as in Figure 3.3 the regulator leaves emissions unconstrained but charges the firm a tax T per unit of e. Show how the first-order conditions from maximizing profits $\pi(p,y,w,a) = py - c(w,y,a) - Te(y,a)$ compare to equation (3.7).
10. Suppose marginal damages due to industrial chlorine emissions into a river system are defined by the equation

    $MD = 2E$.

    where E is the measure of pollution. Marginal abatement costs are defined by the equation

    $MAC = 1000 - \frac{1}{2}E$.

    (a) Calculate the pollution level in the absence of any regulation. If you were a policy maker and were asked to set a target for emissions reduction, how large a reduction would you guess ought to be pursued?
    (b) Calculate the optimal level of pollution. How good was your guess?

    Answers
    (a) In the absence of any pollution, the firm will pollute up to the point where $MAC = 0$. The MAC curve shows the marginal benefit of pollution to the firm, and as long as it is positive it pays for the firm to pollute more. Set $1000 - \frac{1}{2}E = 0$ and solve to get $E = 2000$ units.
    (b) The optimal pollution level (E^*) occurs where $MD = MAC$. Set $2E = 1000 - \frac{1}{2}E$ and solve for E, to get $E^* = 400$. Pollution should be reduced in this case by 80 per cent (1600 units).

11. Now suppose that scientific evidence arises showing that the chlorine release is twice as damaging as previously thought: so the MD curve is actually

    $MD = 4E$.

    Should you order emissions be cut in half (from 400 down to 200)?

Or more? Why or why not?

12. Suppose two firms, 1 and 2, have the following marginal abatement cost curves:

$$MAC_1 = 100 - 3e_1 \quad MAC_2 = 50 - 2e_2$$

Find the least-cost allocation of emissions between the two firms that controls total emissions to 20 units.

13. Suppose the marginal damages function is defined by

$$MD = 2e$$

and the industry MAC function is defined by

$$MAC = 20 - 3e.$$

Calculate the optimal emissions level and the pollution tax which would implement it.

14. Suppose there are 2 firms. The first has an MAC curve given by

$$MAC_1 = 10 - e_1$$

The second has an MAC curve given by

$$MAC_2 = 30 - 3e_2$$

Suppose the regulator wants to reduce emissions by half compared to the unregulated level. What emissions tax is needed? How much does each firm emit? Does each firm cut emissions by the same amount?

15. Suppose there are two firms with marginal abatement cost functions, $MAC_1 = 100 - 3e_1$ and $MAC_2 = 50 - 2e_2$. If the government wishes to control total emissions so that $e_1 + e_2 = 20$ using a tradable permits system, find the equilibrium price and allocation of permits.

16. Suppose there are 2 firms with MAC's

$$MAC_1 = 1000 - e_1$$

$$MAC_2 = 1200 - 2e_2$$

and marginal damages

$$MD = \tfrac{2}{3}E$$

Where

$$E = e_1 + e_2.$$

Find the optimal level of emissions (E^*), plus firm-specific optimal emissions and the level of marginal damages at the optimum.

Answer

Two things must be true at the optimum:

- the *equimarginal condition* must hold, $MAC_1 = MAC_2$
- and the optimality condition must hold, $MAC = MD$

(a) Set $MAC_1 = MAC_2 = M$ and get the market MAC curve:

$$MAC_1 = M = 1000 - e_1 \Rightarrow \quad e_1 = 1000 - M$$

$$MAC_2 = M = 1200 - 2e_2 \Rightarrow e_2 = 600 - \tfrac{1}{2}M$$

Add up to get

$$E = e_1 + e_2$$

$$\Rightarrow E = 1600 - \tfrac{3}{2}M.$$

Note that unregulated emissions $\bar{E}$ occur where $M = 0$, so $\bar{E} = 1600$.

(b) Set $MD = M$ which implies $M = \tfrac{2}{3}E$. Substitute into the expression for E to get

$$E = 1600 - \tfrac{3}{2}(\tfrac{2}{3}E)$$

$$\Rightarrow E = 1600 - E$$

$$\Rightarrow E^* = 800.$$

Optimal emissions are 800.

MD at $E^* = 800$ is $\frac{2 \times 800}{3} = \frac{1600}{3}$.

Then

$$e_1^* = 1000 - \frac{1600}{3} = 466\tfrac{2}{3}$$

and

$$e_2^* = 600 - \tfrac{1}{2}\frac{1600}{3} = 333\tfrac{1}{3}.$$

17. Suppose that

$$MAC_1 = 1000 - 2e_1$$

$$MAC_2 = 1200 - 2e_2$$

$$MD = 3E$$

where

$$E = e_1 + e_2$$

Derive:

- the market (or aggregate) MAC curve
- the optimal emissions level
- the optimal level of emissions for Firm 1 and Firm 2
- the value of an emissions tax that would achieve the optimum.

18. Suppose a firm has a factory that will operate for two periods before closing permanently. It currently has an MAC of

$$MAC = 1400 - 2e.$$

But in the next period, because of some equipment upgrades it will have an MAC of

$$MAC = 1000 - 2e.$$

The government would like the firm to restrict emissions to 300 in each period. The firm offers to keep its total emissions to 600 across the two periods but would like to emit different amounts in each. If the government allows this how much will the firm emit in Period 1 and how much in Period 2?

19. Consider a situation in which there are fifteen polluters all emitting the same pollutant in some region. Suppose a regulator knows the total damage function $TD(E)$ defined over emissions E in that region, but not the aggregate marginal abatement cost function $MAC(E)$. In particular,

$$TD(E) = 5000E + 6.1E^2$$

where E is kilotons per year and TD is measured in dollars per year.

   The current level of emissions is 1000 kilotons annually. Assume that the emissions of each firm can be accurately measured.

(a) If the regulator imposes a pollution tax of \$10,000 per kiloton, what level of resulting emissions would leave her satisfied that this is an optimal policy? Explain your answer carefully. Hint: derive the MD curve and draw a picture of the situation.

(b) Suppose after a few years emissions have settled down to 600 Kt per year. Political constraints arise such that only one further revision to the tax rate can be made. Suggest what the new rate should be.

20. Assume MACs are linear. Suppose a new technology can be adopted at zero cost, which causes the MAC to swing downwards. Also assume that if the firm adopts the technology, the regulator automatically adjusts the standard or tax rate to its new optimal level. Prove that under an emissions tax system, the firm will *always* adopt the new technology, but under a standards system the firm may or may not do so.

21. Consider the same situation as above, but assume now that the regulator is expected to leave the emissions tax or standard constant after the firm adopts the new technology. Will the firm always adopt the innovation under taxes or standards or both?

22. Explain why the possibility of using abatement equipment makes the Pigovian tax approach an inefficient tool for pollution policy.

23. Many policy makers like to emphasize the development of new technology as a strategy for pollution reduction. Describe a case in which adoption of a new pollution control technology might be worse for society, even if the level of emissions falls as a result.

24. To what extent do the mechanisms discussed in Section 4.5 provide an efficient solution to the problem of non-point source pollution? Can you suggest other approaches?

References and Extra Reading

Baumol, William, and Wallace Oates (1988). *The Theory of Environmental Policy.* Cambridge: Cambridge University Press.

Cabe, Richard and Joseph A. Herriges (1992). 'The Regulation of Non-Point-Source Pollution under Imperfect and Asymmetric Information.' *Journal of Environmental Economics and Management* 22: 134–46.

Collinge, Robert C., and W.E. Oates (1982). 'Efficiency in the Short and Long Runs: A System of Rental Emission Permits,' *Canadian Journal of Economics* 15(2): 346–54.

Cornes, Richard (1992). *Duality and Modern Economics.* Cambridge: Cambridge University Press.

McKitrick, Ross R. (1999). 'A Cournot Mechanism for Pollution Control under Asymmetric Information.' *Environmental and Resource Economics* (1999): 353–63.

McKitrick, Ross R., and Robert C. Collinge (2000). 'Linear Pigovian Taxes and the Optimal Size of a Polluting Industry.' *Canadian Journal of Economics* 33(4): 1106–19.

Milliman, S., and R. Prince (1989). 'Firm Incentives to Promote Technological Change in Pollution Control.' *Journal of Environmental Economics and Management* 17: 247–65.

Segerson, Kathleen (1988). 'Uncertainty and Incentives for Nonpoint Source Pollution Control.' *Journal of Environmental Economics and Management* 15: 87–98.

Shortle, James S., and Richard D. Horan (2001). 'The Economics of Nonpoint Source Pollution Control.' *Journal of Economic Surveys* 15(3): 255–89.

5 Information, Uncertainty, and Instrument Choice

5.1 Incentives to Report Truthfully

In a situation of uncertain or incomplete information, regulators often negotiate standards with the party being regulated. The first step in this process is to find out from the polluter, 'what are you capable of doing?' The regulator often does not know what the firm's MAC curve looks like, and it must take seriously the firm's report of its abatement costs. What incentives does the polluting firm have to tell the truth? The answer turns out to depend on the type of policy that will be implemented.

If the regulator is going to set a standard based on the firm's report of its own marginal abatement cost function, the firm has an incentive to exaggerate its control costs. In the Figure 5.1 below, MAC_T is the true MAC function, while MAC_R is what the firm reports. The regulator picks the emissions level where MD equals MAC_R. The compliance cost to the firm is the area under the MAC_T curve.

If the firm reports MAC_T it pays compliance costs shown as the triangle E^*ac. If it reports MAC_R it only pays compliance costs E_1bc because the regulator sets the standard at E_1 rather than E^*. Hence, that the firm knows a regulatory standard will be set based on the information it gives to the regulator gives the firm the incentive to misrepresent its control costs, leading to a higher than optimal pollution level. An important point here is that once the policy is implemented based on the firm's report, no information concerning marginal abatement costs is generated that would signal to the regulator that control costs were exaggerated.

Suppose instead that the regulator is going to impose a tax based

Figure 5.1 Incentives to exaggerate costs under a standard.

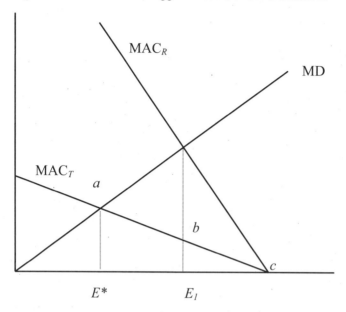

$$E^* \qquad\qquad E_1$$

on what the firm says. It will set the tax rate where MD = MAC. Interestingly, in this case, the firm never has an incentive to over-report its MAC, and in fact may under-report its MAC. Consider the diagram below (Fig. 5.2).

Under a pollution tax the firm's compliance costs are the sum of its tax payments plus the area under the MAC. If the firm reports MAC_T it pays the area $0T^*aE^*$ in tax payments on emissions E^*, plus the area E^*ac in abatement costs, for a total of $0T^*ac$. But look what happens if it reports MAC_R instead. If the tax rate is set at T_1 it can't very well shut down or it would give away the fact that it overstated its MAC. Instead it must go along with the MAC it reported by emitting at E_1. Here its compliance costs have dropped to E_1bc, but it must pay taxes at the rate T_1 on all its emissions, shown by the area $0T_1dE_1$. So its total compliance costs are now $0T_1dbc$, which exceeds $0T_1ac$. Hence the firm is worse off by exaggerating its compliance costs.

5.1.1 Incentives to Under-report under an Emissions Tax

It can be shown that the firm will, in fact, have an incentive to under-

Figure 5.2 Incentives to report costs under an emissions tax.

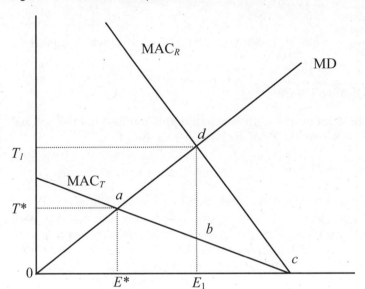

report its abatement costs in the presence of a tax. We cannot prove this with a diagram but it can be shown by re-casting the problem into mathematical form. (Readers who are uninterested in the proof can skip to the next section.)

Define $v = E_1 - E^*$ and $d = T_1 - T^*$. If the firm files a truthful report its total compliance costs are

$$TCC_T = T^*E^* + \pi(\bar{E}) - \pi(E^*)$$

where $\bar{E}$ is the unregulated emissions level and π is the profits function, that is, $\pi_E = MAC$. The firm, by filing a false report about its MAC and then playing along by responding to the tax rate as if its reported MAC is true, would have total compliance costs

$$TCC_R = (T^* + d)(E^* + v) + \pi(\bar{E}) - \pi(E^* + v).$$

Note that $d = MD(E^* + v) - MD(E^*)$. If the firm chooses v to minimize TCC_R we have the first-order condition

$$(E^* + v)MD'(E_1) + T^* + MD(E_1) - MD(E^*) - \pi_E(E_1) = 0$$

where $\dfrac{\partial MD(E_1)}{\partial v} \equiv MD'(E_1)$. Since $T = MD(E^*)$, the above condition reduces to

$$MD(E_1) - \pi_E(E_1) = -E_1 MD'(E_1).$$

Because the term on the right is negative this implies that the optimal value of E_1 is where $MD < MAC$, which is to the left of E^*.

5.1.2 Many Small Firms

If there are many small firms and each one is considering whether or not to exaggerate, the optimal report can be shown to coincide with the truthful one if each firm perceives its influence on the tax rate to be negligible (so $MD' = 0$). It is easier to show this mathematically, rather than using diagrams. Suppose all other firms have made reports such that the tax rate is set at $\tilde{T}$. Denote firm i's privately optimal emissions at this tax level as $\tilde{e}_i$. Now suppose the firm considers changing its report to an MAC that implies a different optimal emissions level $\hat{e}_i = \tilde{e}_i + v$. Assuming it has to follow through on this claim, its total compliance costs will be

$$TCC_R^i = \tilde{T} \cdot (\tilde{e}_i + v) + \pi^i(\bar{e}_i) - \pi^i(\tilde{e}_i + v)$$

where $\bar{e}_i$ is firm i's unregulated emissions level. Maximizing with respect to v the first-order condition is

$$\frac{\partial TCC_R^i}{\partial v} = \tilde{T} - \pi_e^i(\hat{e}_i) = 0$$

and this implies $\hat{e}_i = \tilde{e}_i$ or $v = 0$. Because this is the case for all firms regardless of how $\tilde{T}$ is defined (i.e., it does not assume that all other firms tell the truth) the Nash equilibrium involves telling the truth.

In the case of emission reduction subsidies, the outcome is not as favourable. It turns out that the firm has an incentive to exaggerate its control costs once again. Try to draw out the diagram which demonstrates why this is so. Draw the MD-MAC diagram with the 'true' and the 'reported' MAC curves and compare the firm's net compliance

Figure 5.3 Equivalence of price and quantity instruments.

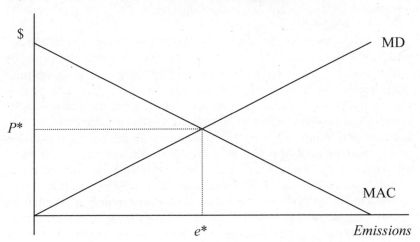

costs. Assume that the firm will be paid a subsidy for each unit by which its emissions fall below the base level. By reporting an artificially high MAC, it raises the equilibrium subsidy rate and reduces the amount of emissions reduction it must do.

5.2 Prices versus Quantities

5.2.1 Equivalence under Certainty

If we knew exactly where the MD and MAC curves sit, we would have a relatively easy task in setting pollution policy. However, this information is not necessarily available. In the previous section we looked at the challenge of giving firms incentives to reveal their marginal abatement costs. In this section we examine the question of which variable should be targeted: the emissions price, or the emissions quantity.

We can broadly classify policy instruments into ones that target prices (including taxes and subsidies) and ones that target quantities (include permits and standards). To achieve an optimal pollution level, if all the relevant curves are known with certainty it does not matter which variable we control.

In Figure 5.3, which shows the aggregate MAC and MD curves, we attain the optimum either by setting the quantity of emissions at e^*, using fixed standards or tradable permits (assuming the fixed standards are efficiently distributed), or by setting a tax at $P*$. There is an evident symmetry between the policies.

Often, however, we do not know the MD and/or the MAC curves with certainty. In such cases we have to make do with an estimate of one or both functions. Because we are sure of making an error of some magnitude in such an exercise, we can also be sure that we will experience some social welfare loss compared to the full-information optimum. How does this affect the symmetry between price and quantity instruments? When we examine the expected social welfare losses due to mismeasurement of pollution damages or abatement costs, it turns out that, in some cases, price controls are preferred to quantity controls, and vice versa in others. In this section we characterize such situations.

The classic analysis of regulation under uncertainty is Weitzman (1974). This section follows Baumol and Oates (1988, Chapter 6). Another survey is Cropper and Oates (1992). Throughout this section we will assume that the lack of information takes a very specific form: that the relevant curves are linear, and that their slopes are known (at least locally in the neighbourhood of the optimum), but that the position of one or the other curve is unknown.

5.2.2 Policy Choice When Damages Are Uncertain

Suppose that the MAC function is known with certainty, but the MD function is not known. The situation is illustrated in Figure 5.4.

The regulator believes that the marginal damages are represented by the curve $MD_{Estimate}$, while in fact the true damages are shown by MD_{True}. What are the consequences of setting policy under such conditions?

If the regulator uses a permits policy, she will force emissions back to the level e_1, which is below the true social optimum at e_2. The social welfare loss compared to the full-information optimum is illustrated by the area between the true MD and the MAC curves from e_1 to e_2, which is triangle abc. On the other hand, if the regulator uses a tax (price) instrument, she will compute the optimal tax rate as P_1, instead of P_2, the true optimal emissions price. In this case the social welfare loss is also triangle abc. Thus, when the MAC function is known but the MD function is unknown, the social welfare losses due to incorrect estimation are the same regardless of whether the regulator uses a price or a quantity instrument.

Figure 5.4 Situation in which marginal damages are incorrectly estimated.

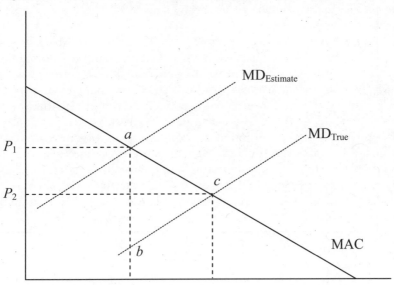

The reason the symmetry is maintained in this case is that the response of polluters to either type of policy is determined by the MAC curve, which is known with certainty. Consequently, both price and quantity instruments generate the same, predictable outcome. What the MD curve tells us is the social costs of the emissions. We are uncertain about the magnitude of the social costs at the policy-induced outcome, but not about where the outcome itself will be. The gap between marginal damages and marginal abatement costs is identical regardless of which instrument got us to the targeted emissions level. In the next example however, the MAC function is uncertain, so the response of firms is not predictable a priori. This will cause the welfare loss due to an incorrect policy target to differ between instrument types.

5.2.3 Policy Choice When the Marginal Abatement Cost Is Uncertain

Suppose that the regulator's information is as illustrated in Figure 5.5. In this case the regulator estimates the $MAC_{Estimate}$ curve while the true control costs are represented by the MAC_{True} curve. If the regulator uses a tax policy, he will set it equal to P_1, and firms respond by emitting

Figure 5.5 Situation in which MAC is incorrectly estimated.

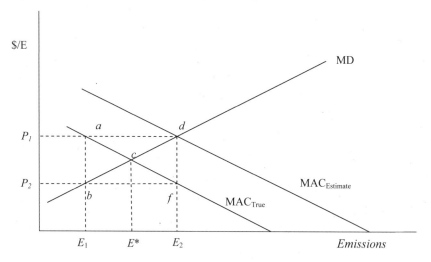

E_1. Thus firms overshoot the optimum and implement too much abatement. The welfare losses of this policy are represented by the triangle *abc*. If instead the regulator uses a quantity instrument, such as a permits auction, he will set the total quantity at E_2, for which firms will bid an equilibrium price P_2. In this case there is too little abatement, and the social welfare costs are shown by the triangle *cdf*.

Which outcome is worse? As drawn, *abc* is a bit bigger than *cdf*, so the mistake under the tax policy is worse than the mistake under the permits policy. That is, given the above situation, a regulator can expect to cause a smaller loss in social welfare due to mis-measurement of the MAC curve under a permits policy than under a tax policy. Is this always the case? No, it depends on the relative slopes of the MD and MAC curves.

5.2.4 Instrument Choice under Uncertainty

Given an uncertain MAC curve, suppose the MD curve is perfectly flat. This would be associated with a linear total damages function. If marginal damages are perfectly flat, we know exactly what the optimum emissions price must be, regardless of where the MAC function lies. Consequently, a tax instrument would be the better option for emis-

Figure 5.6 Welfare analysis of making a mistake when the MAC is nearly flat.

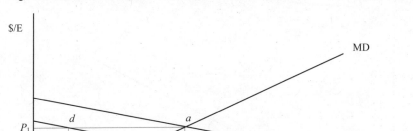

sions control. Conversely, if the MD function were vertical, we would know the optimum quantity of emissions, regardless of where the MAC curve crosses the MD curve. Consequently a quantity instrument would be preferable. In general; therefore, as the MD curve gets steeper, for a given MAC curve slope, our preference moves towards quantity control.

We have drawn a general conclusion from considering the slope of the MD curve, but what about variations in the slope of the MAC curve? Suppose the MAC curve is almost flat as in Figure 5.6. If we pick the quantity E_1 and in so doing make a mistake, the implied price P_1 (i.e., the equilibrium in an emissions trading market) will nevertheless not be far off from the optimal emissions price P^*. But if we pick the price P_1 and in so doing get it wrong, even small mistakes will result in a quantity relatively far off from the optimum, in this case at E_2. Consequently we are better off picking the quantity when the MAC is flat. The diagram shows that the welfare loss associated with an incorrectly chosen quantity is small (area abc) compared to the welfare loss associated with an incorrectly chosen price (area dcf).

Now suppose the MAC curve is almost vertical. In Figure 5.7, again suppose $MAC_{Estimate}$ is estimated, but MAC_{True} is the true location of the curve. If we pick a price (i.e., set a tax at P_2) and make a mistake, the resulting quantity (E_1) will nevertheless not be far off the optimal

Figure 5.7 Welfare analysis of making a mistake when the MAC is steep.

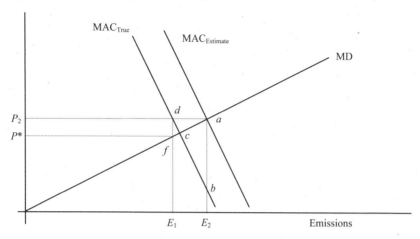

emissions level. But if we pick the quantity E_2 and get it wrong, even small mistakes will result in an implied price relatively far from the optimum P^*. Consequently we are probably better off picking the price in this case. The diagram shows that the welfare loss associated with an incorrectly chosen price is small (area *cdf*) compared to the welfare loss associated with an incorrectly chosen quantity (area *abc*).

These two results can be summarized as follows. Denote the absolute slope of the functions in the neighbourhood of the optimum as $|MD'|$ and $|MAC'|$ respectively. As $|MD'|$ falls or $|MAC'|$ rises, price instruments (taxes) are preferred. As $|MD'|$ rises or $|MAC'|$ falls, quantity controls (permits) are preferred. We can combine the results by defining the ratio:

$$R = \frac{|MD'|}{|MAC'|}. \tag{5.1}$$

If $R = 1$, then neither curve is 'steep' compared to the other, and we would be indifferent between price and quantity instruments. If $R < 1$, and as $R \to 0$ (that is, as $|MD'|$ falls and/or $|MAC'|$ rises), price measures are the preferred instrument. If $R > 1$, and as $R \to \infty$ (that is, as $|MD'|$ rises and/or $|MAC'|$ falls), quantity measures are preferred.

Equation (5.1) can be used even if we do not know the exact slopes, because it only requires that we have an idea of their relative magnitudes. For example, if a policy instrument were to be used for controlling carbon dioxide (CO_2) emissions, most economists who have written on the subject have pointed out that a price instrument is preferable to a quantity instrument (see Jacoby and Ellerman 2004 for a discussion). The reason is that under currently known technology, the MAC for CO_2 emissions is likely very steep. The MD curve is likely very flat, however, since the effect of CO_2 is derived from the global concentration, not each source's emissions. If individual emissions have very little effect on the global concentration, the marginal effect of the first tonne of emissions from any source will be the same as for its last tonne, which implies a flat MD curve. Combining a small value of MD′ and a large value of |MAC′| in (5.1) implies $R < 1$, which indicates that a price policy is preferable.

Review Questions

1. Suppose that the position and shape of the marginal abatement cost curve is unknown and marginal damages are constant. Explain, using a diagram, why a pollution tax system would be preferable to a marketable permits system.
2. Suppose the total damages due to emissions are

$$TD = \frac{1}{4}E^2$$

   and unregulated emissions are 2000 units. The regulator imposes an emissions tax of $800 per unit.
   (a) What resulting emissions level would indicate that this is the optimal tax level, and why?
   (b) Suppose emissions fall to 800 units. Should the tax be raised or lowered?
   (c) Using a linear approximation to the MAC line, what would be the optimal tax rate?
3. Using a diagram, give an example of how the incentives for a firm to reveal its marginal abatement costs change if the proposed instrument for reducing emissions changes.
4. Suppose that a firm's emissions are unobservable. Does that change its potential payoffs from misrepresenting its MAC if the policy proposal is a tax?
5. Use a diagram to show why a firm has an incentive to report a high MAC if the proposed policy is a subsidy of s per unit by which

emissions fall below some benchmark level $\bar{e}$. Is the incentive un-limited? In other words, would the firm report a vertical MAC if it thought it could get away with it?

6. Repeat question 5, but this time suppose that the proposed subsidy is equal to half the firm's total abatement costs.

7. Inefficient policy design can cause the MAC to be steeper than it otherwise would be. How might the use of inefficient policy affect the choice between regulating the emissions price versus quantity?

8. Advocates of large reductions in greenhouse gas emissions some-times claim that such reductions would not only be inexpensive but could even yield net economic benefits (i.e., negative costs), and hence the MAC is very flat and the abatement target ought to be deep. Opponents of such policies warn that deep emission reduc-tions will be extremely expensive (i.e., the MAC is actually very steep), and only a small emission reduction target is appropriate. If each side really believes its own claims, which of the following ought to be supported equally by both sides?

   (a) A tradable permits scheme imposing a deep emissions reduc-tion target.

   (b) An emissions tax at a low level.

   Use a diagram to explain your answer.

9. What important kinds of uncertainty are not covered by the models introduced in this chapter?

References and Extra Reading

Baumol, William, and Wallace Oates (1992). *The Theory of Environmental Policy*, 2nd ed. New York: Cambridge University Press.

Cropper, Maureen L., and Wallace E. Oates (1992). 'Environmental Economics, a Survey.' *Journal of Economic Literature* 30(2): 675–740.

Jacoby, H.D., and A.D. Ellerman (2004). 'The Safety Valve and Climate Policy.' *Energy Policy* 32: 481–91,

Pizer, William A. (1997). 'Prices vs. Quantities Revisited: The Case of Climate Change.' Resources for the Future Discussion Paper 98–02.

Weitzman, Martin (1974). 'Prices *vs.* Quantities.' *The Review of Economic Studies* 41(4): 477–91.

6 Pollution Standards, Monitoring, and Enforcement

6.1 Standards versus Standards

Table 1.2 showed the progress of U.S. motor vehicle emission standards since the 1960s. These standards apply to all new cars. In addition, most U.S. states, and some Canadian provinces, now have motor vehicle inspection and maintenance (I/M) programs. These programs require vehicle owners to undergo an emissions inspection at the time of license renewal, with exceptions in some jurisdictions for late-model cars below certain age limits. The test verifies that the car has functioning air pollution control devices, and that its emissions, in grams per mile or parts per million, are within specified limits.

These regulations are common, but they do not actually target the variable of interest to us. We are not typically interested in the emissions per mile of one single vehicle, but we are interested in the total emissions from all vehicles in a region. In principle, one vehicle that emits a lot per mile is not much of a problem if it is rarely driven. If it were possible to control total emissions per year from all vehicles collectively, would that be more efficient than controlling emissions per mile from each individual car?

The answer is yes, if we are interested in total emissions per year. The damages resulting from motor vehicle emissions result from the total quantity of emissions in a region, not from the variation in emissions per mile across all cars. As we will see in this chapter, it is better to make the target of regulation relate as closely as possible to the quantity of direct interest, that is, the variable in the form in which it enters the total damages function. This is such an important concept that it is worth repeating, with emphasis. *Efficient policy targets the exact variable of inter-*

est, which is usually total emissions. Indirect policy – measures that target variables other than total emissions, is always a costlier way of achieving the emission reduction goal. This is known in the literature as the 'Principle of Targeting' (Dixit 1985, Kopczuk 2003).

This might seem like an obvious point. But many environmental regulations are of indirect form. They are not caps on *levels* of emissions. Sometimes they are caps on *ratios* of emissions to inputs or outputs: for instance, emissions per mile from cars, or limits on the concentrations of contaminants in smoke. And sometimes they are even more indirect, such as prohibitions on certain kinds of vehicles, appliances, or light bulbs.

Many environmental regulations that apply to consumer and industrial products are only indirectly related to the quantities of interest. For example, the European Union and some U.S. states are considering regulations that would effectively ban plasma screen televisions. Environmental protection is a common explanation for these rules. An 11 January 2009 article in the U.K. *Independent*, entitled 'Giant plasma TVs face ban in battle to green England,' begins, 'Energy-guzzling flatscreen plasma televisions will soon be banned as part of the battle against climate change, ministers have told *The Independent*.' The story goes on to explain that large, flat screen televisions use more than twice as much electricity per hour as smaller units based on traditional cathode ray tubes or liquid crystal displays. Likewise, traditional incandescent bulbs use more electricity per hour as compact fluorescent bulbs, which has led the United States, Canada, Australia, and the EU to phase in a ban on incandescent bulbs.

The analysis in this section will lead us to conclude that regulations should be focused as precisely as possible on the variable of interest. With that in mind we can ask whether a ban on a particular kind of appliance, such as a plasma screen television, is likely to be an economically efficient policy option. To answer this question we need to ask what the regulator is actually interested in. Does he or she care what kinds of television sets people own, or what kind of lighting they prefer to use in their homes? The answer is, likely not. We can even go so far as to say that a regulator *should* not care about these things because they are private consumption decisions. If someone prefers the quality of a plasma screen TV and is willing to pay extra for the electricity needed to run it, that is, in principle, no more a matter for public policy than if someone prefers a particular quality of wine and is willing to pay extra to enjoy it. Nor should the regulator be interested in the amount of electricity needed to run the TV, because this is also a private consumption decision and the homeowner has to pay for it. (It is a problem if price controls in the electricity supply process prevent the consumer from paying the marginal cost of electricity production, but the solution to that is to correct the electricity pricing rule, not to regulate the appliances that use the electricity.)

What the regulator is presumably interested are the externalities associated with the electricity-generating process. Indeed, the *Independent* article goes on to say:

> Power consumption goes up as the screens increase in size, so the [government] says that a big plasma model could use four times as much electricity and be responsible for the emission of four times as much carbon dioxide as the biggest CRT.

Hence, the regulator is really concerned about CO_2 emissions, not the type or brand of TV. If that is the case, it would be more economically efficient to regulate CO_2 emissions directly and let people choose whatever type of TV or light bulb they prefer, rather than trying to get at the emissions by regulating the kinds of appliances people use. Trying to achieve a goal for CO_2 emissions via indirect regulations on TV usage is more administratively cumbersome, and is likely to be undermined by the various factors that separate TV usage decisions from the quantity of emissions. For example:

- People can vary the amount of TV they watch. People who purchase a plasma screen TV may not watch it as much as they would have watched a traditional TV, because of the higher electricity costs. Forcing them to use a smaller TV might therefore not save much energy if they run the small TV longer as a result.
- Electricity comes from a variety of sources that produce varying levels of CO_2 emissions. Depending on the time of day, a household may be getting some or most of its electricity from a nuclear power plant, a hydroelectric dam, or even a wind farm, rather than from a power plant burning coal, oil, or natural gas. Switching to a less energy-intensive TV would have little effect on emissions in an area primarily served by nuclear power.

We can therefore venture a prediction that any emission reductions that will be achieved through an indirect regulation, such as a ban on plasma screen TVs or incandescent bulbs, could have been achieved at a lower cost by regulating (or taxing) the emissions directly. In this section we will use a model developed by Helfand (1991) to make this argument more formally, by comparing the costs when ratio standards rather than level standards are used to achieve a target in overall emission levels.

6.1.1 Level Standard versus Emissions Intensity Rule

The first step is to consider the contrast between a 'level' standard, which is written

$$e(y,a) \le e_1 \tag{6.1}$$

and a ratio standard, or emissions intensity rule, which specifies that emissions per unit of output must be below some level. This regulation is written as follows:

$$\frac{e(y,a)}{y} \le z_1. \tag{6.2}$$

To characterize the shape of the boundary (6.2), totally differentiate the equality and set the result equal to zero:

$$\frac{y(e_y \partial y + e_a \partial a) - e \partial y}{y^2} = 0.$$

This rearranges to

$$\frac{\partial a}{\partial y} = -\frac{e_y}{e_a} + \frac{e}{y e_a}. \tag{6.3}$$

The first term on the right of the '=' sign is the slope of (6.1) (see equation 3.4). The second term is negative, because $e_a < 0$. Hence, the slope of (6.2) at every level of y is less than the slope of (6.1), or in other words the locus of points representing equivalent ratios of emissions to output has a shallower slope than the locus of points representing equivalent emissions. However, the iso-intensity line is still upward sloping. We can show this with the following derivation:

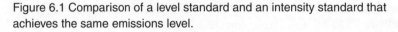

Figure 6.1 Comparison of a level standard and an intensity standard that achieves the same emissions level.

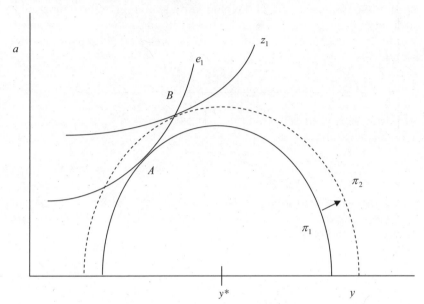

$$-\frac{e_y}{e_a}+\frac{e}{ye_a}>0 \Leftrightarrow \frac{e}{y}<e_y.$$

The second inequality states that average emissions are less than marginal emissions (with respect to output), and because we have assumed $e_{yy}>0$ this must be true.

Putting the two types of constraints together we have the comparison shown in Fig. 6.1.

Figure 6.1 shows the conventional result when a firm complies with a level standard (point A), by finding the tangency point between the iso-profits line π_1 and the iso-emissions line e_1. Now suppose the firm is instead presented with the intensity standard (6.2), represented as line z_1. To make the outcome comparable we set the condition that emissions must also be restricted to e_1 under the intensity standard. So we need to find a point where the iso-profit line is tangent to z_1 but the tangency is located on the line e_1. This occurs at point B, and is associated with profits π_2. It is apparent in Figure 6.1 that by using the intensity

Figure 6.2 Comparison of a level standard with a minimum abatement standard.

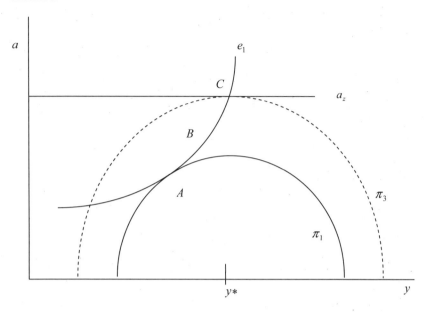

standard to get emissions down to e_1, output increases, abatement increases, and profits decrease.

Now suppose we want to compare a level standard to one that mandates a minimum abatement level

$$a \geq a_z. \tag{6.4}$$

This sort of standard is represented as a horizontal line, and if we again require that the firm operate with emissions e_1 the outcome is as follows. In Figure 6.2, the minimum abatement level is set sufficiently high that a tangency between it and the iso-profit line (which must occur where the slope of the iso-profit line is zero) occurs on the e_1 line. This is at point C, which implies lower profits (at π_3), as well as higher output and higher abatement than before. Point B is indicated as well, indicating that the minimum abatement standard is not only costlier than the level standard, but also costlier than the intensity standard, and while it forces more abatement effort it also induces more output and lower profits. The minimum abatement standard yields output at y^*, identical to the unregulated output level. In a superficial sense this might lead an observer to conclude that this form of regulation was the least disruptive because real output was not affected. But of the regulatory forms examined so far, it is actually the most disruptive, in the sense that it costs the most per unit of emission reduction achieved.

The comparison of points A, B, and C reveals that the cost of a target depends not merely on how stringent it is, but also on the specific form of the regulatory instrument. In the case of both the intensity target and the abatement requirement, the firm is being told not only how much it needs to reduce emissions by, but also *how* to reduce emissions. By adding redundant constraints in this way the cost of the policy goes up. For the purpose of achieving a certain emissions level, the simple level standard is the lowest-cost form of command and control, because it gives the firm the maximum freedom in responding to the target.

This analysis also shows that the shape of the marginal abatement cost function must depend on the nature of the policy. The area under the MAC between the unregulated emissions level and e_1 is equal to the difference between the unrestricted profits π^* and the profits realized under the policy. For A this is $(\pi^* - \pi_1)$, for B it is $(\pi^* - \pi_2)$ and for C it is $(\pi^* - \pi_3)$. Because these are different amounts, the areas under the MACs must differ, and hence so must the MACs themselves.

6.2 Concentration Standards with Many Firms*

The Helfand model only examines a single firm or emitter. We can extend the analysis to look at an economy with multiple firms. This case cannot be treated diagrammatically, but the mathematics is reasonably straightforward. The full model is explained in McKitrick (2000). Consider a regulator confronting n firms, each indexed by i, each of which has a smokestack releasing a total airflow of volume v_i, within which a particular contaminant e_i can be detected. The concentration ratio is

$$r_i = e_i / v_i$$

and the emissions level can therefore be written $e_i = r_i v_i$. The aggregate concentration ratio R for all n firms is given by

$$R = \frac{\Sigma e_i}{\Sigma v_i}$$

where the summation is over $i = 1, \ldots, n$. The cost to the firm of abating output to a specific concentration ratio is $c^i(r)$, a U-shaped function with a minimum of zero at the value of r which the firm would choose without regulation. The regulator typically sets a uniform standard of

$$r_i \leq r^* \text{ for all } i = 1, \ldots, n$$

so as to achieve a given total concentration of the pollutant in the environment.

But suppose the regulator instead solves an optimization problem, namely, minimize the aggregate cost of achieving an aggregate concentration rate R^*. The outcome is as follows. Define $s_i = \frac{v_i}{\Sigma v_i}$, that is, the firm's share in the aggregate airflow of all the regulated firms. Also, note that

$$R = \frac{\Sigma e_i}{\Sigma v_i} = \Sigma r_i \frac{v_i}{\Sigma v_i} = \Sigma r_i s_i.$$

The Lagrangian function for this constrained minimization is

$$L = \Sigma c^i(r_i) + \lambda(\Sigma r_i s_i - R^*).$$

Differentiating with respect to each r_i gives first-order conditions:

$$-\frac{\partial c^i}{\partial r_i} = \lambda s_i. \tag{6.5}$$

The left-hand side can be interpreted as the firm's marginal abatement cost function defined over the concentration of pollution emissions. Note first that (6.5) implies that marginal abatement costs (defined over r_i not e_i) should *not* be equal across firms. Consequently if the regulator wishes to target the aggregate emissions concentration R, an economic instrument, such as a tax or tradable permits, which puts a common price on emission concentrations, will not yield the correct outcome. But a tax based on the relative shares (the s_i's) can be efficient if it is implemented in the form of equation (6.5). Second, note that a uniform concentration standard will not yield an efficient outcome. Because the line c^i is downward-sloping to the left of the minimum point, larger firms (those with large shares s_i) should operate at a higher MAC level, which implies a lower concentration standard; conversely firms with a small airflow should be allowed a higher concentration of contaminant in their emissions.

Here is an illustration of the intuition behind this result. In Ontario, incinerators are restricted to having a total hydrocarbon (THC) concentration of no more than 100 parts per million in the exhaust airflow. In a certain municipality, the garbage incinerator releases approximately 50,000 litres per minute of smoke, with the THC concentration kept within the standard. Nearby, a tire recycling firm had developed a microwave-based process to convert used tires into useable compounds without requiring fuel-based combustion. The process generated a trivial exhaust airflow of about 2 litres per minute (about the rate of an adult breathing) at normal operating levels. But an inspection by the Ministry of the Environment showed that the THC concentration in this airflow was over ten times higher than the legal standard. Consequently, the recycling plant was denied a permit to operate. This result confirms that an efficient set of standards would allow higher concentrations in smaller airflows, if the regulator's target is the aggregate concentration of contaminants.

6.3 Monitoring and Enforcement

If everyone were honest all the time, or if monitoring pollution emissions were cheap and easy, the implementation of pollution policy would be considerably simplified. In practice, monitoring may be costly and/or difficult. The regulator must decide how to obtain maximum compliance subject to a budget constraint that limits monitoring and enforcement activity. A regulator faced with this problem will soon find it involves two separate difficulties: how to get firms to comply with regulations, and how to get them to tell the truth about what they do.

The second challenge arises because a regulator usually needs firms to report their own activities, just as the tax department relies on people to file honest tax returns. Any time someone fills in a form, they are reporting their activities to the government, and the presumption is that they are doing so truthfully. For that matter, any time one does *not* fill in a form, that is a kind of reporting as well. In U.S. states and Canadian provinces, firms are required to report any 'spills' or accidental releases of controlled chemicals in the air or water. For example, businesses in Ohio must report an accidental discharge into the environment to the Ohio Environmental Protection Agency within 30 days of its release, following specific guidelines (see http://www.epa.state.oh.us/dapc/serc/Release_Reporting_2006.pdf).

If a firm does not report a spill on any particular day, that is itself a report, namely 'we had no violations today,' and the regulator needs to decide if it is true. But to inspect all firms every day would require an inspection bureaucracy as large as the private sector itself, and moreover the regulator would then need somehow to ensure that the inspectors make truthful reports, which would require the inspectors themselves be monitored against bribe-taking or favouritism. Because this is both infeasible and an undesirable waste of society's resources, we need to consider how the regulator might structure the economic incentives to encourage truthful reporting and compliance.

If the regulator succeeds in ensuring truthful reporting, it might seem that the compliance problem is solved as well. If firms always report their activity truthfully, they know that they will be caught and punished for any infractions, and if the penalties are severe enough, they will prefer to comply with the regulations. However, in order to induce truthful reporting it may be necessary to trade off some of the severity of the punishment for non-compliance. To accomplish the twin objectives of ensuring truth-telling and compliance the regulator needs to structure the rewards and punishments in a way that can sometime looks odd from the outside. We will see, for instance, that a scheme that induces truth-telling may require a regulator to punish firms it believes are in compliance, and to reward firms it believes are breaking the law!

6.3.1 Standard Enforcement Model

To begin modelling the problem of law enforcement, we develop a very standard crime-and-punishment model. Suppose the payoff from some crime is y, the probability of detection is π, and the fine if caught is F. The expected value of the crime is denoted V, and equals

$$V = (1-\pi)y - \pi F.$$

The would-be criminal has a $(1-\pi)$ chance of getting away with the crime and pocketing the proceeds y, and a π chance of being caught and fined F. The regulator wants to ensure that the crook does not commit the crime, so she must find a way to make the expected value negative. We can rearrange the above to show that

$$V < 0 \quad \Leftrightarrow \quad F > \frac{1-\pi}{\pi} y.$$

Thus, the regulator wants to make F as large as possible, and π as close to 1 as possible. But from the regulator's point of view, it is costly to raise π, and relatively cheap to raise F. Therefore the optimal strategy to control crime at the lowest possible cost is to set

$$\left.\begin{array}{c} F \to \infty \\ \pi \to 0 \end{array}\right\} \; s.t. \quad F > \frac{1-\pi}{\pi} y.$$

In other words, set very high fines along with a low probability of detection. Although this might have been observed historically, it is not the typical strategy today. We tend to observe the punishment variable F to be rather low and trending down over time, and a lot of resources being spent raising π. This is true in pollution policy as well, and as we will see can be explained by considering the uncertainty involved in proving guilt.

Evidence on pollution regulation (e.g., Harrington 1988) has indicated that although the level of fines (or whatever measure of punishment we use), is rather low, actual rates of compliance seem to be quite high. Inspections of firms and audits of emissions routinely show that the vast majority comply with stated regulations. But those who are out of compliance tend not to be fined too heavily. Why do firms comply as much as they do, even if penalties are low?

There have been a number of proposed explanations. Harrington (1988) worked out a model in which firms are tagged as 'dirty' or 'clean.' Dirty firms are inspected more and fined more heavily. Clean firms are inspected less and fined less heavily, but thereafter they are considered 'dirty' until they pass a number of subsequent inspections. Under such a system, firms have an incentive to be considered 'clean.' Apart from good public relations, it is cheaper for them to face fewer inspections and expect lower fines for non-compliance. So most firms attempt to get, and stay, in the 'clean' category. As a result, when such firms are found out of compliance, they pay a small fine, but then move into the other category. This model does succeed in explaining how it could be that firms largely comply but pay small fines if they break the law. However, it has a number of problems, including the fact that, in practice, regulators have not been observed to actually use this sort of 'experience rating' system.

An alternative explanation was proposed by several other authors (see, e.g., Malik 1993) which makes use of the fact that regulators want to encourage truthful self-reporting by firms, in order to cut down on their inspection costs. One way they can do this is to set two different fines: F_1, for firms that truthfully report non-compliance, and F_2 for firms that report compliance but are found to have actually been out of compliance. If the probability of detection is π, the regulator structures the fine system such that

$$F_1 \leq \pi F_2.$$

This makes truth-telling the better strategy. In this case it is better to make F_1 very small, so that π does not have to be so big. In fact, if the regulator wants to maximize the chance that firms will tell the truth, it should set F_1 equal to zero.

As an example, the Ohio Environmental Protection Agency (mentioned above) runs an agency called the Office of Compliance Assistance and Pollution Prevention (OCAPP). This office exists to provide information for regulated firms on how to ensure they are staying within the laws on pollution release. The state is clearly interested in ensuring that firms comply with pollution laws. But firms needing advice or assistance on complying with the laws might be reluctant to contact the government, out of fear that they will inadvertently flag themselves as potential lawbreakers. So the OCAPP web site (http://www.epa.state.oh.us/ocapp/ocapp.html) states: 'OCAPP is a not a regulatory program at Ohio EPA. This means that information obtained by the office is not shared with Ohio EPA inspection or enforcement staff.' By allowing firms to seek assistance on compliance without triggering a fine or a penalty, the government might seem to be rewarding or protecting lawbreakers. But once we look at situations where governments rely on firms to self-report truthfully, this approach makes sense. The concept of an optimal punishment for polluting behaviour can also change in surprising ways, as we see in the next section.

6.3.2 Regulation with Random Pollution and Uncertain Inspections

There are other complications that need to be considered. Firms may not have complete control over their emissions; that is, there is still a possibility of random non-compliance, and inspections are not entirely accurate. Examining these issues requires some additional notation. The following section is based on Malik's 1993 paper.

Figure 6.3 The probability of having low emissions as a function of abatement effort.

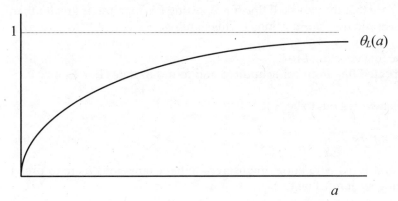

Suppose a firm can have one of two emission levels: low (e_L) or high (e_H). The firm puts abatement efforts a into keeping its emissions low, but can only affect the probability of having low emissions, which is called $\theta_L(a)$. The probability of maintaining low emissions is a concave function of effort a, as shown in Figure 6.3.

The firm files a report r indicating that it either had low emissions $(r = L)$ or high emissions $(r = H)$. The regulator takes action as follows:

1. If the firm reports high emissions it pays a fine F_H.
2. If the firm reports low emissions it pays a fine F_L, and it is selected with probability π for an audit. Audits are assumed to be expensive so the regulator would like to keep the audit frequency as low as possible. The outcome of the audit is a report indicating either low or high emissions, and depends on the firm's true emissions:
   a. If the firm truly has low emissions, there is a probability q_L that the audit will report this, and a probability $(1 - q_L)$ that the audit will report high emissions.
   b. If the firm truly has high emissions, there is a probability q_H that the audit will report this, and a probability $(1 - q_H)$ that the audit will report low emissions.
3. If the audit reports low emissions the firm pays no additional fine.
4. If the audit reports high emissions the firm pays an additional fine F_X for having cheated on its report.

The policy problem is to induce truth-telling. If firms who know themselves to have high emissions are to prefer telling the truth, it must be the case that the expected fine for reporting L is reported is greater than the certain fine of reporting H. This requires:

[fine for reporting L] +
[expected fine from being audited and found in state H] > F_H

which works out to be

$$F_L + \pi q_H F_X > F_H.$$ (6.6)

Also, if firms who know themselves to have emissions L are to prefer saying so, it must be that:

[fine for reporting H] > $[F_L]$ +
[expected fine if audit mistakenly reports H]

which is written out as

$$F_H > (1-\pi)F_L + \pi(F_L + q_L \cdot 0 + (1-q_L)F_X)$$

or

$$F_H > F_L + \pi(1-q_L)F_X.$$ (6.7)

Suppose both (6.6) and (6.7) hold. Then firms will prefer to tell the truth no matter whether their emissions are low or high. What is the cost for the firm of making a unit of abatement effort under this condition? Suppose the abatement cost function is $C(a)$. Expected total costs will be:

$C(a) + \theta(a)$ [expected fine under L] + $(1-\theta(a))$ [fine under H]

which is written as

$$C(a) + \theta(a)[F_L + \pi(1-q_L)F_X] + (1-\theta(a))F_H.$$

The firm wants to choose a to minimize this, which yields a first-order condition:

$$C'(a) = \theta'(a)\big[F_H - (F_L + \pi(1 - q_L)F_X)\big].$$

If this yields an interior solution ($a > 0$), it must be the case that the term in the square brackets is positive. This in turn implies

$$F_H > F_L + \pi(1 - q_L)F_X$$

which is equation (6.7) again. So as long as the firm is engaging in positive levels of abatement effort we are certain (6.7) holds, which means that the firm will tell the truth if it has emissions L. The only reason it would lie about having low emissions is if there was such a high chance of a false accusation about lying that it would prefer to just pay the fine F_H and avoid being audited. In this case it won't bother with abatement effort.

It is a trickier matter to ensure that (6.6) holds, that is, that the firm always tells the truth when in state H. We can rearrange the expression to yield

$$\pi > \frac{(F_H - F_L)}{q_H F_X}. \tag{6.8}$$

Notice that the higher the regulator sets F_H, the higher the probability of audit π must be set. This is a consequence of the need to induce firms to tell the truth. Thus, we expect fines for firms telling the truth about non-compliance not to go 'too high.' The higher F_L is set (assuming it is less than F_H) the lower we can set the audit probability π, but we also need (6.7) to hold, and it is less likely to hold the higher is F_L. Hence, the fines for truthfully reporting low emissions should also be kept small. The penalty for being caught cheating, F_X, should be set as high as possible in order to minimize the need to audit firms. Finally, the less accurate are the audits of firms with high emissions the lower will q_H be, and consequently the audit probability must be higher.

At this point we have shown that the regulator should set only modest penalties for firms that tell the truth, which is why one occasionally hears complaints about how polluters are paying rather small fines for accidental spills and other forms of non-compliance. As long as the truth-telling constraints are working, we should expect to observe low fines: the key is whether we also observe high compliance and self-reporting of non-compliance.

One additional, and unexpected result, is the problem of 'credible commitment.' It arises because the audits are not entirely accurate. Suppose a regulator implements the scheme outlined above, and ensures that conditions (6.6) and (6.7) hold. Then a firm reports L. It is audited, and the audit comes back H. What to do? The regulator is caught in a dilemma:

- The structure of the policy guarantees that the firm was telling the truth
- The audits are known to make mistakes sometimes.

Therefore the regulator should ignore the audit and let the firm off the hook. But if she does this, *she will change the structure of the policy in such a way as to destroy the incentives that got the firms to tell the truth in the first place.* Therefore,

- She must impose the fine, even though she knows the firm is innocent!

This is a paradoxical result. The policy design induces truthful reporting. So why bother auditing? Because without the threat of the audit ($\pi > 0$) firms will not tell the truth. But the audit is not precise. So the regulator may occasionally have to knowingly fine an innocent firm. This raises the problem of credible commitment: can the regulator *really* commit to such a policy? It is hard to say, but it is not likely that the regulator could stay permanently committed to such a policy.

Is there a way around the commitment dilemma? One possibility is to increase the accuracy of the audit, for instance by ordering a second one. Suppose the regulator sets an audit probability π using equation (6.8):

$$\pi = \frac{(F_H - F_L)}{q_H F_X}.$$

Then one day a firm reporting low emissions ($r = L$) is audited and the result comes back H. Knowing that the audit is probably wrong the regulator orders a second audit. But that departs from the policy structure that originally implied equation (6.6). If a second audit is ordered in the event of a finding of H for a firm reporting L, we could show that equation (6.6) should read

$$F_L + \pi \cdot q_H^2 F_X > F_H. \tag{6.9}$$

This implies the audit probability should be

$$\hat{\pi} = \frac{(F_H - F_L)}{(q_H)^2 F_X} > \frac{(F_H - F_L)}{q_H F_X} = \pi.$$

As long as $q_H < 1$ we will have $\hat{\pi} > \pi$. That is, if the regulator plans to use a second audit to verify the first one, then the probability of being audited in the first place must be higher in a system without second audits; otherwise the truth-telling constraints will not hold. Also, the two-audit structure increases costs for the regulator. Not only do more firms need to be audited, but duplicate audits are ordered if the result is H.

There isn't an easy answer here. If audits are not 100 per cent accurate, the regulator will eventually run into the credible commitment dilemma. The outcome will either be a weakening of the truth-telling incentives or an attempt to prosecute a firm that the regulator does not think is guilty. If a firm truly has L emissions then when audits are repeated the expected fine for reporting L is (writing it out in long form):

$$(1-\pi)F_L + \pi[F_L + q_L \cdot 0 + (1-q_L)(q_L \cdot 0 + (1-q_L)F_X)]$$

which means equation (6.7) changes to

$$F_H > F_L + \pi(1-q_L)^2 F_X.$$

The expected size of the unfair fine drops at the rate $(1-q_L)^2$. If audits are 80 per cent accurate, then instead of a 20 per cent chance of an unfair fine there will only be 4 per cent chance. However, this improvement in the system comes at the cost of more audits.

We noted earlier on that a simple crime and punishment model suggests that the cheapest regulatory strategy would be one with a low probability of detection and very high penalties. But now we can begin to see why legal systems have tended in the opposite direction. Courts do not merely try to minimize the occurrence of crime, but they also try to minimize the probability of a false conviction. Knowing that investigations are not 100 per cent accurate, the 'audit' process (which can be viewed as the investigation/prosecution process) tends to get more thorough over time. As in the above model, the result is relatively high compliance rates and relatively low penalties, with severe penalties reserved for those who deny being out of compliance but are convicted anyway. This entails increasing 'audit' probabilities (i.e., increased policing and investigation activity), and occasionally the need for a prosecutor to press charges against individuals he or she believes may not actually be guilty.

Review Questions

1. Consider two ways of defining an emissions standard: a *level* standard that requires emissions be held below some level, as in

   $$e(y, a) \le \hat{e}$$

   and an *emissions intensity* standard, that stipulates emissions per unit of output must be held below some level:

   $$\frac{e(y, a)}{y} \le \hat{z}.$$

   Prove that when graphed in (y, a) space (as in the iso-emissions line) the emissions intensity standard is less steep than the emissions level standard.

2. Suppose the regulator imposes a standard that takes the form of a requirement to use a certain amount of abatement effort a per unit of output y. What would the constraint line look like in (y, a) space? How would the outcome compare to a level standard that achieves the same emissions reduction?

3. Suppose that 1000 firms are subject to pollution regulations. Each one files an annual report indicating whether it was in compliance with regulations or not. Suppose you read the following news item.

   Last year, government records showed that 15 firms reported being out of compliance with pollution regulations. In each case, the firms were hit with heavy financial penalties and, in some cases, managers and/or directors were sent to jail.

   Would this indicate the enforcement system is working well? What extra information would you need in order to decide?

4. Suppose there is a self-reporting requirement in place (as analyzed in Malik 1993). The government wants to 'get tough' on polluters by raising the fine (t_H) for firms which are found to have levels of emissions above permitted levels. Suppose also that emission audits are known to be 95 per cent accurate; that is, when a firm

actually has H-level emissions the audit will report H rather than L 95 times out of 100. Suppose that the maximum payable fine is K. Derive the maximum feasible level of t_H which the government can impose which will still ensure truth-telling in firms' reports.

5. Think of some recent environmental policy announcements you have heard from governments in North America and Europe. Which ones were directly targeted on the variable of interest, and which were indirect? Can you think of ways an indirect policy could be changed to make it more efficient?

6. Suppose you are the director of the Regional Pollution Control Authority. Your inspection staff report that there is a very high rate of compliance with pollution control laws. But a journalist contacts you, saying that based on your published annual reports he has observed that, of the firms that made illegal discharges to the environment, most paid only a small fine or no penalty at all. He wants to know why you go so easy on firms that are polluting. What additional information would you want to give to the journalist to clarify whether the system is working as intended, and whether the small size of the fines is a problem.

7. Suppose that a regulator has structured the inspection and enforcement system so that she is confident firms file truthful reports. Explain the dilemma created if audits are not 100 per cent accurate and an inspection reports that a firm was out of compliance and lied to cover it up.

8. Consider this quotation from Adler (1998): 'Evaluating environmental protection by the number of enforcement actions taken is a bit like rating a mutual fund on the number of stocks bought and sold in a given year. Such actions make for a good bureaucratic bean-counting exercise, but it is a poor proxy for actual results.'

   Do you agree or disagree? Why do you suppose extra prosecutions may not result in greater environmental protection?

References and Extra Reading

Adler, Jonathan (1998). 'Bean Counting for a Better Earth.' *Regulation* (Spring): 40–8.

Dixit, Avinash (1985). 'Tax Policy in Open Economies.' In *Handbook of Public Economics*, Vol. 1, ed. A.J. Auerbach and M.S. Feldstein, pp. 313–74. Amsterdam and New York: North-Holland.

Harrington, Winston (1988). 'Enforcement Leverage When Penalties Are Restricted.' *Journal of Public Economics* 37(1): 29–53.

Helfand, Gloria E. (1991). 'Standards versus Standards: The Effects of Different Pollution Restrictions.' *The American Economic Review* 81(3): 622–34.

Kopczuk, Wojciech (2003). 'A Note on Optimal Taxation in the Presence of Externalities.' *Economics Letters* 80: 81–6.

Livernois, John, and Chris McKenna (1999). 'Truth or Consequences: Enforcing Pollution Standards with Self-Reporting.' *Journal of Public Economics* 71: 415–40.

Kreps, David M. (1990). *A Course in Microeconomic Theory.* Princeton: Princeton University Press.

Malik Arun S. (1993). 'Self-Reporting and the Design of Policies for Regulating Stochastic Pollution,' *Journal of Environmental Economics and Management* 24(3): 241–57.

McKitrick, Ross R. (2000). 'The Design of Regulations Expressed as Ratios or Percentage Quotas.' *Journal of Regulatory Economics* 19(3): 295–305.

McKitrick, Ross (2005). 'Decentralizing a Regulatory Standard Expressed in Ratio or Intensity Form.' *Energy Journal* 26(4): 1–9.

7 Tradable Permits and Quotas

7.1 The Competitive Case

In July 2009 the U.S. House of Representatives narrowly approved a bill sponsored by Congressmen Henry Waxman and Edward Markey to implement a so-called cap and trade system for regulating industrial CO_2 emissions. 'Cap and trade' refers to a tradable permit system in which the regulator sets a cap, distributes permits using some allocation mechanism, and then lets the regulated entities trade their permits among themselves. The European Union has had a CO_2 emission trading system since 2005, and Canada and Australia have proposed to implement ones as well. Prior to the Waxman-Markey bill, the U.S. Congress had voted down several previous cap and trade proposals for greenhouse gases, such as one sponsored by Senators Lieberman and Warner the year before. The Waxman-Markey bill must still pass the U.S. Senate before it becomes law. But the debate around the bill in the House of Representatives put the concept of tradable pollution permits squarely on the front pages of newspapers around the world.

A host of questions arise when setting up markets for pollution permits, such as how they should be distributed and what would happen if a firm were to obtain market power over its competitors. We will look at these issues in this chapter.

In much of the discussion so far we have treated environmental policy as a pricing problem in which we put a tax τ on emissions. If τ is set equal to marginal damages (evaluated at the optimal emissions level) then the result is cost-effective (the equimarginal criterion holds) and efficient (marginal damages equal marginal abatement costs). A firm paying a tax τ on each unit of emissions e will choose emissions to maximize net profits

$$\pi(e) - \tau e$$

which occurs at a point $\hat{e}$ where

$$\pi'(\hat{e}) = \tau \tag{7.1}$$

that is, where the tax equals marginal abatement costs (see Section 4.2). Now suppose the firm does not pay a tax τ, but instead has to hold a permit Q for each unit of emissions, and permits can be bought and sold for a price P. This ought, in principle, to yield a symmetrical result. The firms' problem now is

$$\max_{e} \pi(e) - PQ \text{ subject to } Q = e.$$

Substituting e for Q gives us the same result as (7.1):

$$\pi' = P. \tag{7.2}$$

The mathematical symmetry between the instruments is expressed as $Q = \hat{e} \Leftrightarrow P = \tau$. Hence, the policymaker can control either price (i.e., set a tax on emissions) and let the market determine the quantity, or control the quantity (by issuing a set number of permits) and let the market determine the price. Either method can generate the same outcome.

Tradable permits yield an equimarginal outcome because if any two firms have differing MACs then they have an incentive to exchange permits. For instance, suppose that at its current emissions level firm A has an MAC of $100, and firm B has an MAC of $50. Then it would be mutually beneficial for A to purchase an emissions permit from B for, say, $75. This would require B to reduce emissions by one unit, but it would get paid $75 to do something that costs it $50, so it would come out ahead. The credit thus transferred to firm A would allow it to increase emissions by one unit, which is worth marginal profits of $100, whereas the permit cost $75, so A comes out ahead as well. As long as MACs differ between any two firms, they will be able to find a mutually beneficial trade. Thus, market equilibrium implies the equimarginal criterion must hold: MACs are equal across emission sources. If the number of permits Q is set equal to the optimal emission level E^* the outcome will be efficient as well.

Figure 7.1 Sulfur dioxide permit prices in the United States, 2000–7.

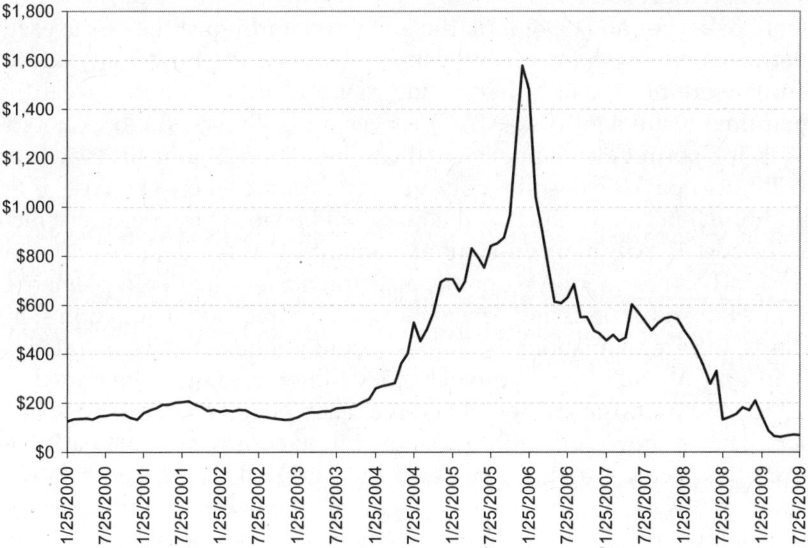

Source: Cantor Fitzgerald Inc. Used with permission.

The outcome of a permits market also provides important informa-tion since it reveals firms' MACs. If the regulator knows the MD curve, then the market price of permits can be used to assess whether the sup-ply of permits is too high (MD > MAC) or too low (MAC > MD).

7.1.1 The U.S. Sulfur Dioxide Market

The most famous tradable permit system in the world is the U.S. sulfur dioxide (SO_2) market, or the Acid Rain Allowance market as it is for-mally known. Its first phase began as a provision of the 1991 U.S. Clean Air Act Amendments. As of 2000 it covered all power generating plants over 25 Megawatts. For many years permit prices were rather low, at around $100 per ton. But as shown in Figure 7.1, that changed when prices spiked to $1,600 per ton in late 2005. As of summer 2009 the price had fallen to under $70 per ton, reflecting the effects of the 2008 credit crisis and global recession.

The EPA runs an annual auction in which 150,000 permits are sold (the EPA calls them 'allowances'), each one allowing 1 ton of emissions.

The total number of permits currently issued each year is just under 9 million tons, most of which are given away free to established emitters. Joskow et al. (1998) took the auction data from some of the early permit auctions and drew bid-ask curves, showing how many allowances were bid for at a descending menu of prices. These reveal the marginal abatement cost (MAC) curves for polluters. As long as bidding for permits is competitive, it can be expected that firms will be willing to pay for permits only up to the point where the cost of an additional permit is equal to the marginal benefit of the permit (which is the cost of marginal emissions abatement). This is a demonstration of the kind of information economic instruments reveal after implementation. Had sulfur emission been controlled by traditional emission standards, information about the MACs would not have been generated.

In 1997 a total of approximately 10.6 million permits were issued, of which 150,000 were auctioned and the rest were given to existing emitters. This is shown in Figure 7.2 as the initial supply curve. A backstop price has been set at $1,500 for new firms and $2,000 for other firms (for simplicity we will use the $1,500 figure as the backstop in the discussion below). Firms can pay the backstop price in lieu of buying permits, making it an effective cap on the permits price.

The market clearing price in the 1997 auction was $106.75. The EPA estimates that in the absence of the SO_2 emission controls, 15.1 million tons of sulfur would have been emitted in 1997 (EPA 1995, Table 3–1). Presumably, in the absence of a control requirement, the price of permits would be zero. This gives us two points on the market MAC curve. A straight line joining (15.1, 0) and (10.6, 106.75) has the (approximate) equation

$$MAC_1 = 359 - 23.8E \tag{7.3}$$

where E measures sulfur emissions in million tons and MAC is measured in U.S. dollars. Equation (7.3) is graphed in Figure 7.2 as the gray dashed line ('initial demand').

Industry and EPA forecasts for average permit prices were between $150 and $300 per ton (Smith et al. 1998), so the prices observed in the initial years of the market were somewhat lower than expected. It turned out that reducing emissions was less costly than had been anticipated. A big reason was deregulation of U.S. rail transportation in the early 1990s, which allowed eastern power companies to buy coal from Wyoming rather than Virginia. Western coal has a lower sulfur

Figure 7.2 Estimated MAC for U.S. sulfur emissions from plants covered by EPA SO$_2$ allowance market.

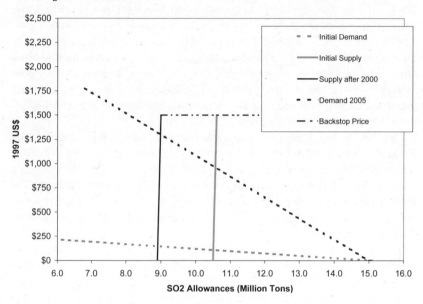

content, so the combination of the installation of smokestack scrubbers and access to Wyoming coal led to sufficient low-cost sulfur emission reductions that demand for permits was low in the early phase of the program.

In Phase II of the program, starting in 2000, allowable emissions were reduced to approximately 9 million tons annually ('current supply,' solid black line). The MAC curve ('initial demand') implies a market price of about $150, which remained the case-up to the end of 2003.

The price did not jump in 2000 when the supply shifted because 'banking' of permits had been permitted from the beginning of the program. Firms can buy permits for use up to 7 years ahead. By the year 2000 firms had banked 11.4 million tons of permits. In effect they had been emitting less than they held allowances for, and in the years to follow they emitted more than they had (current) permits for, thus drawing down their permit reserves.

By the end of 2005, however, the supply of permits was tight and demand (the MAC) had swung upwards to the 'Demand 2005' line in Figure 7.2, pushing the market price up to $1,400, approaching the backstop price of $1,500. This was the result of several factors. In 2003 the U.S. EPA began discussing measures to further reduce air emissions and in January 2004 released what would later be called the Clean Air Interstate Rule, requiring new emission reductions of up to 70 per cent in many eastern states by 2015. Firms began buying up permits in anticipation of tighter market conditions in years ahead. Also, strong demand for energy caused an expansion of the demand for permits. However, prices dropped in the subsequent years as many firms worked quickly to build and install new scrubbers and demand for energy declined with the 2008–09 economic recession.

One lesson from the U.S. market is that the MAC curve is not static. Regulators must have some idea of what market price they consider reasonable before writing down rules for tradable permits markets. In the case of the U.S. system, the backstop price of $1,500 means that the permits supply function becomes horizontal at that price. But it is worth questioning whether marginal damages really are that high.

The comination of a permits supply plus a backstop tax is sometimes called a 'hybrid' instrument. In Section 5.2 we looked at the choice between taxes and permits when the MAC and MD curves are uncertain. In a well-known paper, Roberts and Spence (1977) showed that a combination of tax, subsidy, and permits can provide a better option than one instrument alone.

The hybrid system works as follows. Suppose the regulator offers permits for sale with the following rules:

- L permits will be sold
- Firms can opt to pay the tax τ instead of holding a permit for a ton of emissions
- The regulator will buy back permits at the price s.

The outcome of this arrangement is illustrated in Figure 7.3. The (vertical) supply curve is at emissions L. No one will bid more than τ per unit of emissions, because they can pay that as a tax instead. And no one will sell permits for less than s because they can sell them back to the government for that amount. So the supply function is capped, top and bottom, as shown.

Now suppose we don't know which MAC curve is the right one, or that we have an estimate of MAC_2 at the moment but we anticipate it may change up or down depending on economic and technology

Figure 7.3 Hybrid instrument.

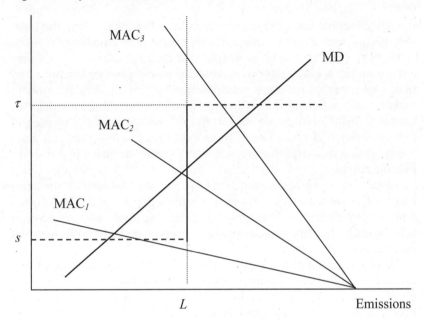

changes in years ahead. If we are committed to emissions at L, the market equilibrium is pretty close to the optimum, given the position of the MD curve. But we run two risks. If abatement becomes much cheaper, falling to MAC_1, we would want to have emissions go down below L. If abatement becomes more expensive, rising to MAC_3, we would want emissions to rise above L. In practice, however, it may be difficult for a regulator to adjust the volume of permits or the tax rate on emissions. That's where the tax/subsidy hybrid policy can help. By offering to buy emission permits back at a price s firms have an incentive to reduce emissions below L when abatement costs fall. And by offering to let firms pay the tax τ instead of holding a permit, it allows emissions to grow if the MAC curve moves far enough out to justify it. In Figure 7.3 you can identify the optimum emission levels associated with the MD curve and MAC_1 – MAC_3. The hybrid instrument tracks the optimum more closely than would a pure permits auction at a quantity of L or an emissions tax of τ, each of which could, on their own, cause very large departures from efficiency.

7.2 Market Power and Tradable Permits*

In settings where one or more firms may exert market power, the tradable permit system may have a disadvantage over emission taxes because of the ability of a large firm to manipulate the price. A uniform emissions tax is equivalent to a perfectly elastic permits supply function, which precludes price manipulation by firms unless the policymaker has previously committed to a pricing rule that ties price to quantity. But if permits are sold in the market then a large buyer can potentially crowd out other firms in order to secure a financial gain. This problem was explored by Hahn (1984) in a dominant player-competitive fringe model.

Suppose there are m firms and all firms but one (indexed #1) are price takers. The regulator distributes L permits. Firm i gets Q_i^0 permits where the superscript 0 denotes the initial holdings. The firm buys or sells permits, and after trading holds Q_i permits. The market price of permits is denoted P.

Each firm has a profit function $\pi^i(e_i)$, which is expressed as a function of emissions. Because firms must hold one unit of permits for each unit of emissions we can rewrite it as $\pi^i(Q_i)$. Firms 2, ..., m are price takers, so by (7.2) they operate where

$$\frac{\partial \pi^i}{\partial Q_i} = P, \tag{7.4}$$

which implies that there are $m - 1$ permit demand functions of the form

$Q_i(P)$, $i = 2, ..., m$.

The dominant player does not choose an emissions quantity in this case; it chooses the optimal permits *price*. Recognizing its influence on the market price it solves

$$\max_P \pi^1(Q_1) - P(Q_1 - Q_1^0)$$

subject to the market clearing constraint

$$L - \sum_{i=2}^{m} Q_i(P) = Q_1. \tag{7.5}$$

Substituting the constraint into the objective function and differentiating yields first-order conditions

$$-\frac{\partial \pi^1}{\partial Q_1} \sum_{i=2}^{m} \frac{\partial Q_i}{\partial P} + P \sum_{i=2}^{m} \frac{\partial Q_i}{\partial P} - \left(L - \sum_{i=2}^{m} Q_i - Q_1^0 \right) = 0. \tag{7.6}$$

We will denote the firm's privately optimal price $\tilde{P}$. Collecting terms in (7.6) gives us

$$\frac{\partial \pi^1}{\partial Q_1} = P \Leftrightarrow Q_1^0 = L - \sum Q_i(P). \tag{7.7}$$

This tells us that if the dominant player's initial allocation (Q_1^0) equals the amount it would choose to buy under a trading system in which it controls the price, then its MAC will equal P, and since, by (7.4), this is also true of all the other firms, then the outcome satisfies the equimarginal criterion. We will denote the price in a competitive, equimarginal outcome P^*.

That means the presence of the dominant player does not preclude a cost-effective outcome, but only if the regulator is able to forecast the exactly correct number of permits to give the large firm. If the large firm ends up buying or selling permits, that indicates that it did not receive its ex post optimal number of permits and the cost-effective outcome will not be attained.

In that case, we can ask what would happen if the amount of permits assigned to the dominant player goes up or down. Note that Firm 1's optimal profits depend on its choice of P, its permit endowment Q_1^0, and the total number of permits L. Hence, we can write it as $\pi^1(P, Q_1^0, L)$. This optimizes profits at the point where $\pi_P^1 = 0$ (the subscript denotes a derivative), and we can differentiate the first-order condition to obtain

$$\pi_{PP}^1 \partial P + \pi_{PQ}^1 \partial Q_1^0 + \pi_{PL}^1 \partial L = 0. \tag{7.8}$$

We can assume that L is constant. Also, note that π_{PQ}^1 is the derivative of (7.6) with respect to Q_1^0, which equals 1. Using these and rearranging (7.8) yields

$$\frac{\partial P}{\partial Q_1^0} = -\frac{1}{\pi_{PP}^1}. \tag{7.9}$$

Because the firm is optimizing profits, $\pi^1_{PP} < 0$. (7.9) thus implies that the higher the initial endowment to Firm 1, the higher will be the equilibrium price.

The total benefit of emissions is the sum of the profit functions. For Firms 2, ..., m, their permit usage is a function of P, as implied by (7.4). The policy objective is to maximize this subject to the emissions constraint (7.5). Suppose Firm 1 took into account all firms' profits along with its own when choosing an optimum. It would then choose P to maximize the total industry profits subject to the emissions constraint. Substituting (7.5) into the objective function yields the unconstrained maximization problem

$$\max_P \pi^1(P, Q^0_1, Q_1 + \Sigma Q_i(P)) + \Sigma \pi^i(Q_i(P)) \tag{7.10}$$

where the summation Σ is over Firms 2, ..., m. The first-order condition is

$$\frac{\partial \pi^1}{\partial P} + \frac{\partial \pi^1}{\partial L} \Sigma \frac{\partial Q_i}{\partial P} + \Sigma \frac{\partial \pi^i}{\partial Q_i} \frac{\partial Q_i}{\partial P} = 0$$

$$\Rightarrow \frac{\partial \pi^1}{\partial P} = -\Sigma \frac{\partial Q_i}{\partial P} \left(\frac{\partial \pi^1}{\partial L} + \frac{\partial \pi^i}{\partial Q_i} \right) \tag{7.11}$$

Because for each firm emissions are a decreasing function of P, and profits increase with emissions, the expression on the right side must be positive (noting the minus sign in front of the summation). Hence, the competitive price P^* would be where

$$\frac{\partial \pi^1}{\partial P^*} > 0. \tag{7.12}$$

If Firm 1 did not optimize the profits of the rest of the industry it would choose a price $\tilde{P}$ where $\pi^1_P = 0$. The profit function is concave, and (7.12) therefore implies that the competitive price P^* is less than the distorted price $\tilde{P}$.

7.3 Auction versus Quotas

Looking back at Figure 7.2, the current volume of U.S. sulfur permits is 9 million, and the price as of mid-2007 was about $600 per ton. This implies that the total market value was around $5.4 billion, and the total abatement cost can be approximated as the area under the MAC up to 15 million tons, which is $1.8 billion (assuming a current market price of $600). Some advocates of tradable permits point to the $5.4 billion market as an argument for setting up tradable permits for other types of air emissions, such as CO_2. You might hear people say things like: 'The market for CO_2 emission permits could be worth a trillion dollars globally by 2010. Unless the United States ratifies the Kyoto Protocol it risks being shut out of this valuable market.'

The statement doesn't make sense, because the market value of the permits only arises as a result of the limits on emissions, which are costly for society to impose. The $5.4 billion permits market represents the rental values of the permits. This is not new wealth; rather, it is a transfer of capital valuation away from the owners of the firms doing the emitting towards the holders of the emission permits.

In the absence of the emission limits imposed by the permits market, the MAC would be zero, and the profits of the emitters would be higher. This would be reflected in their share prices. When the tradable permits system is implemented, in which 9 million permits trade at $600 each, total abatement costs of $1.8 billion come off the annual market value of the firms and $5.4 billion in share value is shifted away from the owners of the firms towards the holders of the permits. If the owners of the firms are assigned the permits, this transfer is neutral for them. If the permit recipients are not the same as the emitters' shareholders, then wealth is transferred. But at no point is new wealth created by the policy.

If the reduction in emissions generates benefits that exceed the costs, then the policy would pass a social welfare cost-benefit test and would be worth implementing. But that is a different analysis than simply pointing to the volume of trading on the permits market and thinking that the $5.4 billion represents a 'new' market or an overall economic opportunity. If that were true, we could make ourselves arbitrarily wealthy by limiting all sorts of activities and issuing tradable permits for them. Such permit markets might be worth many billions of dollars (assuming the limits could be enforced), but it would not be new wealth. It would be a reallocation of existing wealth into the hands of whoever received the initial allocation of permits, accompanied by deadweight losses reflecting the loss in profits associated with complying with the cap imposed by the permits system By imposing an artificial scarcity on emissions, the tradable permit market creates 'scarcity rents' which equal the permit price times the number of permits. However, scarcity rents are created by any policy that limits a valuable activity. If the emission limits were imposed in the form of standards, rents would still be created; it would just be harder to identify them because the policy does not give rise to the data necessary to value them. In the case of the U.S. sulfur dioxide market we know the price because it is observed in daily trading. This makes it easy to estimate the size of the scarcity rents, but it does not imply that scarcity rents are only created by a permits system.

The question of what happens to the scarcity rents is very important for evaluating the overall cost of emissions control policy. If the rents are not captured, they accrue to whoever gets the permits. If the government hands out the permits free of charge then the holders of permits get the rents. If the government auctions all the permits to the highest bidders, the government collects the rents and can use them to generate social welfare by lowering other taxes. In principle, the second approach should have a lower social cost than the first one, even though the outcome in terms of emissions control is the same.

Some authors distinguish these two cases by referring to freely distributed permits as 'quotas,' as opposed to 'permits' or 'credits' which are auctioned off. In principle, the economic costs of quotas are higher than (auctioned) permits because the rents are not captured by the government, and hence cannot be used to improve welfare by reducing other taxes. The two systems are identical in economic terms if we compare quotas to auctioned permits where the proceeds from the auction are handed out as a lump-sum to households, or if the economy happens not to have any tax distortions. Barring these two unlikely situations, quotas are costlier to implement than auctioned permits or emission taxes. This is a relatively new topic in environmental economics, and to explore it further requires developing some models of tax policy, which is done in the next chapter.

The issue of auction versus quotas has attracted the interest of U.S. policymakers who are thinking about implementing a tradable permits system for carbon dioxide. In June 2008 I testified on the costs of climate policy before the U.S. House of Representatives Committee on Energy and Air Quality. A few months later I was contacted by then-chair Hon. John Dingell with a set of follow-up questions. One of the questions concerned how the costs of implementing the policy would be affected by auctioning rather than giving away the permits. My responses to Chairman Dingell's questions are posted online at http://rossmckitrick.weebly.com.

Review Questions

1. Suppose MD = 2E and MAC = 20 – E. The government sells $Q = 10$ emission permits. It also sets a 'backstop' emissions tax at $T = 7$. That is, firms can either hold a permit or pay the fee to emit. What will be the outcome of this policy, and how would it compare to the optimal outcome?

2. Suppose the $MD = \frac{1}{3}E$ and there are two firms with MACs of $MAC_1 = 100 - \frac{1}{2}e_1$ and $MAC_2 = 150 - e_2$. Note that $E = e_1 + e_2$. Prove that the unregulated emissions level is 350. Prove that the optimal emissions level is 175, and that if an optimal tradable permits system were in place, Firm 1 would emit 250/3 units and Firm 2 would emit 275/3 units.

3. One important application of tradable permits is called *banking*, in which a firm can purchase permits today to be used at some point in the future. Suppose there is an industry which releases a pollutant e. In 4 years the pollutant will be banned entirely and no emissions will be allowed (with or without a permit). At present, emissions are unregulated. The firm's profit function with respect to emissions is

$$\pi(e) = 100 + 100e - \frac{1}{2}e^2.$$

The regulator announces a plan to phase out emissions according to the following schedule.

Year	Total Allowable Emissions
1	75
2	50
3	25
4	10

and 0 thereafter.

So, for instance: for 1 year starting today, the firm can emit 75 units. Then in the year after that, the firm can emit 50 units. And so forth.

Consider the discount rate to be zero. Banking would allow the firm to emit less than the allowable limit in one year, and save the unused allowances in order to emit ore than the allowable limit in another year. Assume that emissions after year 4 are not permitted even if the firm holds a permit. Calculate the optimal banking strategy for this firm, and the amount it saves compared to the no-banking case. Explain your answer.

4. Suppose we have $MD = 2E$ and $MAC = 200 - 2E$. If we are uncertain about the positions of the MD and MAC curves, would a price instrument be preferred to a quantity instrument in order to minimize the social welfare costs of making a mistake?

   Now suppose the government auctions 50 permits, and also sets a backstop price of $80, meaning that firms could pay the fee of $80 per unit of emissions rather than hold a permit. What will be the outcome? Contrast it graphically with the optimum.

5. Suppose a firm has an MAC given by $MAC = 1000 - E$. Currently, emissions are unregulated. The government plans to phase out all emissions over the next 4 years. It announces a schedule of annual allowable emissions, but the firm is permitted to bank permits, meaning that if it emits less in one year than it holds permits for, it can save the unused permits for use in a subsequent year. The schedule is as follows:

Year 1	Year 2	Year 3	Year 4
1,000	700	400	0

   After Year 4 the pollutant is banned outright and permits from earlier years cannot be used.

   Also, the regulator announces a 'backstop price' of $600, meaning that if in years 1 to 4 the firm wants to emit more than it holds permits for it can do so at a cost of $600 per unit.

   Derive the firm's optimal banking strategy, its level of emissions in years 1 to 4, and the amount paid in 'backstop' charges, if any. Assume the firm uses a discount rate of 0.

6. Suppose there is a polluting industry consisting of one large price-setting firm and a competitive fringe. The regulator would like to issue tradable permits for controlling pollution. Because of the potential for the large firm to monopolize the permits market, the regulator decides to issue permits only to the competitive firms, forcing the large firm to buy its permits from the competitive firms. Will this ensure a competitive market outcome? Explain why or why not.

7. Why do you suppose the price of sulfur dioxide(SO_2) permits rose and fell so much since 2000 (see Figure 7.1)? If the purpose of the emissions trading market is to put the optimal price on emissions, does this volatility suggest a problem in the policy design?
8. Can the owners of firms in an industry actually be made better off by introducing a tradable quota scheme? Explain how this could happen, and where the 'new money' comes from.
9. In the early days of the European carbon permits market, politicians expressed surprise that utilities that had been given free permits nonetheless raised the price of energy they were selling to consumers. They had expected that firms who got free permits would 'absorb the cost' of emission reductions without passing them to consumers on in the form of higher energy prices. Explain why policymakers should have expected firms to pass on higher prices to consumers regardless of whether permits were auctioned or given away.
10. In what way is a tradable permits market like a cartel system for firms in an industry?

References and Extra Reading

Burtraw, Dallas, Allan Krupnick, Erin Mansur, David Austin, and Deirdre Farrell (1997). 'The Costs and Benefits of Reducing Acid Rain.' Resources for the Future Discussion Paper 97–31.

Cramton, P., and S. Kerr (2002). 'Tradeable Carbon Permit Auctions: How and Why to Auction Not Grandfather.' *Energy Policy* 333–45.

Dinan, T.M., and D.L. Rogers (2002). 'Distributional Effects of Carbon Allowance Trading: How Government Decisions Determine Winners and Losers.' *National Tax Journal* 55(2002): 199–222.

Energy Information Administration (1998). 'Impacts of the Kyoto Protocol on U.S. Energy Markets and Economic Activity.' Washington: mimeo. Available online at: http://www.eia.doe.gov/oiaf/kyoto/pdf/sroiaf9803.pdf.

Energy Information Administration (2007). 'Energy Market and Economic Impacts of a Proposal to Reduce Greenhouse Gas Intensity with a Cap and Trade System.' Washington, DC: Office of Integrated Analysis and Forecasting, January.

Hahn, Robert W. (1984). 'Market Power and Transferable Property Rights.' *Quarterly Journal of Economics* 99(4): 753–65.

Joskow, Paul L., Richard Schmalensee, and Elizabeth M. Bailey (1998). 'The

Market for Sulfur Dioxide Emissions.' *American Economic Review* 88(4): 669–85.

Paltsev, Sergey, John M. Reilly, Henry D. Jacoby, Angelo C. Gurgel, Gilbert E. Metcalf, Andrei P. Sokolov, and Jennifer F. Holak (2007). 'Assessment of U.S. Cap-and-Trade Proposals.' National Bureau of Economic Research Working Paper 13176, June.

Parry, I.W.H. (2003). 'Fiscal Interactions and the Case for Carbon Taxes over Grandfathered Carbon Permits.' Resources for the Future Discussion Paper 03–46.

Parry, I.W.H. (2004). 'Are Emission Permits Regressive?' *Journal of Environmental Economics and Management* 47(2004): 364–87.

Pizer, William A. (1997). 'Prices vs. Quantities Revisited: The Case of Climate Change.' Resources for the Future Discussion Paper 98–02.

Roberts, Marc J., and Michael Spence (1976). 'Effluent Charges and Licenses under Uncertainty.' *Journal of Public Economics* 5:193–208.

Schmalensee, Richard, Paul L. Joskow, A. Denny Ellerman, Juan Pablo Montero, and Elizabeth M. Bailey (1998). 'An Interim Evaluation of Sulfur Dioxide Emissions Trading.' *The Journal of Economic Perspectives* 12(3): 53–68.

Smith, Anne, Jeremy Platt, and A. Danny Ellerman (1998). 'The Costs of Reducing Utility SO_2 Emissions: Not as Low as You Might Think.' *Public Utilities Fortnightly* 15 May; longer edition released as MIT Discussion Paper, 17 August.

U.S. Environmental Protection Agency (EPA) (1995). *Human Health Benefits from Sulfate Reductions under Title IV of the 1990 Clean Air Act Amendments.* Washington, DC: Office of Air and Radiation, November.

8 Emission Taxes and the General Equilibrium Model of Emission Pricing

8.1 Review of Basic Concepts

At this point we have already covered most of the basics of emission taxes. We first introduced the terminology in Section 1.2.2. In Section 2.3 we defined marginal damages, which is the concept that guides valuation of pollution reduction. In Chapter 3 we developed the marginal abatement cost curve, showing that there is a basic symmetry between targeting the quantity of emissions and the price of emissions, making emission taxes an effective control device. In Chapter 4 we looked at the way in which emission taxes allocate abatement activity across firms according to the equimarginal condition. In Section 4.2 we derived the key result that firms respond to an emissions tax by moving to the level of emissions where the tax rate equals the marginal abatement cost level. We also looked at the effect of taxes on long-run efficiency (entry-exit) and adoption of new pollution control technology. Section 4.7 explained the difference between emission taxes and Pigovian taxes, and critiqued the simple analysis often found in introductory textbooks. In Chapter 5 we looked at the way emission taxes change the incentives for firms to reveal information about their abatement costs, and the way uncertainty affects whether taxes or emission caps are the most appropriate instrument. In Section 7.3 we discussed the issue of scarcity rents under tradable permits, which corresponds closely to the issue of emission tax revenue. We will see in this chapter that the way emission tax revenue is recycled into the economy has a large effect on the overall cost of the policy.

Having established all these basic results, only a brief introduction is needed at this point before developing the general equilibrium analysis on which this chapter focuses. Firms' profits π_i are defined as a function of their emitting activity e_i. Emitting activity itself is a function of an emissions tax τ, so we can write the sum of profits as $\sum \pi_i(e_i(\tau))$ and the total damages as $D(E(\tau))$, where $E = \sum e_i$. Then a compact way to describe the optimal emissions tax problem is to maximize social welfare W with respect to τ, where

$$W = \sum \pi_i(e_i(\tau)) - D(E(\tau)). \tag{8.1}$$

The first-order condition is

$$\sum \frac{\partial e_i}{\partial \tau} \left(\frac{\partial \pi_i}{\partial e_i} - \frac{\partial D}{\partial E} \right) = 0. \tag{8.2}$$

Setting the term in brackets to equal zero, we obtain the usual solution that marginal abatement costs should equal marginal damages, where the latter are defined over the sum of emissions E.

One important wrinkle to the emissions tax story is that the outcome for a firm is not affected if a certain level of emissions is set as a threshold below which no tax is paid, as long as the threshold is below the resulting emissions level. For example, suppose that a firm is charged τ per unit of emissions, but only on those emissions above a base level. The firm's optimization problem is now

$$\max_{e_i} \pi(e) - \tau(e - \hat{e})$$

and since $\hat{e}$ is fixed, this has the usual solution

$$\frac{\partial \pi}{\partial e} = \tau.$$

However, if the resulting emissions level, which we will denote e^*, is less than $\hat{e}$, the resulting profits would be less than could be obtained by simply setting $e^* = \hat{e}$.

The outcome is illustrated in Figure 8.1.

If the tax rate τ is charged, the resulting emissions level would be e^*. If the payment threshold is $\hat{e}_1$ then the resulting emissions level will be e^* and the tax bill will be

$$\tau(e^* - \hat{e}_1).$$

Figure 8.1 Emission taxes and payment thresholds.

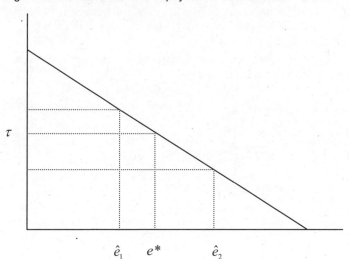

$$\hat{e}_1 \qquad e^* \qquad\qquad \hat{e}_2$$

If the threshold is $\hat{e}_2$ then the firm will not emit at e^*, but will continue up to the threshold level and will pay no taxes.

8.2 Deadweight Loss

To go further in the analysis of emission taxes it will be helpful to review the basic terminology of taxation and deadweight loss. In Figure 8.2 we have a standard demand-supply diagram.

The initial competitive equilibrium is at quantity Q^*. Adding the unit tax t causes the buyer's price to rise from P^* to P^B and the seller's price to fall to P^S, and the new equilibrium is at Q_t. The deadweight loss is the shaded area, representing the loss in consumer surplus and producer surplus which does not accrue as revenue for the government. The deadweight loss is often referred to as the 'excess burden' of the tax system, and if the tax rate is raised the additional deadweight loss is the 'marginal excess burden' or MEB. It can be shown that with linear demand and supply lines, the MEB rises with the square of the tax rate. A related term is the 'marginal cost of public funds' (MCPF). This is the welfare cost per dollar of additional revenue. Estimates of the MCPF in the U.S. tax system range from 1.2 to 4.0 for many of the principal revenue-raising taxes (see Browning 1987; Fullerton 1991). A MCPF of

Figure 8.2 Deadweight loss in a standard demand-supply diagram.

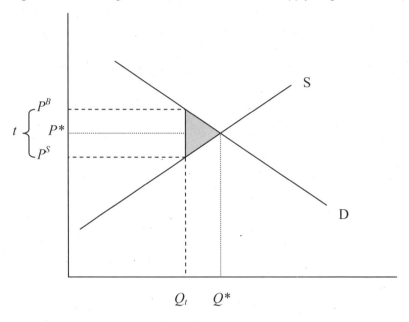

1.2 implies that $1.20 of consumer and producer surplus must be destroyed for every $1 of public revenue at the margin.

8.3 Revenue Recycling and Tax Interaction Effects

Section 8.2 shows, more or less, the standard public finance view: taxes cause welfare losses over and above the revenues they raise, by driving a wedge between buyers' and sellers' prices. But environmental economics offers an alternative story: a tax on marginal damages resulting from externalities *improves* welfare, by internalizing the social cost of emissions. It did not take long before people suggested that these two results ought to be put together. Suppose we levy environmental taxes, which raise money and improve welfare. We could then use the money to reduce other, distorting taxes at the margin, which reduces the excess burden of the tax system and thus provides an additional increase in welfare. This is called the 'double dividend' argument: environmental taxes provide two benefits, one from reducing pollution, the other from reducing distortions in the tax system (assuming the

Figure 8.3 The revenue recycling effect.

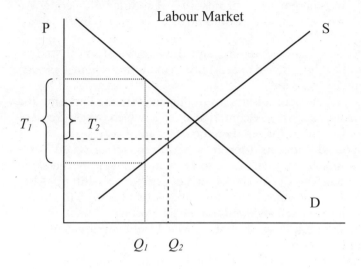

revenue from pollution taxes is 'recycled' by reducing other tax rates). Applying this logic to a simple tax reform model, Lee and Misiolek (1986) concluded that environmental taxes should typically be higher than marginal damages, to take into account the additional benefit from the tax offset. In its more extreme form, the double dividend hypothesis was sometimes held to imply that *any* environmental tax is welfare improving, even if we do not know what are the benefits of reducing pollution, because the pollution tax reduces environmental damages while revenues from such taxes allow for a reduction in the excess burden of the rest of the tax system.

This story, however, is not quite right. It is not the case that *any* reduction in pollution improves net welfare (it depends on the MAC as well as MD), and in addition, taxes on polluting goods exacerbate the excess burdens of other taxes. This latter point is rather subtle and was missed for a while. The so-called 'tax interaction' effects may equal or exceed the 'revenue recycling' benefit from reducing other taxes.

Figure 8.3 illustrates the point as follows. Suppose the demand for labour is along line D, and the supply of labour is along line S. Initially the labour tax is T_1, and the total tax bill is T_1Q_1. If this is the only source of tax revenue, then the government raises

$$T_1Q_1 = G$$

as revenue. Now suppose a pollution tax t is imposed on (post-tax) emissions E, and the government raises tE in additional revenue. We might be able to argue that this would finance a reduction in the labour tax to T_2, because $T_2Q_2 + tE = G$.

The reduction in the labour tax, and the additional social welfare brought about by the reduced excess burden in the tax system, has been called a 'double dividend.'

But there is an element missing from this analysis. By imposing the emissions tax, firms must pay compliance costs, which raise the cost of their output. Consumer prices therefore rise, and because the rate of return to labour declines as a result of higher consumer costs, workers require a higher nominal wage to be willing to supply the same amount of labour. This causes the labour supply curve to shift up. Also, the increased costs of other goods will cause other markets to shrink, although for now we will just focus on the labour market.

Consider Figure 8.4. If we start at tax rate T_2 and employment level Q_2, a shift in the labour supply curve from S to S' would, on its own, reduce the amount of money being raised through labour taxes. In order to maintain total revenues of G, the government would have to increase the labour tax. When the labour supply curve shifts up, the labour tax revenue falls to T_2Q_3, which is less than T_2Q_2. If $T_2Q_2 + tE = G$ then

$$T_2Q_3 + tE < G.$$

In order to keep the budget balanced, it will be necessary to raise the labour tax to some new level T_3 (which is not shown on Fig. 8.4).

So now, as a result of introducing a tax on pollution, two offsetting changes occur elsewhere in the tax system. First, the revenue recycling effect (RE) allows the policy maker to reduce another tax. But simultaneously, the (tax) interaction effect (IE) requires other taxes to increase. Which one will be stronger?

Parry (1995) used a graphical model with two markets to show that the IE will typically be stronger than the RE. This implies that if the regulator is optimizing the emissions tax with respect to both the pollution damages and the excess burden of the tax system, he or she will typically want to set the emissions tax below the classical solution point where MD = MAC. The key mechanism is that the real wage rate goes down when an emission tax is imposed. If workers are paid w per unit, but consumer costs go up as a result of the emissions tax, the nominal wage rate has to increase to keep the labour supply constant.

Figure 8.4 The tax interaction effect.

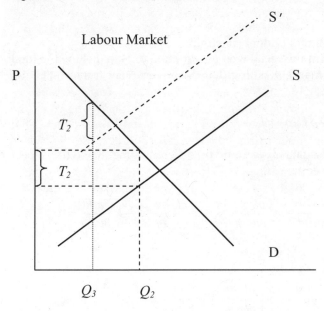

We can draw more precise conclusions by representing the case mathematically, as follows. Suppose there is a productive sector that employs labour L at nominal cost w per unit, to produce a total product

$$\rho f(L)$$

where ρ is the selling price. A tax on labour is imposed at the rate t, implying sector profits

$$\rho f(L) - w(1+t)L.$$

A second sector only uses emissions e to generate profits $\pi(e)$, and the damages are $D(e)$. The government needs to raise an amount G, using an emissions tax τ and the labour tax t. The budget constraint is therefore

$$\tau e + t w L = G. \tag{8.3}$$

This rearranges to an expression for the labour tax rate:

$$t = (G - \tau e) / (wL),$$

which implies, for revenue-neutral tax shifts,

$$\frac{\partial t}{\partial \tau} = -\frac{e}{wL} \tag{8.4}$$

along the government budget constraint.

We can augment the social welfare equation (8.1) to include the total surplus in both markets, noting that the government transfers, G, net out the tax terms:

$$W = \pi(e) - D(e) + pf(L) - wL. \tag{8.5}$$

The optimal emissions tax is found by differentiating (8.5) with respect to τ and setting equal to 0:

$$\frac{\partial W}{\partial \tau} = \frac{\partial \pi}{\partial e}\frac{\partial e}{\partial \tau} - \frac{\partial D}{\partial e}\frac{\partial e}{\partial \tau} + pf'\frac{\partial L}{\partial w}\frac{\partial w}{\partial t}\frac{\partial t}{\partial \tau} - w\frac{\partial L}{\partial w}\frac{\partial w}{\partial t}\frac{\partial t}{\partial \tau} - L\frac{\partial w}{\partial t}\frac{\partial t}{\partial \tau} = 0.$$

Because $pf' - w = wt$, using (8.4) this reduces to

$$\frac{\partial W}{\partial \tau} = \frac{\partial e}{\partial \tau}(MAC - MD) - \frac{te}{L}\left(\frac{\partial L}{\partial w}\frac{\partial w}{\partial t}\right) + \frac{\partial w}{\partial t}\frac{e}{w} = 0.$$

Denote the labour supply elasticity as $\eta = \frac{\partial L}{\partial w}\frac{w}{L}$ and the elasticity of the nominal wage rate with respect to the labour tax rate as $\psi = \frac{\partial w}{\partial t}\frac{t}{w}$. Note that $\eta > 0$ and $\psi < 0$. The above expression implies that welfare is optimized where

$$(MAC - MD) = \frac{\psi\eta e - \mu e / t}{\partial e / \partial \tau} = \frac{\psi e(\eta - 1/t)}{\partial e / \partial \tau}. \tag{8.6}$$

Note that the denominator, $\partial e / \partial \tau$, is negative. The numerator will be positive if $\eta < 1/t$, implying that the optimal tax rate will be where MAC < MD. Because $0 < t < 1$, this means that $\eta \le 1$ is a sufficient condition, and if, for example, $t = 0.3$ the labour supply elasticity could rise as high as 3.33 and the right-hand side would still be negative.

(8.6) can be rearranged further by denoting the elasticity of emissions with respect to the tax rate as ε:

$$\varepsilon \equiv \frac{\partial e}{\partial \tau}\frac{\tau}{e}.$$

Then welfare is optimized where

$$(MAC - MD) = \frac{\psi\tau(\eta - 1/t)}{\varepsilon}.$$

Assuming that $\eta < 1/t$ and the other elasticities are non-zero, this expression yields some straightforward implications. First, any positive emissions tax $\tau > 0$ implies there should be a gap between MAC and MD at the optimal tax level. Second, the gap should be larger (ceteris paribus) the smaller is ε; that is, the steeper is the MAC. Third, the less sensitive the nominal wage rate is to the labour tax (i.e., smaller ψ), the smaller the optimal gap between MAC and MD.

The key issue in this analysis is the presence of a pre-existing distortion in the economy resulting from the structure of the rest of the tax system. The fact that the emissions tax raises revenue for the government (as would a permits auction) means that offsetting tax reductions can occur. But suppose the policy was a set of emission standards, or tradable permits subject to free distribution. If the permits are given away or 'grandfathered' (rather than being auctioned), as is the case in the U.S. sulfur dioxide market, then the amount τe accrues as *scarcity rents* to the permit holders, and the government does not raise as much additional revenue (the only additional revenue raised by the government is income taxation of the scarcity rents). Therefore it has no money to fund tax reductions to offset the IE. As mentioned in the previous chapter, when tradable permits are grandfathered rather than auctioned they are sometimes called *quotas*. In the presence of a distorting tax system, a quota market is more expensive, from society's point of view, than an emissions tax or a permits auction, because the interaction effects arise under both policies, but the revenue recycling effect is much weaker or non-existent under a quota system.

So, the presence of other taxes in the economy makes two differences to the standard (partial equilibrium) analysis. First, it breaks down the symmetry between taxes and tradable quotas because of the way the scarcity rents (τe) are distributed. In other words, a tradable quota system does not have the same overall economic costs as an emissions tax, even if the resulting emission levels are identical for both instruments. Second, it implies that the conventional optimal pricing rule ($\tau = MD$) may not hold. We will prove this latter point in a general equilibrium framework in the next section.

On the issue of the asymmetry between taxes and quotas, Parry, Wil-

Figure 8.5 Optimal emissions control taking policy costs into account.

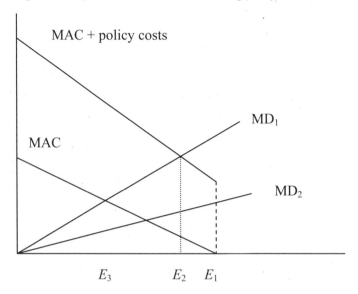

liams, and Goulder (1999) used analytical and numerical modeling to show that, in the case of U.S. carbon dioxide emissions, at a labour tax rate of 40% the tax interaction effect was so strong that under tradable quotas the first unit of emissions reduction would cost at least $18 (U.S.) per ton. If quota rents are not themselves subject to taxation the marginal cost of the first unit of emissions reduction would be over $29 per ton. But if emissions are taxed and the revenues are used to reduce labour taxes the marginal cost of emission reductions begins at zero. For a 20 per cent reduction in emissions, an emissions tax would have a marginal cost of just over $60 per ton, whereas tradable quotas would have a marginal economic cost of over $100 per ton.

These results suggest that, if marginal damages of CO_2 emissions were, say, $10 per ton, any amount of emissions reduction would be welfare reducing under a tradable quota scheme. This seems counterintuitive, because Figure 8.5 shows the MAC reaching the horizontal axis at E_1, and it is clearly optimal to reduce emissions at that point, ceteris paribus. The point of the tax interaction literature is that the distortions in the economy resulting from the tax system create a hidden category of *policy costs*. If these are taken into account, our standard

MAC curve for a policy that does not achieve full revenue recycling should be redrawn as shown in Figure 8.5. If the marginal damages are MD_1, the diagram would imply emissions should be reduced to E_3 if we only consult the MAC curve. But if we do not achieve revenue recycling we need to refer instead to MAC + *policy costs*, which implies that emissions should be reduced by a lesser amount, to E_2, and the tax rate necessary (which follows the MAC curve) would be less also. If marginal damages are MD_2, we would not be able to justify reducing emissions at all as long as we use an instrument that has policy costs associated with it.

The other question raised by considering the nature of the tax system is how externalities should be taxed in an economy in which there are pre-existing tax distortions. The partial equilibrium model above only hints at the solution. A more complete treatment was provided in an elegant analysis first presented by Agnar Sandmo in the *Swedish Journal of Economics* in 1975.

8.4 The Sandmo Model of Optimal Taxation in the Presence of Externalities*

In this section we tie together many of the themes developed thus far by asking: What is the optimal tax, in a general equilibrium setting, on a commodity whose consumption generates externalities, when there are distortionary taxes elsewhere in the economy? This is the question tackled in the Sandmo model.

Consider an economy with n consumers, all of whom are identical. There are $m + 1$ consumer goods. The amount of good i consumed by each consumer is denoted x_i. The total consumption across n consumers is denoted X_i. x_0 is the amount of labour supplied. The total time endowment is normalized at unity, so leisure demand is $1 - x_0$. Consumption of the mth good generates an externality in linear proportion to total consumption. The individual utility function is written

$$u^j = u(1 - x_0, x_1, ..., x_m, X_m) \tag{8.7}$$

and the aggregate utility is nu^j. Production occurs through a linear technology frontier:

$$\sum_{i=1}^{m} a_i X_i = X_0 \tag{8.8}$$

where the a_i's are input-output coefficients, showing the amount of labour required to produce a unit of that commodity. The left-hand side shows the aggregate labour requirement to produce all m commodities and the right-hand side shows the aggregate labour supply. Note that no capital or savings appear in this model.

8.4.1 First-Best Allocation

The Pareto-optimal allocation of production and consumption will solve the following constrained optimization (the 'planner's problem'):

$$\max_{x_i} L = nu(1 - x_0, x_1, ..., x_m, X_m) - \alpha\left(-X_0 + \sum_{i=1}^{m} a_i X_i\right). \tag{8.9}$$

The first-order conditions are:

$$\frac{u_i}{u_0} = a_i \qquad (i = 1, ..., m - 1) \tag{8.10}$$

and

$$\frac{u_m}{u_0}\left(1 + n\frac{u_{m+1}}{u_m}\right) = a_m. \tag{8.11}$$

(The equations here numbered 8.10 and 8.11 correspond to equations 5 and 6 in Sandmo's article). Equation (8.10) indicates that, for each good, the marginal rate of substitution in consumption should equal the marginal rate of transformation of labour into that commodity. Equation (8.11) is analogous to the familiar Samuelsonian rule for public goods. The second term in the brackets is the sum across individuals of the marginal rates of substitution between X_m, the public externality, and x_m, the private benefit from consuming good m. The marginal rate of substitution between labour and production of good m should exceed the marginal cost of producing good m (expressed in labour units) by an amount reflecting the aggregate disutility caused by consumption of good m.

These are the first-order conditions for an optimally 'planned' economy. What we now want to do is examine the first-order conditions in a competitive economy, that is, one in which agents individually choose production and consumption levels in response to market prices. Then, we will see if there is a tax system that can cause the competitive outcome to correspond with the planner's optimum.

8.4.2 Decentralized Competitive Outcome

We first need to define price and tax terms. Consumers pay prices $P = (P_0, P_1, ..., P_m)$, firms receive prices $p = (p_0, p_1, ..., p_m)$, and the difference is the set of unit taxes $t = (t_0, t_1, ..., t_m)$, hence $P_i = p_i + t_i$. It is a feature of optimal taxation models that we can normalize one consumer price and one producer price to unity; by doing so we automatically set one tax rate to zero. We will make labour the numeraire good, hence $P_0 = p_0 = 1$ and $t_0 = 0$. The consumer's budget constraint is

$$\sum_{i=1}^{m} P_i x_i = S + x_0 \tag{8.12}$$

where S is a lump-sum transfer from the government to each consumer. As price-takers, consumers solve their utility maximization problem at

$$\frac{u_i}{u_0} = P_i. \tag{8.13}$$

Producers must operate where

$$p_i = a_i. \tag{8.14}$$

The left-hand side of (8.14) shows the additional revenue from one more unit of production. The right-hand side shows the marginal cost of production, in particular the additional units of labour needed to produce another unit of output, multiplied by the wage rate (in this case 1). If the selling price exceeded the marginal cost, the firm would expand production until the selling price falls, and if the selling price were below marginal cost the firm would reduce output until the selling price rises. Since marginal cost and average cost are the same in this model, (8.14) is a zero-profit condition that describes the equilibrium production level.

To force an outcome in the decentralized case that coincides with the Pareto optimum, it must be the case that equations (8.13) and (8.14) correspond with (8.10) and (8.11). This requires a tax system that yields the following pricing conditions:

$$P_i = p_i \quad \text{for all } i = 1, \ldots, m-1, \tag{8.15}$$

and

$$P_m\left(1 + n\frac{u_{m+1}}{u_m}\right) = p_m. \tag{8.16}$$

Equation (8.15) implies that unit taxes on each good should be zero, except for the m-th good. (8.16) implies that the buyer's price should exceed the seller's price (because $u_{m+1} < 0$). Define

$$\theta_m = -n\frac{u_{m+1}}{u_m} \tag{8.17}$$

which is, in this context, marginal social damages from consumption of good m. Since, by (8.16), $P_m(1-\theta_m) = p_m$ we have

$$\theta_m P_m = P_m - p_m = t_m. \tag{8.18}$$

Thus, (8.18) implies that the unit tax on m should equal marginal social damages, converted into money at P_m, the current relative price between (the consumer's cost of) m and labour.

At this point it might seem odd that we have derived a solution where the optimal tax equals MD, yet in the previous section we derived a result showing that this result is likely incorrect. But recall that the tax interaction effects drove the previous results, and there are none in the Sandmo model (so far). The competitive outcome only coincides with the planner's outcome when all unit taxes are zero and, in that case, the externality tax is equal to marginal damages.

Lump-sum transfers S do not matter one way or the other because they drop out of all first-order conditions. Also, there is no reason to subsidize other goods, that is, set a tax rate $t_i < 0$ on goods other than m, due to the externality on good m, even if the other goods are substitutes for m. This result emerges clearly in the ideal world of our general equilibrium model, but in the world of policymaking, the idea of subsidizing 'clean' alternatives has considerable popularity. Recent years have seen heavy subsidies in North America and Europe for alternative energy sources like wind, solar, and biofuels, as well as for purchasing hybrid and flexfuel vehicles, compact fluorescent bulbs, and so on. But regardless of the magnitude of the eternality associated with good m it is inefficient to manipulate the prices of other goods. As with the principle of targeting discussed in Section 6.1 above, the efficient form of an emissions tax is to price in the externality on m, but not to subsidize substitute commodities.

Another point that could easily be shown in this framework is that no compensation payments should be made to the household in response to the overall externality. We have not discussed compensation payments thus far, but the concept will emerge in the next chapter when we examine legal instruments for pollution control. An interesting contrast emerges between a rights-based and a policy-based framework. In the court system, payment for damages goes from the polluter to the victim. But in the optimal policy framework, if we added to the consumer's budget a payment cX_m, where c is a compensation payment for the total externality, the above analysis would yield $c = 0$ as a feature of the optimum; that is, there should be no compensation. Although c is not a term in the Sandmo model itself, the extension is explored formally in Chapter 4 of Baumol and Oates (1988).

Setting the emissions tax equal to marginal damages is a *first-best* outcome. But it may not be the case (and likely is not) that emission taxes suffice to balance the government budget. The only other option in the above setup is to use lump-sum taxes S, which are generally ruled out in practice. So we must explore a *second-best* situation, in which lump-sum taxes are arbitrarily ruled out and instead positive taxes are levied on other goods. This will introduce the interaction effects discussed earlier, with the predictable result that the optimal price on the externality will no longer coincide with marginal damages.

8.4.3 Optimal Second-Best Tax System

It will facilitate the analysis to work with the indirect utility function rather than the direct utility function. This is the function we get if we substitute the Marshallian demand functions (which are functions of prices and income alone) back into the utility function. Hence, we define $u(x(P)) \equiv v(P)$, where the absence of a subscript indicates a vector. Differentiate v with respect to price k to get

$$\frac{\partial v}{\partial P_k} = -u_0 \frac{\partial x_0}{\partial P_k} + \sum_{i=1}^{m} u_i \frac{\partial x_i}{\partial P_k} + nu_{m+1} \frac{\partial x_m}{\partial P_k}. \tag{8.19}$$

When the consumer solves the utility-maximization problem subject to a linear budget constraint the first-order conditions are:

$$u_i = \lambda P_i$$

where λ is the Lagrange multiplier. Substitute these into (8.19) to get

$$\frac{\partial v}{\partial P_k} = -\lambda \frac{\partial x_0}{\partial P_k} + \lambda \sum_{i=1}^{m} P_i \frac{\partial x_i}{\partial P_k} + n u_{m+1} \frac{\partial x_m}{\partial P_k}. \qquad (8.20)$$

Now note that the total differential of the consumer's budget constraint with respect to the k-th price is

$$-\frac{\partial x_0}{\partial P_k} + \sum_{i=1}^{m} P_i \frac{\partial x_i}{\partial P_k} + x_k = 0. \qquad (8.21)$$

Rearrange this as follows:

$$x_k = \frac{\partial x_0}{\partial P_k} + \sum_{i=1}^{m} P_i \frac{\partial x_i}{\partial P_k}$$

and substitute into (8.20) to get

$$\frac{\partial v}{\partial P_k} = -\lambda x_k + n u_{m+1} \frac{\partial x_m}{\partial P_k}. \qquad (8.22)$$

Now let us introduce the government. Suppose the government needs to raise revenue T. Its budget constraint is

$$\sum_{i=1}^{m} t_i X_i = n \sum_{i=1}^{m} (P_i - p_i) x_i = T. \qquad (8.23)$$

We are using a utilitarian social welfare function, which is written

$$W = n v(P). \qquad (8.24)$$

The government's tax design problem is to maximize W subject to (8.23). Rather than doing the maximization with respect to the tax rates it will turn out to be easier to do it with respect to the consumer price P. (Because the producer prices are determined by the input-output coefficients, the choice of P automatically determines t as well.) The Lagrange function is

$$L = nv(P) - \beta\left[n\sum(P_i - p_i)x_i - T\right].$$

The first order conditions (with respect to P_k) are:

$$n\frac{\partial v}{\partial P_k} - \beta\left[n\sum(P_i - p_i)\frac{\partial x_i}{\partial P_k} + nx_k\right] = 0.$$

The n's cancel out. Also, we can replace $\frac{\partial v}{\partial P_k}$ with (8.22) and $(P_i - p_i)$ with t_i. This yields:

$$-\lambda x_k + nu_{m+1}\frac{\partial x_m}{\partial P_k} - \beta\left[n\sum t_i\frac{\partial x_i}{\partial P_k} + x_k\right] = 0 \tag{8.25}$$

for $(k = 1, ..., m)$.

Buried in this series of equations is the optimal tax system. We want to solve it for the t's. We will need to use matrix notation to do this. Rewrite (8.25) as

$$-\lambda\mathbf{x} + nu_{m+1}\nabla_p x_m - \beta\mathbf{J}^*t - \beta\mathbf{x} = 0$$

where

$$\mathbf{x} = \begin{bmatrix} x_1 \\ \vdots \\ x_m \end{bmatrix}, \quad \nabla_p x_m = \begin{bmatrix} \frac{\partial x_m}{\partial P_1} \\ \vdots \\ \frac{\partial x_m}{\partial P_M} \end{bmatrix}, \quad \mathbf{J}^* = \begin{bmatrix} \frac{\partial x_1}{\partial P_1} & \cdots & \frac{\partial x_m}{\partial P_1} \\ \vdots & \ddots & \vdots \\ \frac{\partial x_1}{\partial P_m} & \cdots & \frac{\partial x_m}{\partial P_m} \end{bmatrix},$$

and t is the vector of tax rates. Then

$$-(\lambda + \beta)\mathbf{x} + nu_{m+1}\nabla_p x_m = \beta\mathbf{J}^*t$$

or

$$\mathbf{J}^*t = \frac{-(\lambda + \beta)}{\beta}\mathbf{x} + \frac{1}{\beta}nu_{m+1}\nabla_p x_m.$$

Denote the determinant of $\mathbf{J}^*$ as $\mathbf{J}$ and let J_{ik} be the co-factor of element j_{ik}. Then by Cramer's rule,

$$t_k = -\left(\frac{\lambda + \beta}{\beta}\right)\frac{\sum x_i J_{ik}}{\mathbf{J}} + \frac{1}{\beta}nu_{m+1}\frac{\sum\frac{\partial x_i}{\partial P_i}}{\mathbf{J}}$$

which further reduces to

$$\theta_k = (1-\mu)\left[-\frac{1}{P_k}\frac{\sum x_i J_{ik}}{J}\right] \qquad (8.26)$$

for $k = 1, \ldots, m - 1$; and

$$\theta_m = (1-\mu)\left[-\frac{1}{P_m}\frac{\sum x_i J_{im}}{J}\right] + \mu\left[-n\frac{u_{m+1}}{u_m}\right], \qquad (8.27)$$

where θ_k is the ad valorem tax rate, i.e. $\theta_k = \frac{t_k}{P_k}$, and $\mu = -\lambda/\beta$.

Equation (8.27) tells us that the externality component of the tax is additive, and moreover that it only enters the formula for the m-th good, not for any of the others. This indicates that our earlier point about not subsidizing substitutes to the dirty good is sufficiently general as to carry over to the second-best analysis.

What does the weighting parameter μ signify? Recall that $\mu = -\lambda/\beta$. The variable λ is the Lagrange multiplier from the consumer's optimization problem, and hence shows the marginal utility of (private) income. The variable β is the Lagrange multiplier from the social welfare maximization problem. It shows the social welfare change from raising the government's revenue requirement, or in other words, the aggregate marginal disutility of adding one dollar to public income. Thus

$$-\frac{\lambda}{\beta} = -\frac{\partial u/\partial[\text{Private Income}]}{\partial u/\partial[\text{Public Income}]}. \qquad (8.28)$$

In words, μ = the marginal rate of substitution between public and private income. In an economy with no tax distortions, the value of a dollar lost to the private sector exactly equals the value of the dollar gained by the public sector, so in this case we would have $\mu = 1$. Then Equations (8.26) and (8.27) would collapse to the first-best solution. The only non-lump sum tax would be the one on good m, and it would be equal to marginal social damages. This, as we saw earlier, corresponds to the case where there is no excess burden in the tax system. The classic prescription of $\tau = MD$ applies in the ideal world where there are no distortions from the existing tax system.

If there are distorting taxes, however, the marginal value of private income differs from the marginal value of public income. Because of the deadweight loss triangle, a dollar's worth of incremental public income costs more than a dollar's worth of private welfare. To keep welfare unchanged, the marginal utility associated with the public spending would have to be greater than the marginal utility of the foregone private consumption. Hence, the denominator in (8.28) must be larger than the numerator, or $\mu < 1$, when there are tax distortions in the economy. From (8.27) this implies that the optimal environmental tax should be smaller than it would be in the first-best case. This completes a point introduced in Section 8.3, where we said that the presence of other taxes in the economy undermines the classical rule $\tau = MD$.

The parameter μ is very close to the concept of the marginal cost of public funds, because it is approximately true that $\mu = 1/MCPF$. If the MCPF rises towards infinity (taxes get extremely distorting and burdensome), then μ approaches 0. By (8.27), the efficient tax system would be based only on revenue-raising components, and the environmental component on good m would vanish. This is somewhat counter-intuitive, and indeed goes against the double-dividend argument that in economies with very distorting tax systems we should raise pollution taxes and lower other taxes. It turns out that the opposite is true: in very distorting tax systems we should not raise pollution taxes; other things being equal we should lower them. The reason is that as the level of distortions in the tax system rise, all public goods – including environmental protection – get more costly and optimal provision levels go down. Suppose the externality in this case were a benefit, rather than a cost. Then the 'tax' would be negative one – a subsidy. But if the tax system were heavily distorting, we would intuitively expect that the subsidy for provision of the external benefit should be scaled back. In the same way, the tax places a cost on the externality and in that sense provides a public good, namely environmental cleanliness. But in doing so it increases the distortions in the market for the m-th good, and if these distortions are already severe, we will not want to exacerbate them, even to improve environmental quality. The focus of the tax system would shift to raising revenue.

If we make one further simplification we can generate a bit more insight. Suppose the cross-price derivatives are zero, that is,

$$\frac{\partial x_i}{\partial P_i} = 0 \quad \text{for all } i \neq j.$$

Define $\varepsilon_k = \dfrac{\partial x_k}{\partial P_k} \dfrac{P_k}{x_k}$. Then

$$\theta_k = (1-\mu)\left[-\frac{1}{\varepsilon_k}\right] \tag{8.29}$$

for $k = 1, \ldots, m - 1$; and

$$\theta_m = (1-\mu)\left[-\frac{1}{\varepsilon_m}\right] + \mu\left[-n\frac{u_{m+1}}{u_m}\right]. \tag{8.30}$$

Equation (8.29) is a standard optimal tax equation showing that the tax rate on a good should be higher, the smaller is the magnitude of its own price elasticity. Equation (8.30) shows that the optimal tax on a good which generates an externality is a weighted sum of two components: the revenue-raising component and the externality.

8.4.4 Pollution Taxes and Deadweight Loss

Estimates of the marginal cost of public funds are quite variable depending on the narrowness of the tax and differences between definitions of excess burden. Mayshar (1991) reports a range from around 1.1 to 1.8 for some principal U.S. taxes. Suppose we take a central estimate to be around 1.3. We can relate the results of this section to those in Section 8.3 by noting that the environmental portion of the tax in equation (8.30) is approximately 77 per cent of MD. The optimal externality charge is less than the actual value of marginal damages, as a result of the interactions with the rest of the tax system.

Another point that emerges in this model is that, in response to externalities from one good, we should adjust the price of that good, but not other goods. This echoes a point made in Chapter 6 as well, namely that environmental policy should focus on the variable of interest as directly as possible, rather than on related goods. If we have priced the externality directly we should not also subsidize substitutes. As noted above, this point seems to be easy to miss, because so many governments subsidize alternative energy sources out of concern about the environmental impacts of fossil fuel-based power generation.

Finally, note that the environmental component will be additive on top of the revenue-raising component. If the government had previously determined that the existing taxes are the necessary 'revenue-raising' taxes, and the externality were 'newly discovered,' then we would add to the existing tax an amount approximately equal to MD/$MCPF$.

This analysis by no means takes away from the idea that environmental taxes are good tools for dealing with externalities. Recall that distortions in the tax system raise the cost of all forms of environmental protection, whether achieved through pricing or non-price instruments. In the case of non-price instruments, such as standards, no revenue is contributed to the government except indirectly through taxation of the scarcity rents generated by emissions controls. Because the absence of new revenue precludes a revenue recycling effect, such instruments are even costlier to the economy. Hence, the Sandmo model contains an unstated generalization, which to my knowledge has not been emphasized in the literature: in the presence of distorting taxes the optimal emissions level is higher than it otherwise would be, and if emissions control policy is not revenue raising (with the revenues dedicated to reducing other taxes) the optimal emissions level is even higher still.

8.5 Subsidies

In a simple sense, subsidies should work just the same as taxes do, except for the presence of a constant term. Suppose that in the absence of regulation a firm emits $\bar{e}$. If the firm is confronted with an emission tax t its profits are $\pi(e) - \tau e$. The optimal emissions level occurs where

$$\pi'(e) = \tau.$$

Suppose instead that the regulator promises to pay the firm s for each unit by which its emissions fall below $\bar{e}$. Then the firm's profits are:

$$\pi(e) + s(\bar{e} - e). \tag{8.31}$$

But this rearranges to

$$\pi(e) - se + s\bar{e}.$$

The last term, $s\bar{e}$, is a lump-sum. So when the firm chooses its optimal emissions under (8.31), it goes to where

$$\pi'(e) = s.$$

If $s = \tau$, the first-order condition is identical to that for an emissions tax. Hence the outcome for the individual firm will be the same.

For the *industry* however, the outcome may not be the same. At the optimal emissions level under the tax system (call it e^τ), the firm earns

$$\pi(e^\tau) - \tau e^\tau.$$

Under the subsidy system, the firms earns

$$\pi(e^s) - se^s + s\overline{e}.$$

The policy which yields identical emissions for each firm sets $s = \tau$. But this policy yields different profits for each firm in the industry because firms earn more under the subsidy scheme. And because profits attract entrants, there will be more firms in the industry under the subsidy scheme than under the tax scheme. If each firm emits the same amount under either policy, but there are more firms under the subsidy policy, total emissions are higher under the subsidy scheme than under the tax scheme.

It is even possible that the subsidy plan can increase total emissions. Suppose there are n firms and that all firms are identical. The total emissions are

$$E = ne.$$

The effect of the subsidy s is

$$\frac{dE}{ds} = n\frac{\partial e}{\partial s} + e\frac{\partial n}{\partial s}.$$

We know that $\frac{\partial e}{\partial s}$ is negative, but $\frac{\partial n}{\partial s}$ is non-negative. Hence $\frac{dE}{ds}$ may be positive or negative.

The only way to avoid attracting entrants is to offer the subsidy only to existing firms. But this creates an advantage for incumbents which can be used strategically to keep out potential competitors. The way to avoid this, in turn, is to give the subsidy to all current and future firms regardless of whether they enter or exit. But this is computationally impossible, and would be infeasible to implement. There may be cases in which entry is ruled out just by circumstance. For instance, emissions might be tied to the operation of gas or oil wells, or mines, and the total number of these is fixed by extraction permits. In this case the subsidy system can still yield an efficient outcome.

Review Questions

1. Suppose a firm's marginal abatement cost curve is $MAC = 30 - E$. The government sets an emissions tax of $t = 17$, and says it will only charge the firm for emissions over 10 units. What will be the outcome, and how much will the firm pay in taxes?

2. Suppose now the government charges a tax of $t = 20$, but raises the threshold to 15 units. What will happen to emissions, and will the firm's tax bill go up or down?

3. For the model summarized in equation (8.6), what would be the optimal gap between MD and MAC be if the nominal wage rate w does not change in response to a change in the labour tax t?

4. For the model summarized in equation (8.6), how does the optimal gap between MD and MAC change as the MAC gets steeper?

5. One firm has a MAC of $MAC_1 = 1400 - e_1$. Another has $MAC_2 = 1200 - \frac{1}{3}e_2$. Marginal damages are $MD = E$ where E is total emissions. Find the total unregulated emissions, the optimal emissions levels for each firm, and the optimal emissions tax.

6. Suppose a government imposes a tax t on the smoke emissions from the power plants in its jurisdiction. It is then proposed that even more progress could be made on emission reductions by using the tax proceeds to subsidize wind energy production. Do you think this is a good idea? Why or why not?

7. In cases where the MAC is steep, a tax equaling MD, with a suitable adjustment for tax distortion effects, would only yield a small reduction in emissions. A regulator observing this might conclude that the emissions tax was a flawed policy, and propose deeper reductions using tradable permits or direct regulation. Is it true that the emissions tax was a flawed approach under the circumstances?

8. Other things being equal, if the marginal excess burden of the rest of the tax system rises, should emission taxes be adjusted up or down in response? Explain why.

9. In what sense does an optimal emissions tax function like an environmental 'supply curve' in the economy?

10. One concern about environmental taxes is that they may be *regressive*, in other words that they may fall disproportionately heavily on low-income households. Can you give examples of taxes where this may be a problem? How might it be remedied, and might the measures taken to deal with it detract from the efficiency of the tax instrument?

References and Extra Reading

Browning, E. K. (1987). 'On the marginal welfare cost of taxation.' *American Economic Review* 77: 11–23.

Fullerton, Don (1991). 'Reconciling Recent Estimates of the Marginal Welfare Cost of Taxation.' *The American Economic Review* 81(1): 302–8

Lee, D. R., and W. S. Misiolek (1986). 'Substituting Pollution Taxation for General Taxation: Some Implications for Efficiency in Pollution Taxation.' *Journal of Environmental Economics and Management* 13: 338–47.

Mayshar, Joram (1991). 'On Measuring the Marginal Cost of Funds Analytically.' *American Economic Review* 81(5): 1329–35.

Parry, Ian, Roberton C. Williams III, and Lawrence H. Goulder (1999). 'When Can Carbon Abatement Policies Increase Welfare? The Fundamental Role of Distorted Factor Markets.' *Journal of Environmental Economics and Management* 37: 52–84.

Parry, I.W.H. (1995). 'Pollution Taxes and Revenue Recycling.' *Journal of Environmental Economics and Management* 29: S64–S77.

Sandmo, Agnar (1975). 'Optimal Taxation in the Presence of Externalities.' *Swedish Journal of Economics* 77: 86–98.

Walls, Margaret, and Jean Hanson (1996). 'Distributional Impacts of and Environmental Tax Shift: The Case of Motor Vehicle Emission Taxes.' Resources for the Future Discussion Paper 96-11, February.

9 Bargaining and Tort Law as Solutions to Externalities

9.1 Introduction

Up to now we have focused on government interventions for externalities. Another category of policy that primarily involves courts, rather than legislators, is known as *tort law* under the British and American common-law tradition, and the *Law of Delicts* under the French civil code. Each is a form of jurisprudence that addresses torts, or harm done by one party (the 'tortfeasor') against a victim, where there is no contract between them to govern the payment of costs. In this chapter I will focus on the common law approaches used in systems derived from the British common law, which includes the United States and Canada outside Quebec.

Under common law, several categories of tort have been defined that are relevant to the control of pollution. A *nuisance* tort occurs when one person's activity interferes with another's right to reasonable enjoyment of his or her property. This can take the form of smells, smoke, obstruction of view, and so on. If one person's actions cause an invasion of another's property, for instance by waste runoff or air pollution, this may be considered a *trespass*, which is also a tort. There does not need to be a specific law prohibiting nuisance or trespass for them to be considered torts, because the categories exist under longstanding common-law traditions.

If a victim sues a tortfeasor and the court upholds the complaint, the tortfeasor is said to be *liable*. Liability may arise because the tortfeasor failed to meet a *negligence* standard, which means he or she failed to exercise a sufficient level of *due care*. Under a negligence rule, if damages occurred but the tortfeasor can show he or she exercised due care, he or she is not liable for damages. Alternatively, if the standard is *strict liability*, the court will hold the tortfeasor liable if any damages can be proven to have occurred, regardless of the care taken by the tortfeasor to prevent them.

Remedies may include an *injunction* that forbids continuation of the action causing the tort, and/or the court may order the tortfeasor to pay *damages* to the victim to compensate for losses. By issuing a ruling the court assigns rights. If the complaint is upheld the court effectively assigns rights to the victim. If the complaint is dismissed the court effectively assigns rights to the tortfeasor.

Suppose a farmer observes that a neighbouring garbage incinerator is spraying soot and waste on his fields. He goes to court and sues for an injunction. The court agrees that the soot constitutes a trespass and orders the incinerator to shut down. In this case an externality was dealt with and no law was required, except for the common law of torts.

The story does not necessarily end there, however. The court has assigned the right to the farmer not to have soot blowing onto his field. But the incinerator may want to negotiate a contract with the farmer, and it might propose a bargain. After all, it would be very expensive for the incinerator to shut down, and it might not cost very much for the farmer simply to leave the injured section of his farm uncultivated. Or the incinerator may be able to reduce the emissions somewhat by spending money on abatement, but not eliminate them entirely. In that case it might be better (from an overall efficiency point of view) for the incinerator to continue operating while paying the farmer an agreed-upon sum in compensation for the smoke damages, or even for the incinerator to buy the field from the farmer. The situation is illustrated in Figure 9.1.

Initially emissions are at $\overline{E}$. Total damages are given by the area under the MD curve, which add up to $a + b + c$. Now the court issues an injunction forbidding the emissions, so they fall to zero (E_0). The farmer is better off but the garbage incinerator is worse off. Suppose the incinerator goes to the farmer and offers a deal: Allow us to increase emissions to E^*, in exchange for compensation of

$c + \frac{1}{2}d$.

The farmer gets $c + \frac{1}{2}d$ and incurs c in damages, so he is better off by $\frac{1}{2}d$. The firm pays $c + \frac{1}{2}d$ for the right to emission that earn it profits of $c + d$, so it too is better off by $\frac{1}{2}d$.

Figure 9.1 Bargaining directly over the level of an externality.

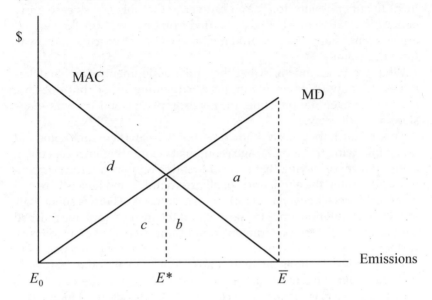

This proposal yields the optimal emissions level at E^*. Would they keep bargaining and end up at a different target? Not in this example. If the firm wants to increase emissions further, it has to offer a payment at least as high as the MD curve, but it only earns an amount down on the MAC curve, so it is unwilling to do so. If the farmer wants the firm to reduce emissions below E^*, he knows the firm would incur the cost according to the MAC line. But the maximum benefit to the farmer of further emission reductions is on the MD line, so it is not worth enough to the farmer to cover the firm's costs. Even if emissions did go below E^*, the firm would then be willing to bid up to the amount on the MAC line for the right to increase emissions again, and this would exceed the amount of compensation required by the farmer, as shown on the MD line. So they will tend to arrive back at E^* after bargaining.

Let us now back up and suppose that the court had decided in favour of the incinerator. Suppose it held that the farmer had not established that the smoke is a nuisance or trespass and refused to issue an injunction. Now the firm has the rights, and it emits at $\overline{E}$. The farmer could then go to the incinerator and offer to pay it to reduce emissions. By

similar reasoning, suppose the farmer offers the firm $b + \frac{1}{2}a$ as induce-
ment to cut emissions to E^*. You can verify that this makes each party
better off (relative to where they started from) by $\frac{1}{2}a$. Also, they would
arrive at emissions E^* and would not have an incentive to bargain away
from this point.

What we have shown is that the initial assignment of rights determines the flow of payments under a bargaining phase, but does not
change the eventual outcome. In this example we end up with emissions at E^* either way.

This result is popularly known as the 'Coase Theorem.' Some authors, following the late Chicago economist George Stigler, restated it in
a strong form by saying that in a competitive economy, direct bargaining will result in the elimination of all externalities, and hence there will
be no difference between private and social costs. There is some logic
to this interpretation: once the farmer and the incinerator have finished
bargaining to E^*, the government cannot improve on the outcome by
further policy intervention. But that is only true for the two parties to
the bargaining. If the incinerator smoke affects many other parties as
well there may be a need for a policy measure, unless the victims can
coordinate in a class action (see Section 9.2.1). This interpretation, however, goes further than the theory supports, and further than Coase's
own argument. Coase did argue that if there are no costs to bargaining and information is perfect, then one-on-one externalities will be
resolved by direct negotiation, there will be no need for regulation or
pollution taxes, and the outcome will be optimal regardless of who has
the initial rights. But he also added the corollary that because not all externalities can be dealt with by direct bargaining, therefore transaction
costs are not zero and information is not perfect in all the instances that
matter.

Coase's article was published in 1961. There has been a lot of discussion since then about what he really meant, and what it means for
environmental policy. Where externalities involve one injurer and one
victim it is quite reasonable to argue that government regulation is not
necessary, and instead the individuals should work out a solution under the supervision of the courts in a context of clear property rights
and liability rules. In practice, that happens every day. The regulator
does not need to have any prior information about damages, abatement
costs, and so on. The two parties involved have that information and
will bring it to bear on the problem themselves. Hence, liability law as
a means of protecting the environment is sometimes motivated on the

grounds that the regulator does not have the information necessary to achieve as good an outcome as the one that can be achieved by direct bargaining.

The role of property rights as a means of protecting the environment has been limited, however, for several reasons. First, in many important cases there are multiple victims and/or multiple tortfeasors, so coordinating litigation is difficult. Second, pollution damages are often uncertain and courts may have difficulty identifying efficient outcomes. Third, the payment of compensation to victims makes the outcome different from the analysis of optimal taxes or tradable permits. If victims can choose their level of exposure, this feature of the tort law approach can lead to inefficiencies. We will look at each of these issues in turn.

9.2 Multiple Victims and Joint Tortfeasors

9.2.1 Multiple Victims

If there are multiple victims of a tort, for instance if a factory pollutes the water supply of a large region and causes injury to m households, the victims have to coordinate their efforts at suing the polluter. Because of the free-riding problem they may be unable to engage in the collective action needed to bring a suit to court on behalf of all victims.

In principle, courts do not need to hear from all victims. A single plaintiff can initiate a lawsuit, and if the connection between cause and effect is clear enough, each victim would face a private incentive to sue. However, in order to facilitate joint cases, which are more efficient for the court and may result in a more accurate summation of damages, courts can certify *class actions*, in which a single plaintiff acts on behalf of a larger, identifiable group, and the lawyers are paid on the basis of the expectation of an award that covers all the group members rather than just one. However, to certify a class action, a court needs to be convinced that the issue is class-wide rather than individual. Courts have ruled that plaintiffs need to show that their claims cannot be pursued individually, that the causal links proving damage can be established on a class-wide basis rather than individually, and that the defence would not entail individual arguments. So it can be an expensive undertaking to certify a class action.

9.2.2 Joint Tortfeasors

One of the most interesting – and difficult – challenges confronting civil courts over the past few centuries has been the adjudication of cases involving *joint tortfeasors*, in which two or more individuals are jointly responsible for an injury. Examples include a group of firms collectively polluting an airshed or watershed; a succession of landowners, each of which contaminates the site and groundwater; a hazardous workplace at which employees work for a hierarchy of subcontractors, subsidiaries, firms, and holding companies. In each case, liability for damages is not obviously confined to one party. Because the injury is often indivisible, the court must decide which of the injurers should be held liable, under what circumstances, and for how much of the value of the damages, and it must apportion responsibility in a way that is fair ex post and provides a deterrent ex ante to future potential injurers. Courts have thus far failed to determine a universally satisfactory rule for adjudicating such disputes. Different doctrines, each giving rise to different ex ante incentives, have been tried and discarded over time. Rules have changed when those in use are found to be manifestly unfair or impractical. Nor are economists entirely satisfied with the current approaches to joint tortfeasor cases (see reviews in Cooter and Ulen 1988, and Miceli and Segerson 1991).

Negligence and strict liability doctrines developed where one party is wholly responsible for damages. One of the earliest complications to arise came about from recognizing that sometimes the victim is partly responsible for the extent of the injury. An early case (in which a drunken man fell from a horse upon running over some debris left in the road by a neighbour) led to a ruling that *contributory negligence*, in which the victim's carelessness or activities contributes to the injury, is a *bar to recovery*, that is, it rules out any right of the victim to be paid damages by the tortfeasor. This constituted a severe restriction on plaintiffs. Courts soon began to weaken the doctrine. A later modification assigned responsibility to the party who had the 'last clear chance' to avoid the accident, and shielded from liability a party whose portion of blame was trivially small.

Common-law courts in the twentieth century moved away from the rule of contributory negligence towards a doctrine of *comparative fault*. This is the rule that if two or more individuals are responsible for the injury, the court should apportion blame and divide up the damage claim respectively. Because the victim may bear some percentage of the responsibility, the total which can be claimed from the tortfeasor may be reduced, but the contributory negligence does not make a complete bar to recovery. Some places have added stipulations that comparative fault cases are dismissed if the victim is 50 per cent or more responsible (see North 1996).

Where comparative fault has been applied, the courts have had a difficult time deciding on an appropriate rule for apportioning liability. Sometimes the division is arbitrary, and sometimes it is based on comparisons of associated activity levels. A famous case in this regard involved the anti-miscarriage drug diethylstilbestrol (DES), which was shown to be carcinogenic in the children of its users two decades after its ingestion (Cooter and Ulen, 1988, pp. 339–40). Victims sued the manufacturers after the symptoms appeared. The court found the pharmaceutical firms jointly liable, and they were ordered to pay claims according to their respective shares of sales at the time that the drug was being taken.

Comparative fault can place an onerous burden on a victim, however, because he or she may have to sue dozens or hundreds of individuals to collect the full value of damages, depending on the number of tortfeasors. And if any of the injurers is insolvent or if their portion of the blame is so small that the award will not cover litigation costs, some of the damages may never be recovered. Consequently, many legislatures have implemented a rule of *joint and several liability*, under which a victim can sue any *one* of the injurers for the *entire* amount of the damages. This allows the victim to go after the injurer with the 'deep pockets,' increasing the chance of full recovery of damages. Under an early version of joint and several liability, the defendant found liable for the damages caused jointly by all the tortfeasors could not sue the other parties to make them contribute to the cost of paying the claim. But many jurisdictions have since begun to allow such litigation, called *contribution actions*.

Other cases have led courts to use other rules, and new rules are regularly proposed to deal with emerging case law, including environmental damages. But the situation is in flux, with no clear agreement as to whether a universally correct rule for joint tortfeasor liability exists. Nor is it clear whether the new 'rule of contribution' is more or less efficient than the old rule of joint and several liability without contribution, although it strikes most observers as being more fair.

9.2.2.1 NEGLIGENCE

In order to further analyse the outcomes of legal systems from an economic point of view we need to develop a mathematical version of the graphical tools used above. It is customary (Cooter and Ulen 1988; Shavell 1987) to model damages and costs as functions of the level of precaution taken by agents. However, it will be easier to relate the liability problem to the environmental economics literature by focusing on the level of the activity (or emissions) in which agents engage, which gives rise to the external damages. The externality-generating activity level of agent i will be denoted e_i, and referred to as 'emissions.' Total emissions $\Sigma_i e_i$ are denoted E. Denote the total emissions of all firms except those of firm i as E_{-i}, that is, $E_{-i} = E - e_i$. The gross private benefit to each firm of producing e_i is given by a profit function $\pi_i(e_i)$. Social costs associated with the activity are summarized by the convex, increasing damage function $D(E)$. The planner's social welfare function is the sum of private benefits minus the social costs of the activity:

$$W(e_1, ..., e_n, n) = \Sigma_i \pi_i(e_i) - D(E). \tag{9.1}$$

The optimal emission levels (denoted with *) are determined by the set of n first-order conditions:

$$\frac{\partial \pi_i(e_i^*)}{\partial e_i} = D'(E^*). \tag{9.2}$$

The entire setup should be familiar by now. The optimal number of firms, n^*, is defined where the last firm to enter the externality-generating industry adds nothing to net social welfare W. Assume for simplicity that this occurs at an integer value of n, hence

$$W(\cdot, n^*) - W(\cdot, n^* - 1) = \pi_n(e_n^*) - [D(E^*) - D(E_{-n}^*)] = 0. \tag{9.3}$$

Equations (9.2) and (9.3) implicitly define the long-run socially optimal level of externality-generating activity per firm and the optimal number of firms.

A variable which has been set to the privately optimal level (from the firm's perspective) will be denoted throughout by placing a ^ on top of it. So, for instance, $\hat{e}_i$ will denote the firm's preferred emissions level, and e_i^* will denote the optimal level from society's point of view. The purpose of our analysis is to see whether the incentives created by the courts' rules cause these two terms to equal one another.

Firms weigh the benefits of their activity against the liability costs $C_i(e_i)$ which are determined by the particular rules imposed by courts and/or legislators. They are assumed to be increasing in e_i. Net profits are

$$\pi_i(e_i) - C(e_i). \tag{9.4}$$

Each firm chooses an activity level where

$$\frac{\partial \pi_i(\hat{e}_i)}{\partial e_i} = C'(\hat{e}_i). \tag{9.5}$$

The last firm to enter earns zero expected profits:

$$\pi_m(\hat{e}_m) - C(\hat{e}_m) = 0. \tag{9.6}$$

The letter m will be reserved throughout this chapter to denote that firm which earns zero profits upon entering under liability rule C, when all other firms are emitting according to (9.5). In general it will be the case that $\hat{m} \neq n^*$.

A negligence rule imposes a requirement of reasonable care in order to shield a firm from liability. Assume that the rule stipulates that an emissions level of e_i^R is the reasonable care threshold. Then the firm's expected profits are:

$$\pi_i(e_i) = \begin{cases} \pi_i(\hat{e}_i), & \hat{e}_i \leq e_i^R \\ \pi_i(\hat{e}_i) - C(\hat{e}_i), & \hat{e}_i > e_i^R \end{cases}. \tag{9.7}$$

If it were possible to set firm-specific due care requirements, a negligence rule that would yield efficiency would involve setting

$$e_i^R = e_i^*$$

and

$$C(e_i) > \pi_i(e_i)$$

for all firms.

This would, in effect, present firms with no penalty up to e_i^*, and a sufficiently expensive penalty above e_i^* that firms would not exceed that level. But to implement this solution the regulator must have absolute knowledge of all the functions in (9.7), which is unrealistic. Use of liability law as a regulatory tool is often motivated by the belief that the regulator does *not* have this information. If it did, it could implement the correct outcome through direct regulation, or through emission taxes. Without such information, negligence standards are not much help if we are trying to achieve an efficient distribution of emission levels.

9.2.2.2 STRICT LIABILITY WITH APPORTIONMENT

We will assume apportionment is based on proportionate emissions levels. Each firm expects that the court will assign it the share e_i / E of total damages, hence firm i will maximize

$$\pi_i(e_i) - \frac{e_i}{e_i + E_{-i}} D(E). \tag{9.8}$$

The first-order condition for (9.8) is

$$\frac{\partial \pi_i(\hat{e}_i)}{\partial e_i} - \frac{\hat{e}_i}{\hat{E}} D'(\hat{E}) - \frac{\hat{E}_{-i}}{\hat{E}^2} D(\hat{E}) = 0. \tag{9.9}$$

This shows that the firm takes two considerations into account when deciding its emission levels. First, it only expects to pay a fraction (e_i/E) of the actual damages. On this basis it would aim to operate where $\pi_i'(e_i) > D'(E)$, that is, it would over-emit. But at the same time, it expects all other firms to choose their emission levels subject to the same condition. To the extent that other firms increase their emissions, the damages attributed to firm i increase also, and it will tend to scale back its emissions to limit this. Hence, there are incentives to both raise and lower the firm's emissions. To compare the private optimum $\hat{e}_i$ to the social optimum e_i^*, re-write (9.9) as

$$\frac{\partial \pi_i(\hat{e}_i)}{\partial e_i} - D'(\hat{E}) = \frac{\hat{E}_{-i}}{\hat{E}} \left(\bar{D}(\hat{E}) - D'(\hat{E}) \right) \tag{9.10}$$

where $\bar{D}(\hat{E}) = D(\hat{E})/\hat{E}$, that is, average damages. Suppose that the damage function is a straight line out of the origin. Then average damages always equal marginal damages, and the right-hand side of (9.10) equals zero. In that case, (9.10) corresponds to (9.2), implying $e_i^* = \hat{e}_i$. In other words, the apportionment rule can lead to correct firm-specific behaviour if the total damages function is linear. This result was first derived in Polinsky (1980). Now suppose instead that the damage function is convex, so marginal damages exceed average damages. Then the right side of (9.10) is negative, so at $\hat{e}_i$, marginal benefits (or marginal abatement costs) are less than marginal damages. This implies that privately optimal emissions by each firm exceed the socially optimal level as defined in (9.2), that is, $\hat{e}_i > e_i^*$.

To summarize, if there are multiple contributors to an externality, assigning liability according to proportionate emissions will only lead to efficient behaviour by each source if the damage function is linear and passes through the origin. In the case of convex damages, where marginal damages are increasing, firms will generate excess emissions.

We can also show that the correct number of firms will enter the industry under an average-contribution apportionment rule only if damages are linear. Under the strict liability rule, the last firm entering (denoted as firm m) will just earn zero profits:

$$\pi_m(e_m) - e_m \overline{D}(\hat{E}) = 0. \tag{9.11}$$

The change in the social welfare function at this point is

$$\Delta_m W_m = \pi_m(e_m) - D(\hat{E}) + D(\hat{E}_{-m}). \tag{9.12}$$

(9.11) and (9.12) can be combined to yield

$$\Delta_m W_m = e_m\, D(\hat{E})\big/\hat{E} - \hat{E}\, D(\hat{E})\big/\hat{E} + \hat{E}_{-m}\, D(\hat{E}_{-m})\big/\hat{E}_{-m}$$

which reduces to

$$\Delta_m W_m = -\hat{E}_{-m}\left(\overline{D}(\hat{E}) - \overline{D}(\hat{E}_{-m})\right). \tag{9.13}$$

This expression can only equal zero if average damages are constant at the point where firm m enters, that is, $\overline{D}(\hat{E}) = \overline{D}(\hat{E}_{-m})$. Otherwise, increasing average damages implies that the right-hand side of (9.13) is negative, and hence at m the social welfare function is sloping downwards. This implies that a greater-than optimal number of firms have entered the industry, each one emitting greater-than-optimal levels of pollution.

One way of dealing with the propensity for firms to over-emit under an apportionment liability rule is to have legislatures instruct courts to apply *punitive damages*. If the law stipulates a version of the so-called rule of the reciprocal (Cooter 1991), the ratio of the plaintiff's total award to the value of damages would be, in this case, E/e_i. This will cause each firm's private profit function (9.4) to correspond to net social benefits, and each firm that operates will generate the optimal emissions. The last firm to enter will be the one that earns

$$\pi_m(\hat{e}_m) - D(\hat{E}_m) = 0. \tag{9.14}$$

But where (9.14) holds, $\Delta_m W_m = D(\hat{E}_{-m}) > 0$. If the social welfare function is upward sloping this implies that the equilibrium number of firms is too low. Hence, punitive damages might correct the short-run (firm-specific) incentives under the proportionate damage system, but too many firms will exit the industry. The possibility that punitive liability might drive out firms undertaking efficient levels of the damaging activity is a concern among analysts of contemporary tort liability. An example in the product liability context is the decision by the G.D. Searle company in the 1980s to withdraw its intrauterine birth control device from the market, even though independent experts considered it a safe product, after a competitor (the A.H. Robins Company) was bankrupted by liability proceedings over the Dalkon Shield (see Cooter and Ulen 1988, p. 373). The above result explains how the use of punitive damages to induce efficient firm-specific behaviour simultaneously creates long-run inefficiency by inducing the exit of efficient firms.

It is possible to extend this framework to consider joint and several liability with contribution actions. In that case the model requires some tools of game theory to account for the interactions among firms. A firm has to decide how likely it is to be sued directly, and if it is either launching or facing a contribution action it has to apportion amounts across other firms. At that point it again becomes difficult to ensure efficient levels of emissions unless the damage function is linear, or unless the court is able to impose rather complicated cost burden formulae. Some additional development is given in Miceli and Segerson (1991).

9.3 Contests over Damages*

In the previous section we ignored the fact that court trials involve uncertain outcomes. Scholars in the economics of law have modeled the court process using *contest success functions* (Skaperdas 1992).

Suppose that by hiring legal counsel at a unit cost w, the firm i can reduce the expected value of the damages by some factor $\rho_i(L_p, L_i)$, where L_p is the amount of legal services employed by the plaintiff and L_i is the amount of legal services hired by the defendant. A reduction in the expected value of the damages can come about in several ways. First, defence counsel may cast sufficient doubt on the plaintiff's evidence, or the defendant's own direct culpability, as to make it uncertain once the suit is underway that the plaintiff can pass the 'balance of probabilities' test. Second, the lawyer for the defendant may use procedural delays to postpone well into the future the date at which the actual damages must be paid, reducing their present value to the defendant. Third, the defendant's counsel may aggressively move against the plaintiff, through countersuits or threats of legal action, and intimidate the plaintiff into either withdrawing or settling out of court for a reduced amount. On the use of countersuits for intimidation see Hurley and Shogren, (1997), and see Cooter and Rubinfeld (1989) on out-of-court settlements. Finally, legal counsel can shelter the defendant's assets so that only a limited amount of money remains accessible to the court to make good on a damage award (Pitchford 1995). Sheltering strategies are limited by law, and can be risky for lawyers and clients if a court subsequently discovers assets that were not disclosed.

The success of these strategies can be summarized by the function $\rho_i(L_p, L_i)$. Its properties are:

(C.1) $0 \leq \rho_i \leq 1$; $L_p > 0, L_i > 0 \Rightarrow 0 < \rho_i < 1$ (i.e., ρ_i is bounded between 0 and 1, with the inequalities strict for positive amounts of plaintiff and defendant effort);

(C.2) $\rho_i(0, L_i) = 0$;

(C.3) $\rho_i(L_p, 0) = 1$ (i.e., failure to hire any legal counsel in the court ensures one's defeat);

(C.4) $\dfrac{\partial \rho_i(L_p, L_i)}{\partial L_i} < 0$; $\dfrac{\partial^2 \rho_i(L_p, L_i)}{\partial L_i^2} > 0$ (i.e., there are decreasing returns to the defendant's use of legal services. An analogous condition, not shown, would apply to the plaintiff).

The damages attributable to the defendant, if it is found liable, are

$$D(E) - D(E_{-i})$$

which we denote $\Delta_i D$. Hence its expected profits are

$$\pi_i - wL_i - \rho_i \Delta_i D. \tag{9.15}$$

This assumes the 'American Rule,' where each party to the lawsuit pays his or her own expenses. (The alternative is the British Rule, where the loser pays the legal fees for both parties). We will ignore the negligence rule, because as we saw above there is no way to construct a uniform due care requirement that achieves long-run efficiency in this kind of model (Polinsky 1980) and the regulator cannot be expected to have enough information to implement efficient firm-specific negligence rules. In the strict liability setting, we are interested in two issues. First, do the firms that operate generate the optimal emissions level, and, second, does the right number of firms continue to operate?

We can show that with uncertainty in the trial process, such that $\rho_i < 1$, there will be too many firms, each emitting too much. The firm (i.e., the defendant) optimizes over e_i and L_i, taking the legal expenditures of potential plaintiffs as given, yielding first-order conditions,

$$\pi_i'(e_i) - \rho_i D'(E) = 0 \tag{9.16}$$

and

$$-\frac{\partial \rho_i}{\partial L_i} = w / \Delta_i D, \tag{9.17}$$

where w is the unit cost of legal services. Since $w > 0$, any firm which generates positive emissions will have a positive demand for legal representation, and consequently the expected value of the plaintiff's proportionate recovery of damages will be less than unity. As w increases (counsel gets costlier) or $(D(E) - D(E_{-i}))$ decreases (the value of damages declines), the firm moves to a point on $\rho_i(L_p, L_i)$ with a steeper (negative) slope, which corresponds to a lower demand for legal services. This is shown in Figure 9.2

As long as $\rho_i < 1$, (9.16) implies that the firm will operate where marginal damages exceed marginal abatement costs. The social welfare function is still (9.1); because we do not count legal expenses as a benefit or cost, they are just transfers among agents in this framework. If (9.3) holds true then

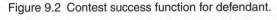

Figure 9.2 Contest success function for defendant.

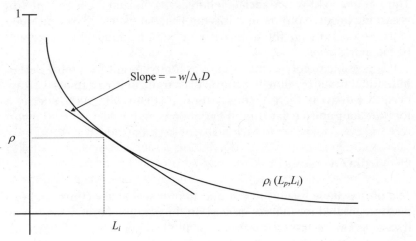

$$\pi_i(e_i^*) = \Delta_i D(E^*). \tag{9.18}$$

We want to know whether firm n^* is actually the marginal firm, or whether it is still earning positive profits, in which case further entry would occur. The profits of firm n are given by (9.15). If we substitute in (9.18) we can rearrange this expression to

$$\pi_n = (1 - \rho_n)\Delta_n D(E) - wL_n. \tag{9.19}$$

To evaluate the sign of (9.19) suppose that firm n is taken to court. It could avoid the lawsuit by offering to pay the maximum award the plaintiff could hope to achieve, which in this case is damages less the plaintiff's legal costs (wL_p). Hence, if the case goes ahead the maximum fraction the defendant expects to pay is

$$\rho_n < \frac{\Delta_n D - wL_p}{\Delta_n D},$$

which rearranges to

$$(1 - \rho_n)\Delta_n D - wL_p > 0. \tag{9.20}$$

If the defendant expects to use as much legal effort as the plaintiff (i.e.,

$L_n = L_p$) then (9.20) implies that the expression in (9.19) is positive. Thus, at the point where social welfare is maximized the marginal firm is earning positive profits, and this implies that there will be continued entry. So not only are the firms each emitting too much, but there will be too many firms.

It is possible to correct the incentives for over-emitting on the part of individual firms, by allowing courts to charge punitive damages. However, as we saw in the previous section, it is very difficult to specify a formula for punitive damages that both gets individual behaviour correct and does not result in excessive exit from the industry.

9.4 Victim Overexposure

The next issue is related to the question of whether victims ought to be compensated for injuries ex post. In the Sandmo optimal tax model (presented in the last chapter), and in all the other models of externalities we have examined, no payments are made to victims in compensation for the damages they experience. A charge is placed on the polluter, but the damages themselves are incurred without compensation. By contrast, the tort law system assumes that the damage fee paid by an injuring party will be paid to the victim. This can cause an inefficient outcome if the victim exploits the expectation of compensation and over-exposes himself or herself to damages. The problem arises only when the victim, prior to the injury, exercises some control over the size of the injury, in anticipation of some form of damage compensation being paid. It does not arise if the compensation can be set up as a 'lump sum' amount, but it is hard to do this in a sensible way.

To illustrate this problem, suppose a potential victim can build his house in one of two locations, x and y. x is very close to a smoky factory, while y is far away. Because of the environmental laws in that region, the victim has the right to full compensation for smoke damage incurred. We illustrate the choice to be made in the Figure 9.3. The marginal damages associated with the locations x and y are as drawn. The MAC function for the smoky factory is also shown. The unregulated emissions level is e_1. If the victim chooses location x, he can force the polluter to emit at e_x. Here, the polluter's liability is $g + h$, and the total abatement costs are $c + d + f$, for a total cost of $c + d + f + g + h$. The victim suffers damages $g + h$, but is paid compensation $g + h$, for a net cost of zero. If the victim chooses location y, he can force the polluter to emit at e_y. The polluter's liability is $h + d$ and abatement costs are c, for a total

Figure 9.3 Victim overexposure.

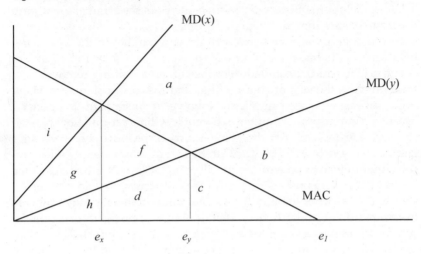

cost of $c + d + h$. The victim suffers damages $h + d$, but is paid $h + d$ in compensation and so is no worse off.

The problem is that the victim is indifferent between x and y, since he expects full compensation payments for any damages. But the firm, which has to make the payments, is not indifferent: it prefers the victim to locate at y, at which it incurs costs which are less by the amount $f + g$. The potential for the victim to inflict an inefficient outcome on the polluter may not be that worrisome however. In this case it would pay the polluter to offer the victim some amount z, where $0 < z < (f + g)$, to induce the victim to locate at y. Because the victim is indifferent between x and y, the payment z could be arbitrarily small, so the firm can secure the preferred outcome at a low cost in this case. And because we are assuming that direct bargaining is possible, it seems reasonable that such a solution would be sought by the parties.

Now consider which optimum the victim would prefer if no compensation payments were expected. From society's perspective, the total net benefit is the area under the MAC less the area under the MD. For location x this is area i. For location y this is area $i + f + g$. Social welfare is higher if the victim chooses location y. The loss in each situation to the victim would be the damages incurred in a Coasian equilibrium. For x these would be $g + h$, while for y they would be $h + d$. Which is worse? The first is, in effect, light damage up close, while the second is heavy damage far away. The victim would prefer y to x if $d < g$. To ensure y is chosen, the polluting firm could possibly arrange a side payment z to ensure that $(d - z) < g$.

To illustrate these results, we can draw a parallel to the late twentieth century 'liability crisis' in the United States. Over the twentieth century, U.S. courts extended doctrines of strict liability to cover new areas, such as the sale of commodities and the hiring of labour. Many such transactions now implicitly involve an insurance component, because one party or the other is potentially liable for a later damage claim. The trouble is that the proliferation of product and workplace liability has led to moral hazard problems, in which people who perceive themselves to be entitled to full compensation for damages take less precaution against mishap than they otherwise would. So, for instance, the threat of liability has forced many motel and hotel owners to remove diving boards from their swimming pools; transit fares in some U.S. cities now include liability insurance costs which account for as much as 17 per cent of the ticket cost; new ladders in the U.S. are up to 25 per cent more expensive due to the insurance premiums carried by the manufacturer, and so on (see Viscusi 1991 for these examples). Related to this problem is the observation that safety regulations occasionally induce such extreme reductions in precautionary behaviour as to more than offset the intent of the law. When child-proof caps were made mandatory on drug containers, hospitals subsequently reported *increases* in child poisoning rates, which was attributed to the careless storage of medicine containers induced by the fact that, since the drugs were in hard-to-open bottles, parents expected their children to be safe even if they took less care. When seatbelts were made mandatory in the 1970s, incidents of speeding, dangerous driving, life-threatening collisions, and pedestrians being struck all increased, which was again attributed to the fact that belted occupants took more risks in their driving, expecting the seatbelt to keep them safe in the event of collision (again, see Viscusi 1991 for these examples). Hence, the above model is not implausible in suggesting that victims may willingly increase their exposure to pollution hazards if they acquire an expectation that they will be compensated.

Review Questions

1. In the Coasian bargaining example, suppose the court is unable or

unwilling to assign rights between the farmer and the firm. Is it still possible that the optimal emission level might be reached?

2. Equation (9.15) assumes each party pays its own court costs. In the British (and Canadian) system, the court typically assigns costs to the losing party. Hence ρ_i not only denotes the fraction of damages the defendant expects to pay, but also the fraction of total legal costs the defendant expects to pay. Assume that each party chooses its legal services independently, so $\partial L_p / \partial L_i = 0$. Write down the form of (9.15) that would apply under the British rule and derive the first-order conditions. Show that the firm will tend to hire more legal services under the British rule. Will the expected emissions of each firm be higher or lower?

3. Suppose a developer can build a subdivision at the north end of his property or the south end. The north site is adjacent to an ethanol plant that generates foul odours that can be measured in units averaged over a year. Previous court cases have assessed the value of nuisance damages for adjacent properties at $800 per odour unit per year, which would be split among the homeowners in the subdivision. The ethanol firm's MAC is

$$MAC = 1500 - e$$

where e is the level of odour units averaged over a year. The south end of the property is costlier to build on and the road access is worse, adding one million dollars to the cost of building the subdivision. But from there the homeowners would only be able to smell the ethanol plant occasionally. They would still have reduced enjoyment of their property, incurring damages at a rate previous courts have assessed at $200 per odour unit per year. Suppose the developer offers to build at the south end in exchange for $1,250,000 from the ethanol plant. The developer would be better off, but would the ethanol plant be willing to pay this much?

4. Explain the difference between a negligence liability standard and a strict liability standard.

5. Explain what 'contributory negligence' is and why it led to rulings that have seemed unfair in retrospect.

6. Why does the comparative fault rule place a potentially onerous burden on plaintiffs when there are joint tortfeasors?

7. Explain why the apportionment rule gives firms the incentive to emit the efficient amount only if the damage function is linear and

passes through the origin. If the damage function is convex will firms tend to emit too much or too little?

8. If the court is empowered to assess punitive damages to establish an incentive that induces individual firms to emit the optimal level, what might happen to the number of firms in the industry?

9. Recently some environmental groups have tried suing fossil fuel producers for damages related to climate change, in particular things like hurricanes on the U.S. coast and sea-level changes. What kinds of hurdles would you expect such groups to face trying to certify a class-action lawsuit, and obtaining a damage award?

References and Extra Reading

Brown, John P. (1973). 'Towards an Economic Theory of Liability.' *Journal of Legal Studies* 2: 323–50.

Brubaker, Elizabeth (1995). *Property Rights in Defence of Nature.* Toronto: Earthscan.

Coase, Ronald H. (1960). 'The Problem of Social Cost.' *The Journal of Law and Economics* 3 (October) DOI: 10.1086/466560.

Cooter Robert D., and Daniel D. Rubinfeld (1989). 'Economic Analysis of Legal Disputes and Their Resolution.' *Journal of Economic Literature* 27 (September): 1067–97.

Cooter, Robert D. (1991). 'Economic Theories of Legal Liability.' *Journal of Economic Perspectives* 5(3): 11–30.

Cooter, Robert D., and Thomas Ulen (1988). *Law and Economics.* Glenview: Scott, Foresman and Company.

Dewees, Don (1992). 'The Role of Tort Law in Controlling Environmental Pollution.' *Canadian Public Policy–Analyse de Politiques* 18(4): 425–42.

Diamond, Peter (1974). 'Single Activity Accidents.' *Journal of Legal Studies* 3: 107–64.

Ewerhart, Christian, and Patrick W. Schmitz (1998). '*Ex Post* Liability vs. *Ex Ante* Safety Regulation: Substitutes or Complements? Comment.' *American Economic Review* 88(4): 1027.

Hurley, Terrance M., and Jason F. Shogren (1997). 'Environmental Conflicts and the SLAPP.' *Journal of Environmental Economics and Policy* 33(3): 253–74.

Kolstad, Charles, Thomas S. Ulen, and Gary V. Johnson. (1990). '*Ex Post* Liability vs. *Ex Ante* Safety Regulation: Substitutes or Complements?' *American Economic Review* 80(4): 888–901.

Kornhauser, Lewis, and Richard Revesz (1994). 'Multidefendant Settlements: The Impact of Joint and Several Liability.' *Journal of Legal Studies* 23: 41–76.

Landes, William, and Richard Posner (1980). 'Joint and Multiple Tortfeasors: An Economic Analysis,' *Journal of Legal Studies* 9: 517–56.

Meiners, R., and B. Yandle (1998). 'Common Law Environmentalism.' *Public Choice* 94: 49–66.

Menell, Peter (1991). 'The Limitations of Legal Institutions for Addressing Environmental Risks.' *Journal of Economic Perspectives* 5(3): 93–114.

Miceli, Thomas J. (1997). *Economics of the Law.* Oxford: Oxford University Press.

Miceli, Thomas, and Kathleen Segerson (1991).' Joint Liability in Torts: Marginal and Infra-Marginal Efficiency.' *International Review of Law and Economics* 11: 235–49.

North, Michael B. (1996). 'Recent Developments.' *Tulane Law Review* 70: 1165–79.

Ordover, Janusz (1978). 'Costly Litigation in the Model of Single Activity Accidents.' *Journal of Legal Studies* 7: 243–61.

Pitchford, Rohan (1995). 'How Liable Should a Lender Be? The Case of Judgement-Proof Firms and Environmental Risk.' *American Economic Review* 85: 1171–86.

P'ng, I.P.L. (1987). 'Litigation, Liability and Incentives for Care.' *Journal of Public Economics* 34: 61–85.

Polinsky, A. Mitchell, and Daniel L. Rubinfeld (1988). 'The Welfare Implications of Costly Litigation for the Level of Liability.' *Journal of Legal Studies* 17: 151–64.

Polinsky, A. Mitchell. (1980). 'Strict Liability vs. Negligence in a Market Setting.' *American Economic Review* 70(2): 363–7.

Priest, George. (1991). 'The Modern Expansion of Tort Liability: Its Sources, Its Effects and Its Reform.' *Journal of Economic Perspectives* 5(3): 31–50.

Shavell, Steven. (1984). 'A Model of the Optimal Use of Liability and Safety Regulation.' *Rand Journal of Economics* 15(1984): 271–80.

Shavell, Steven. (1987). *Economic Analysis of Accident Law.* Cambridge, Mass.: Harvard University Press.

Skaperdas, Stergios (1992). 'Cooperation, Conflict and Power in the Absence of Property Rights.' *American Economic Review* 82(4): 720–39.

Stigler, George (1966). *The Theory of Price*, 3rd ed. New York: Macmillan.

Tietenberg, Tom (1989). 'Indivisible and Toxic Torts: The Economics of Joint and Several Liability.' *Land Economics* 65(4): 305–19.

Usher, Dan (1998). 'The Coase Theorem Is Tautological, Incoherent or Wrong.' *Economics Letters* 61: 3–11.

Viscusi, V. Kip (1991). 'Product and Occupational Liability.' *Journal of Economic Perspectives* 5(3): 71–92.

10 International Trade and Pollution

10.1 Pollution Havens and Environmental Dumping

After numerous successful rounds of trade liberalization since the 1960s, international trade has risen steadily in recent decades. A new aspect to this pattern is the formation of free trade deals between developed and undeveloped countries, such as the entry of Mexico into the North American Free Trade Agreement (NAFTA). Also, developing countries are actively seeking foreign direct investment as a vehicle for domestic growth. This sometimes leads to the concern that companies engaged in pollution-intensive production will deliberately locate in poor countries to evade high pollution standards, then export goods to the developed countries (who retain stringent pollution standards) at a larger profit than would otherwise have been possible. This is called the 'pollution haven hypothesis' (PHH).

It is closely related to the concept of *environmental dumping*, which is the idea that companies emit excess pollution by locating in a country with lax pollution standards, thereby reducing their cost of production and gaining an unfair advantage in trading relations. This possibility was a major issue during debates over NAFTA. Such concerns have led to calls for *environmental tariffs*, which are punitive levies on imports from alleged pollution havens to compensate domestic producers for the competitive disadvantage of operating under higher pollution standards, and to punish nations for trying to lure industries by relaxing emission standards.

Do countries try to obtain trade advantages this way? For a long time economists have found that the empirical evidence fails to support a relationship between the stringency of a country's pollution policy and its trade flows or rate of foreign investment. However, these phenomena are hard to measure and more recent econometric evidence is divided on the question.

10.1.1 Trade Flows and Pollution

A series of studies over the 1980s and 1990s by economists at the World Bank (see the archive 'New Ideas in Pollution Regulation' at http://go.worldbank.org/T0CB1ZIDU0) looked at changes in the composition of traded goods over time, asking whether the share of 'dirty' production in a national economy was rising, and whether this change could be attributed to trade liberalization. Dirty production includes capital- and resource-intensive production like iron and steelmaking, industrial chemical manufacturing, petroleum refineries, petroleum and coal production, and so on. Lucas and colleagues (1992) surveyed evidence from 80 countries from 1960 to 1988 and found that dirty production as a share of GDP fell in developed countries and rose in undeveloped countries. They point out that this is consistent with the PHH. Low and Yeats (1992) looked at export composition over the interval 1965–1988, and found the share of dirty goods in exports from developed countries fell over that time, but rose among low-income countries. Other studies reaching similar conclusions are discussed in Copeland and Taylor (2004).

As Copeland and Taylor point out, although this evidence is *consistent* with the PHH, it is also consistent with predictions from models in which there are no pollution havens. A simple way to categorize the effects is as follows. Suppose there are two types of goods being produced: x, which is 'dirty' or pollution-intensive, and y which is 'clean.' The world price for each is denoted p_x^o, p_y^o respectively. The total value (or scale) of a country's output is

$$S = p_x^o x + p_y^o y. \tag{10.1}$$

Assume emissions e arise only from production of x, and emissions intensity is z, that is, $e = zx$. The (value) share of dirty production is $\phi_x = p_x^o x / S$. Hence, pollution can be written

$$e = Sz\phi_x / p_x^o. \tag{10.2}$$

Take the log of (10.2) and differentiate to get

$$\hat{e} = \hat{S} + \hat{z} + \hat{\phi}_x \qquad\qquad (10.3)$$

where $\hat{e} = de \,/\, e$ (the percentage change). We are assuming the price of x does not change. Equation (10.3) factorizes a change in emissions into three components:

1. $\hat{S}$ is the *scale effect*, the percentage growth in total output. If everything else stays constant we expect that this is positive. If real output grows while emissions intensity and the share of dirty goods in production stays the same, emissions will grow.
2. $\hat{z}$ is the *technique effect*, capturing the change in the emissions intensity of production. Again, if all else is constant, an increase in emissions intensity will increase emissions.
3   $\hat{\phi}_x$ is the *composition effect*, indicating the share of dirty goods in total production.

Whether increased trade flows cause total pollution to rise depends on how trade liberalization affects each of these three factors. In a simple MD-MAC model, if trade liberalization increases the rate of return to the emitting activity we expect the MAC curve to shift to the right, increasing pollution (whether unregulated or optimally regulated) through the scale effect. If trade liberalization also increases real incomes, say by reducing consumer prices and increasing the return to factors, we expect income to rise, increasing the demand for environmental quality and thereby shifting the MD curve to the left. This would, via an optimal policy mechanism, reduce z, the emissions intensity, causing the technique effect to work opposite to the scale effect.

The change in the composition effect will depend on the country's comparative advantage. In general we expect that wealthy countries have a comparative advantage in capital-intensive production and poor countries have a comparative advantage in labour-intensive production. Because the most pollution-intensive industries tend to be capital intensive, the composition effect will, ceteris paribus, cause an increase in pollution in developed countries following trade liberalization, and a decrease in pollution in poor countries.

Hence, there are three potentially offsetting effects. In their own empirical work, Copeland and Taylor (with Werner Antweiler, 2001) examined changes in urban SO_2 concentrations around the world and used macroeconomic data to estimate separate scale, technique, and composition effects. They find that the coefficients have the expected signs, including a positive effect on pollution as the capital-intensity of the economy increases. However, when expressed in elasticity form they add up to nearly zero:

$$\frac{\hat{e}}{\hat{S}} + \frac{\hat{e}}{\hat{z}} + \frac{\hat{e}}{\hat{\phi}_x} = 0.3 - 2.1 + 1.6 = -0.2.$$

Each term on the left shows the percentage change in pollution concentrations resulting from a percentage change in a right-hand side variable in (10.3). The authors also estimate the elasticity of SO_2 levels with respect to a change in trade intensity ((Exports + Imports)/GDP). According to the PHH, the elasticities should be higher in poor countries, but the data do not support this. There is little relationship between income and the pollution elasticity of trade openness, and what little relationship there is appears to be positive: trade liberalization tends to have a slight positive effect on pollution in developed countries (via the composition effect) and a slight negative effect in poor countries. This is consistent with a positive linkage between pollution and capital-intensive production.

This also suggests that the early studies focusing on the trends in pollution-intensive production may have missed the underlying dynamics. Because economic growth involves capital formation, the data may have merely shown that low-income countries were experiencing more rapid relative growth in their capital stocks than high-income countries. This could have happened even without any pollution haven mechanisms at work.

10.1.2 Foreign Direct Investment and Pollution

The question of whether or not industries migrate to avoid environmental regulation can only be resolved by looking at the data. Copeland and Taylor (2004) provide a review of some of the work done by World Bank economists, and others. While some examples exist of pollution-related industrial flight, statistical evidence of systematic migration in search of lower environmental standards has proven elusive, despite many attempts to identify such effects.

Wheeler (2000) looked at three large developing countries (China, Brazil, and Mexico) during intervals in which they experienced sharp increases in foreign direct investment. If these countries were using lax pollution standards to attract investment, there should be an accom-

Table 10.1 Changes in foreign investment and particulate pollution
in three developing countries (Wheeler 2001).

		Change (%)
Particulate Pollution	China	−32.3
	Brazil	−36.4
	Mexico City	−55.0
Foreign Direct Investment	China	+1011.1
	Brazil	+875.0
	Mexico City	+225.0

Note: The time spans are: China 1987–95, Brazil 1989–97, Mexico City 1985–97.

panying increase in air pollution. In all three countries, foreign direct
investment, measured in real U.S. dollars, grew by hundreds of per cent
(see Table 10.1). But particulate pollution fell. Across 50 Chinese cities,
average particulate levels fell by 32 per cent. Across the major cities
in Brazil's São Paolo state, particulate levels fell by 36 per cent, and
in Mexico City, the proportion of particulate readings above the legal
standard fell by 55 per cent.

Evidence has been found that high-income countries are specializing
in cleaner goods and low-income countries are specializing in relatively dirtier goods, but the stringency of environmental regulation does
not seem statistically linked with relocation of existing manufacturing
plants. Mani et al. (1996) looked at the factors which determined location decisions for 418 new industrial investments in fourteen states
throughout India in 1994. After taking account of differing labour costs,
power supply quality, population, literacy, and so on, they found that
variations in stringency of enforcement of environmental laws had no
effect on the probability of locating in that region. Interestingly, higher
government spending on environmental quality in a state has a positive effect on the location decision. The authors suggested that the environmental spending variable might be acting as a proxy for better
overall government administration in that area.

It is not implausible that environmental regulation may have little effect on plant location decisions, because other business factors typically outweigh pollution control expenses. Compliance costs under even
stringent environmental regulation are typically quite small (less than 3

per cent and often less than 1 per cent of revenues) so other cost factors (labour, energy, capital, taxes) will generally dominate a transnational firm's location decision.

The jury is still out on this issue, though. One problem is that trade policy and income growth are jointly causal, so a country's openness to trade cannot be assumed to be strictly exogenous. Studies that have controlled for endogeneity of trade and pollution policy have sometimes found significant (though still small) relationships between pollution policy and industry location decisions, but they don't appear to be very robust (e.g., Smarzynska and Wei 2001). A further survey and analysis is in Brunnermier and Levinson (2004).

10.2 Trade Liberalization and the Environment

10.2.1 Model Set-up*

In order to explore the theory of trade and the environment, we'll set up a simple model based on Copeland and Taylor (2004). There are two goods, x and y. As before, y is 'clean,' and is produced using labour L_y and capital K_y. x is 'dirty,' and is also produced using labour and capital (L_x, K_x). We can distinguish between *potential* and *actual* output using the standard iso-emissions, iso-profit diagram as follows in Figure 10.1.

In Figure 10.1 the potential output is x^*, which is the unregulated level of the dirty good. The locus of tangencies under progressively tighter emission constraints is the line wx^*. If the firm must constrain emissions to e then the actual output level will be x. Suppose we parameterize the relationship between actual and potential output using the equation:

$$x = e^\alpha (x^*)^{1-\alpha} = e^\alpha (F(K_x, L_x))^{1-\alpha} \tag{10.4}$$

where $0 < \alpha < 1$. If α is close to 0, then x stays close to x^* as e rises, which implies the locus of tangencies looks like the steeper of the two dashed lines in Figure 10.1. If α is close to 1, then as e falls x falls quickly in response. This implies a tangency locus like the lower dashed line.

Because (10.4) is a Cobb-Douglas function, if emissions level e is attained in response to an emissions tax τ (remember the output-abatement locus will be the same under a level standard or under a tax) then the share of emission tax revenues in total value-added from production of x will equal α. This implies:

Figure 10.1 Actual output and potential output of x.

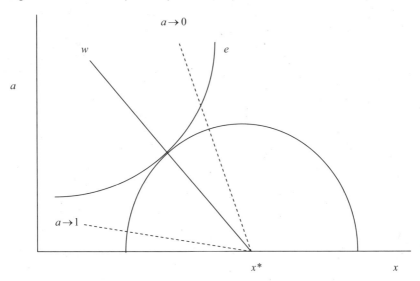

$$\alpha = \frac{\tau e}{p_x x} \Rightarrow z = \frac{p_x \alpha}{\tau} \tag{10.5}$$

where z is emissions intensity, that is, the ratio of emissions e to output x. Equation (10.5) shows that emissions intensity z falls as τ goes up and rises as the selling price of x goes up.

The remainder of the production side of the economy can be specified and yields the usual result that outputs are functions of relative prices and factor endowments:

$$x = x(p, \tau, K, L) \tag{10.6}$$

$$y = y(p, \tau, K, L).$$

In (10.6) we have set the price of y as the numeraire, so $p = p_x / p_y = p_x$. The total value of output in the economy is given by (10.1), which, in a competitive setting, corresponds to the outcome from maximizing the value of national income subject to a given level of emissions e. In other words the national income G is the level that maximizes the value of output subject to a technology constraint $T(K,L,e)$:

$$G(p,K,L,e) = \max_{(x,y)}\{px + y \mid (x,y) \in T(K,L,e)\}. \tag{10.7}$$

This is a common way of setting up national economic models for use in applied trade theory, and it represents the GDP-formation process as if it were the profit function of a single large firm. As such, (10.7) inherits all the properties of neoclassical profit functions, including, by Hotelling's rule,

$$\tau = \frac{\partial G}{\partial e}. \tag{10.8}$$

This is simply a restatement at the national level of the previously derived result that in response to an emissions tax, firms operate where τ = MAC, and the MAC is the derivative of the profit function with respect to emissions. Hence (10.8) is the 'demand curve' for emissions in this economy.

The consumer side of the economy is handled using an expenditure function $I = m(p,e,u)$, which shows the amount of income I required to achieve utility u at prices p in the presence of emissions e. It is convenient to invert the expenditure function to an indirect utility function:

$$I = m(p,e,u) \Leftrightarrow u = V(I,p,e).$$

We define marginal damages as the change in income required to maintain utility given a small increase in e, while holding p constant. This is written as $dV = V_I dI + V_e de = 0$, which gives us:

$$\frac{\partial I}{\partial e} = -\frac{V_e}{V_I} \tag{10.9}$$

The right-hand side is Roy's identity. Equation (10.9) defines an ordinary MD curve, which in this context is like a 'supply' curve for emissions.

Finding the equilibrium in this economy involves assuming a functional form for V and imposing an income constraint. We assume that there are N identical consumers and each one has an indirect utility function of the form

$$V(I,p,e) = v\left(\frac{I}{B(p)}\right) - h(e) \tag{10.10}$$

where v is an increasing function and B is a price index that deflates income. This imposes separability between emissions and goods consumption, which will make the remainder of the analysis easier. The income constraint is

$$I = G(p,K,L,e)/N. \tag{10.11}$$

If we maximize (10.10) while substituting (10.11) in for income, taking p as fixed (at world prices) we get $V_I G_e / N + V_e = 0$, which implies (using 10.8)

$$\tau = N\left(-\frac{V_e}{V_I}\right) = N \cdot MD. \tag{10.12}$$

In other words, the optimal emissions tax should be set equal to the sum of marginal damages. Because there are no other taxes in this economy this is the expected solution.

10.2.2 Welfare Analysis*

We are interested in the welfare effects of trade liberalization, so we need to distinguish between total domestic supply of x, denoted X^s and per capita domestic demand, denoted x^d. Using (10.7) we know that total production is $X^s = G_p$, implying that per capita domestic production is

$$x^s = G_p / N. \tag{10.13}$$

Domestic demand can be derived applying Roy's identity to (10.10):

$$x^d = -\frac{V_p}{V_I}.$$

It will be convenient to use the fact that $V_I = V'/B$, or $B = V'/V_I$. Because $V_p = V' \cdot (-IB'/B^2)$ this implies

$$x^d = \frac{IB'}{B}. \tag{10.14}$$

Now suppose trade opens up, and as a result the relative price of x

changes. The welfare effect can be derived by differentiating V:

$$du = V' \left[\frac{BdI - IB'dp}{B^2} \right] + V_e de.$$

Divide both sides by V_I, the marginal utility of income. Since $I = G/N$ we have the following:

$$\frac{du}{V_I} = \frac{V'}{V_I} \left[\frac{1}{B} \frac{G_p}{N} dp + \frac{1}{B} \frac{G_e}{N} de - \frac{1}{B^2} IB'dp \right] + \frac{V_e}{V_I} de.$$

Using $B = V'/V_I$ this rearranges to

$$\frac{du}{V_I} = \left(\frac{G_p}{N} - \frac{IB'}{B} \right) dp + \left(\frac{G_e}{N} + \frac{V_e}{V_I} \right) de,$$

and using (10.12–14) this gives us

$$\frac{du}{V_I} = (x^s - x^d) dp + \frac{1}{N} (\tau - N \cdot MD) de. \tag{10.15}$$

The left-hand side shows the utility change as a fraction of the marginal utility of money, which can be interpreted as a shadow price. The welfare effect decomposes into two parts. The first defines the classical gains from trade. If a country is a net importer then $x^s < x^d$ so the term in the brackets is negative. Trade liberalization will reduce the import cost ($dp < 0$), so the product is positive. If the country is a net exporter, the term in the brackets is positive and trade liberalization will increase the world price, so again the welfare effect is positive.

The second term represents the effect from the emissions change. If an optimal policy is in place, that is, (10.12), then the term in the brackets is zero and trade liberalization must improve welfare. If the emissions tax policy is not optimal, then the effect on welfare is ambiguous. If trade liberalization causes emissions to rise, but emissions are undertaxed, the combination is negative and offsets the gains from trade.

Note that in (10.15), if emissions are controlled by tradable permits, $de = 0$, and in this case the gains from trade would not be diminished even if there are too many permits sold, so the price is less than marginal damages. This is an interesting asymmetry between permits and taxes.

Equation (10.15) shows that if optimal environmental policy is in place, trade liberalization is welfare-improving. If environmental policy is not optimal, trade liberalization may reduce welfare. But in that case the solution is not to avoid trade liberalization, it is to improve environmental policy, so that the gains from trade may also be realized.

10.2.3 Environmental Effects of Trade Liberalization: Pollution Haven Hypothesis versus Factor Endowment Hypothesis

The model outlined in the previous section describes an economy with two goods, a dirty one (x) and a clean one (y). Each country will have supply functions of the form (10.6), implying the existence of *relative* supply functions:

$$R(p,\tau,K,L) = \frac{x(p,\tau,K,L)}{y(p,\tau,K,L)}.$$
(10.16)

Of course we are just dividing x by y. The reason for doing so is that it allows for a more compressed presentation of the trading relationship. We will use (R^N, R^S) to denote, respectively, relative supply curves for the *North* (i.e., the rich, capital-intensive economy) and the *South* (i.e., the poor, labour-intensive economy).

For each country there will also be a relative demand curve, denoted D, which for convenience we will assume is the same in each country.

Prior to trade, the North has a comparative advantage in production of x, so its relative supply curve sits below and to the right of that of the South. This implies a lower autarky relative price in the North p^N (see Figure 10.2). Each country produces the relative supply indicated by the intersection between demand D and their respective relative supply curve, so the North produces more and the domestic price is lower. When trade opens up between the economies, the price difference between the North and the South creates an impetus for trade, which flows until the price is equalized between regions. This occurs at p^W where the world supply curve intersects the world demand curve, along the world relative supply curve. The world supply curve is determined by assuming the North and South face the same ·price.

For the North, trade increases the selling price of x/y from p^N to p^W, allowing production to increase to where p^W intersects the North's relative supply curve R^N. This implies that the North now exports the

Figure 10.2 Opening trade between North and South.

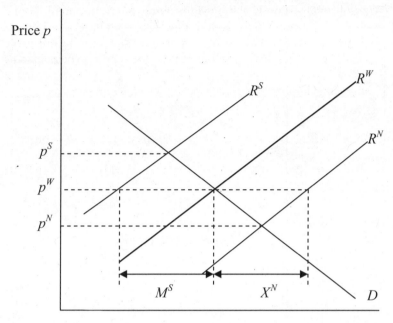

Relative Supply (x/y)

fraction X^N. Relative supply in the South falls to where R^S intersects the world demand curve, implying the South now imports the fraction M^S.

Because the relative supply of x has grown in the North and declined in the South, Figure 10.2 implies that trade will cause pollution to grow in the North and decline in the South as a result of trade liberalization. However, this runs opposite to the PHH, which conjectures that trade liberalization will cause pollution to increase in the South. With two opposite prediction from rival theories, it should be possible to use data to test which is more likely to be true. What we need is to identify how pollution changes in response to openness to trade, and see if it tends to go in different directions in rich-versus-poor countries, and if so where it tends to go up following trade liberalization. If the factor endowment hypothesis, as shown in Figure 10.2, is correct, then pollution should go up in rich countries and down in poor countries following trade liberalization.

Figure 10.3 Elasticity of emissions with respect to trade liberalization, versus relative income, from Copeland and Taylor (2004).

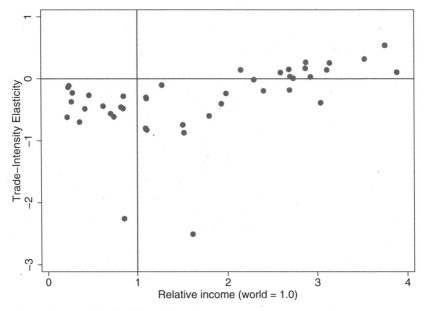

Source: Data provided by Werner Antweiler.

There is some support in the data for this. Figure 10.3 reproduces Figure 9 from Copeland and Taylor (2004). On the vertical axis is shown the elasticity

$$\frac{\%\Delta(SO_2)}{\%\Delta(trade)},$$

the percentage change in average urban SO_2 concentrations given a 1 per cent increase in openness to trade (as measured by (exports + imports)/GDP). As you move into relatively higher-income countries, the elasticity goes from negative to positive. In wealthy countries, trade liberalization is associated with increased SO_2 levels, and vice versa for relatively poor countries. This is an area where more empirical work is needed, looking at other air contaminants, and looking at emissions as well as concentrations.

Review Questions

1. Explain why the formation of free trade agreements between wealthy and poor countries has been a point of concern for those advocating stricter environmental regulation.
2. What is the pollution haven hypothesis? If it is correct, what patterns would we expect to observe in international trade data?
3. The derivation of equation (10.15) assumed that emissions only cause a domestic externality. Suppose pollution travels across borders, so that domestic welfare is

$$V(I,p,e) = v\left(\frac{I}{B(p)}\right) - h(e + e')$$

where e' is emissions from the rest of the world. Discuss how the definition of the optimal tax might change, and what sorts of complications might arise when we try to determine if trade liberalization will lead to welfare gains.
4. Using equation (10.5) explain why, in the presence of an emissions tax, emissions intensity rises as the relative price of the dirty good goes up.
5. Some European leaders have proposed adding special tariffs on imports from countries that do not impose strict controls on carbon dioxide emissions. Discuss whether this might or might not be justified from an economic point of view.

References and Extra Reading

Antweiler, Werner, Brian R. Copeland, and M. Scott Taylor (2001). 'Is Free Trade Good for the Environment?' *American Economic Review* 91(4): 877–908.

Brunnermier, Smita B., and Arik Levinson (2004). 'Examining the Evidence on Environmental Regulations and Industry Location.' *Journal of Environment & Development* 13(1): 6–41.

Cole, Matthew A., and Robert J.R. Elliott (2003). 'Determining the Trade-Environment Composition Effect: The Role of Capital, Labor and Environmental Regulations.' *Journal of Environmental Economics and Management* 46(3): 363–83.

Copeland, Brian, and M. Scott Taylor (2004). 'Trade, Growth and the Environment.' *Journal of Economic Literature* 42(1): 7–71.

Low, Patrick, and Alexander Yeats (1992). 'Do 'Dirty' Industries Migrate?' In *International Trade and the Environment* (Patrick Low, ed.), pp. 89–104. Washington. DC: World Bank.

Lucas, Robert E.B., David Wheeler, and Hemamala Hettige (1992). 'Economic Development, Environmental Regulation, and the International Migration of Toxic Industrial Pollution 1960–1988.' World Bank Policy Research Working Paper Series #1062, December.

Mani, M., S. Pargal, and D. Wheeler (1996). 'Does Environmental Regulation Matter? Determinants of the Location of New Manufacturing Plants in India in 1994.' World Bank Discussion Paper, November.

Smarzynska, Beta and Shang-Jin Wei (2001). 'Pollution Havens and Foreign Direct Investment: Dirty Secret or Popular Myth?' National Bureau of Economic Research Working Paper No. 8465, September.

Wheeler, David (2000). 'Racing to the Bottom? Foreign Investment and Air Quality in Developing Countries.' World Bank Development Research Group Discussion Paper, November.

11 Sustainability and Optimal Growth

11.1 Introduction

Terms like 'sustainable' and 'sustainability' are popular but imprecise buzzwords. The economic treatment of sustainability begins by defining the term in the context of a dynamic economic model, then derives the conditions that indicate whether an economy is on a sustainable path. We are also interested in determining whether consumption can be sustained when output depends on non-renewable resources.

Roughly speaking, sustainability means that future utility, which depends on produced goods as well as environmental services, is not diminished by current consumption. Because the total consumption stream is generated by a return on a total social capital stock, encompassing physical, human, and natural capital, the theory of sustainable consumption is an application of capital theory. The definition and measurement of sustainability has been addressed many times in the economics literature (see, e.g., Solow 1991, Hartwick 1978). The empirical side of this literature concerns the development of national statistics that can indicate whether the economy is on a sustainable path. Hartwick (2000), Hamilton (2001), and Cairns (2001) are some further contributions on this theme.

This chapter will first review the basic definitions of environmental sustainability, yielding a relationship between currently observable data and the discounted stream of potential future consumption. A method will then be described for constructing national measures to track sustainability. Some comments will be made on proposals for so-called genuine progress indicators,' whose lack of theoretical foundation makes their interpretation problematic. Then we will look at the question of whether optimal growth paths are sustainable, and vice versa.

For intuition regarding the definition of sustainability, suppose a financial bond costing $1,000 earns 5 per cent annually. As owner of the bond you could consume $50 each year forever without depleting your capital. If the value of the bond is W and the rate of return is r then maximum sustainable consumption (MSC) each year is rW. But by saving a bit today, one can invest in additional principal and thereby increase potential consumption in every subsequent year. Denote current consumption as C, investment as $\dot{W}$, current income as Y, and the interest rate as r. Then the budget constraint each period is

$$Y = rW = C + \dot{W}. \tag{11.1}$$

We are interested in measuring the total potential consumption path from this moment forwards. The discounted present value of future consumption is defined as:

$$U = \int_{t=0}^{\infty} C(s)e^{-rs}ds. \tag{11.2}$$

For now we can ignore the distinction between real and nominal consumption by assuming the price of C is fixed at 1. For an economy in which utility depends only on current consumption, (11.2) provides a definition of wealth. Later on we will introduce a utility function, but the intuition won't change.

In a steady state, if our wealth has been built up to an optimal level W^*, we could consume rW^* each period forever. Because we are no longer investing, rW^* will therefore equal the steady-state consumption C^*. It is easy to prove that the discounted stream of utility is equivalent to wealth when we are in the steady state, by using the formula for a perpetuity: $C^* = rW^*$, so $W^* = C^*/r^*$. Or, we can do the integration in (11.2):

$$\int_{t=0}^{\infty} C^* e^{-rs}ds = C^* \left(\frac{-1}{r}\right)\left(e^{-rs}\Big|_0^{\infty}\right)$$

$$= \frac{C^*}{r}$$

$$= W^*.$$

In other words, in the steady state, the budget constraint $rW^* = C^*$ reminds us that real wealth is the discounted value of future consumption possibilities. 'Wealth' that does not provide for current or future consumption is not, in the end, wealth.

It may not be the case, however, that the optimal consumption path leads us to accumulate some constant, positive amount of wealth W^* and then cease saving at that point. A consumption path chosen strictly on the grounds of economic optimization might lead to zero wealth (and consumption) at some point in the future. Thus, choosing an optimal consumption/savings path is not necessarily the same as choosing a sustainable, or constant-consumption path, as we will see later.

11.2 Net National Product

What we want to do now is examine whether currently observable data is informative about real wealth, even outside the steady state. If so, then it tells us something about a potentially permanent consumption stream that current wealth could provide.

The term *Net National Product* (NNP) denotes Gross National Product (GNP) minus depreciation expenses and 'set-asides.' We will denote all forms of productive capital as K. If the rate of depreciation is δ, net investment is gross investment I minus depreciation δK, and this gives us the actual change in the capital stock at time t:

$$\dot{K}(t) = I(t) - \delta K(t). \tag{11.3}$$

Real income is the amount of consumption which the capital stock K can generate without being depleted. This is called 'Hicksian' income, after Sir John Hicks, the twentieth-century economist who helped lay the foundation for national income accounting. If the marginal product of capital is determined in a competitive market, it will equal the interest rate r. Then sustainable, or Hicksian, national income is rK. Income can either be consumed or devoted to net investment, so the national budget constraint is:

$$rK(t) = C(t) + \dot{K}(t). \tag{11.4}$$

As before, we can start from equation (11.4) and show that at some initial time 0, the capital stock equals the discounted present value of future consumption. In the previous section we saw that this was true when we were in an optimal steady state, but it turns out to be true whenever net national product is measured using the Hicksian definition of national income (11.4), and is fully allocated between consumption and investment.

The following derivation is from Wilcoxen (1989). Rearrange (11.4) and multiply both sides by e^{-rt} to get

$$(\dot{K}(t) - rK(t))e^{-rt} = -C(t)e^{-rt}. \tag{11.5}$$

Note that

$$\frac{d}{dt}K(t)e^{-rt} = e^{-rt}\dot{K}(t) - rK(t)e^{-rt} = (\dot{K}(t) - rK(t))e^{-rt}$$

and hence (11.5) can be re-written:

$$\frac{d}{dt}K(t)e^{-rt} = -C(t)e^{-rt}. \tag{11.6}$$

Now integrate both sides from time $t = 0$ to infinity:

$$\int_{t=0}^{\infty} \frac{d}{ds}K(s)e^{-rs}ds = -\int_{t=0}^{\infty} C(s)e^{-rs}ds$$

$$K(\infty)e^{-r\infty} - K(0)e^{-r0} = -\int_{t=0}^{\infty} C(s)e^{-rs}ds.$$

Thus,

$$K(0) = \int_{t=0}^{\infty} C(s)e^{-rs}ds. \tag{11.7}$$

At time zero, the value of a nation's capital stock equals the discounted present value of the stream of consumption it will generate. This result depends on (11.4), in which we defined national income in Hicksian terms, and (11.3), in which we defined net investment. It is evident that defining sustainability requires an economic model. The maximum sustainable income is Hicksian income, and real wealth is the total productive capital stock, which must also equal the real value of future consumption. Capital that does not generate future consumption has no real value.

By defining wealth using (11.2) we have treated consumption and welfare each period as if they were the same thing. It is preferable to work with utility functions rather than consumption directly, so we will re-derive some results in terms of optimal intertemporal utility maximization, rather than consumption maximization. We have also ignored the role of prices, but by introducing a utility function we are able to introduce a relative price for consumption and a shadow value of capital in a convenient way.

We will assume that the optimal planning problem is solved at time 0. We will also leave unspecified the production possibility frontier between consumption and investment, but assume that it is a convex set and the shadow price of capital is variable over time. Define the intertemporal social objective function

$$V(0) = \int_{t=0}^{\infty} e^{-rt} U(C(s)) ds. \tag{11.8}$$

The intertemporal utility maximization problem at the start of time 0 is:

$$\max_{\{C(t)\}} \int_{t=0}^{\infty} e^{-rt} U(C(s)) ds \tag{11.9}$$

subject to $\dot{K}(t) = I(t) - \delta K(t)$

$(C(t), \dot{K}(t))$ feasible each period;

given $K(0)$.

The Hamiltonian equation for this problem is

$$H(t) = U(C(t)) + \lambda \dot{K}(t) \tag{11.10}$$

where λ is the shadow value of capital. This represents the marginal utility of one more unit of capital. At time $t = 0$, the marginal value of capital in equation (11.8) is $V_K(0)$. More generally, the shadow price of capital at time t is $V_K(t)$. Also, equation (11.3) plus the national accounting identity $(Y = C + I)$ implies $\dot{K}(t) = Y(t) - C(t)$. So we can re-write (11.10) as

$$H(t) = U(C(t)) + V_K(t)(Y(t) - C(t) - \delta K(t)).$$

Along the optimal path for (11.9), current consumption is optimally traded off against future consumption, implying $H_C = 0$, which gives us

$$U_C(t) = V_K(t). \tag{11.11}$$

Finally, the Hamilton-Jacobi equation in dynamic optimization tells us that, along the optimal path,

$$rV = \max_{\{C\}}[U(C) + V_K \dot{K}]$$

where the time arguments have been dropped for convenience. When the optimal consumption level is substituted into the Hamilton-Jacobi equation, and we use (11.8) and the result in (11.11), we get

$$r \int_{t=0}^{\infty} e^{-rt} U(C^*(s)) ds = rV^* = U(C^*(t)) + U_C(t)\dot{K}(t). \tag{11.12}$$

The term on the right-hand side is the utility value of the optimal current consumption level plus current investment valued using the marginal utility of an extra unit of consumption. The left-hand side is r times the discounted value of all future consumption, which corresponds to the middle term.

How do we interpret (11.12)? Note that (11.8) defines the economy's 'true' wealth: in effect, the real wealth of a nation is its capacity to generate utility into the perpetual future. The left-hand side of (11.12) is the rate of return on true national wealth, which corresponds to the meaning of 'Hicksian' income: the amount of consumption that leaves capital intact, where capital is valued with welfare-relevant weights. The right-hand side of (11.12) is the utility value of consumption plus net investment. In other words this is the utility value of NNP. As a side-note, if the utility function is linear ($U = C$) and the consumption good is the numeraire (so the price of investment goods p equals U_C), equation (11.12) corresponds to equations (10) and (11) in Weitzman (1976).

The curious thing about equation (11.12) is that it suggests that current data (namely net national product) can reveal an economy's *permanently sustainable consumption level*. This works because the terms on the right-hand side of (11.12) are current observations (dated at time t) whereas the term on the left includes the discounted present value of all *future* consumption as long as we follow the optimal path. Having established the equality of these terms, we can use the right-hand side to compute the left-hand side.

There are many assumptions being made to support this result, and some authors have criticized it as very unrealistic. For instance, the relative cost of capital and consumption would change if we actually tried to exploit the above result by consuming all our Hicksian income, so the result is inherently overstated. Also the terms in the derivation above might relate to the theoretical concept of NNP, but actual NNP data from national statistical agencies involve a set of approximations and assumptions that depart from the theory (see Usher 1994).

But at least (11.12) gets us started at thinking about how to measure and test for sustainability. It is important, however, to keep some related concepts separate.

- Cairns (2002) has pointed out that Hicksian income is not the same as sustainable income; rather, it is a 'stationary equivalent' to sustainable income. It tells us the constant amount we could consume forever, given our current social capital stock. But many different income paths are 'sustainable' in the sense that they yield non-decreasing future consumption possibilities, and the optimal consumption path may not be a permanently sustainable one.
- Early researchers on this topic were interested in the problem of non-renewable resources: could an economy generate constant consumption in the future even while depleting a non-renewable resource stock? Back in 1974 Robert Solow proved that it could, as long as certain conditions were met regarding the elasticity of substitution in production. John Hartwick later showed (1977) that an economy satisfying the Solow conditions could remain on a constant consumption path by investing all non-renewable resource rents in renewable capital. This is called the 'Hartwick rule.' Optimal paths do not necessarily obey the Hartwick rule. Others have since shown that the optimal consumption path yields a constant consumption path under the Hartwick rule only if the social planner is maximizing a Rawlsian social welfare function. Otherwise the Hartwick rule is not a necessary condition for the optimal consumption path defined by (11.12). We will look at this issue in Section 11.5.

11.3 Measuring Sustainability

Both equations (11.7) and (11.12) can, in principle, supply a method for measuring 'sustainability.' If we add to (11.12) a measure of the change in the value of non-marketed capital (e.g., resources and environmental quality) then a non-decreasing NNP implies a non-decreasing stream of future consumption possibilities. Using (11.7) we can also examine the 'net savings' in a year, and argue that as long as the total value of the capital stock is increasing, future consumption possibilities are not being diminished.

If we overestimate current investment, our published NNP or total savings statistics will overstate sustainable future consumption and vice versa. On one hand, many people worry that we are using up natural and environmental resources without properly accounting for them, which means that we are overstating investment (by understating depreciation). On the other hand, some people point out that we generally understate investments in human capital, because we do not account for current and future productivity gains arising from education and training.

A great deal of attention has been paid to finding ways of including resource and environmental stocks in the national accounts. The aim is to get NNP closer to the right-hand side of equation (11.12). Weitzman and Lofgren (1997) examined a simple economy with a growing stock of productive labour and a capital stock that includes resources and the environment. They calculate (very roughly of course) that the ratio of sustainable consumption to current NNP is about 1.4; that is, our NNP statistics, on net, understate the true sustainable consumption level by about 40 per cent.

11.3.1 Green Net National Product and Net Savings

To develop an empirical method for measuring net savings we must differentiate among capital types, and use discrete time approximations.

Call financial wealth (measured in dollars) W. Denote physical capital (including land and marketed resources) as K, its price as p_K, and its value as $V(K) = p_K K$. This measure is included the national accounts of most advanced economies. Denote non-marketed resources (including environmental quality) as N, and their value as $V(N) = p_N N$. Although some economies have measures of resource and environmental stocks, these are typically not included in national accounts. Denote human capital as H, and its value as $V(H) = p_H H$. Human capital is difficult to define and quantify. A conventional measure among labour economists is average schooling. However, there is too much heterogeneity in quality and relevance of schooling and it is confounded with local capital availability and other regional variables, so it is thought to be a poor measure. Mulligan and Sala-i-Martin (1995) proposed instead a labour income-based human capital (LIHK) measure that controls for heterogeneity of schooling, experience, health, capital availability, and so on. The measure turns out to be easy to compute: it is the average (across all locations) of the local ratio of total labour income per capita divided by the labour income of a person with zero years of schooling. This latter item is not observed directly but can be computed using something called a Mincer regression. This involves identifying the labour market return to years of schooling then extrapolating back to zero years.

Each type of capital generates a unique net rate of return r_i ('net' implies an adjustment is made for capital depreciation). We can invest in each type of capital, and thereby increase the level available for the future.

Assume that the price of consumption is the numeraire, so the national Hicksian budget constraint can be written:

$$r_W W + r_K V(K) + r_N V(N) + r_H V(H) = C + \Delta W + \Delta V(K) + \Delta V(N) + \Delta V(H)$$
$$= MSC. \tag{11.13}$$

MSC denotes maximum sustainable consumption. The first terms are the rates of return on the different capital stocks. The terms to the right of the first equal sign represent the disposition of income between consumption and net investment. The equality with MSC reminds us that we could perpetually consume our entire net returns to existing capital if we wanted to.

As stated above, if we want to measure 'sustainability' there are two options. The 'green net national product' approach uses the middle form of the above equation. Ordinary net national product is defined as consumption plus net investment:

$$NNP = C + \Delta W + \Delta V(K). \tag{11.14}$$

If we add in the value of the change in non-marketed capital $\Delta V(K)$

and human capital $\Delta V(H)$ we get 'green NNP,' which reveals our true maximum sustainable consumption:

$$GNNP = C + \Delta W + \Delta V(K) + \Delta V(N) + \Delta V(H). \qquad (11.15)$$

Three important points are:

- If in one year there is no change in $V(N)$ (either because $\Delta N = 0$ or the change in p_N exactly offsets the change in N), then $GNNP$ reduces to ordinary NNP with an adjustment for human capital change.
- N only includes those forms of 'natural' capital that generate returns in the form of consumption (or utility) for people.
- The expressions above use stock *values*, not *quantities*.

Using the $GNNP$ criterion we would conclude that the economy is on a sustainable path as long as $GNNP$ is not declining. That is, as long as augmented NNP is not diminishing over time we are not reducing the maximum sustainable consumption level. In practice it would make sense to measure $GNNP$ in per-capita terms to ensure average MSC is not declining.

Another way of measuring sustainability uses equation (11.7), the equality between the value of the capital stock today and the value of the future consumption stream it can generate, discounted by the rate of return. Maintaining future consumption possibilities is what we mean when discuss 'sustainability,' so a suitable indicator of sustainable growth would be positive net savings:

$$\Delta W + \Delta V(K) + \Delta V(N) + \Delta V(H) \geq 0. \qquad (11.16)$$

If this condition holds true then the future consumption stream is not diminished by current consumption. This ought to be evaluated in per-capita terms. Recent criticism of the green NNP approach suggests the net savings measure is preferable. In practice people who work on environmental accounting have focused on this measure (e.g., Hamilton 2001).

When changes in pollution and resource stocks are evaluated along-side changes in the value of the human capital stock, human capital tends to dominate the accounts. The human capital stock is a large quantity, the rate of return to which yields observed income and earnings for all workers in the economy. Because wages and salaries make up about two-thirds of annual national income, if the rate of return to human capital is 5 per cent, that means the human capital stock is about $(0.67/0.05 =)$ 13 times the size of gross national income. Small fluctuations in annual earnings will lead to large changes in the value of the human capital stock.

By contrast, amenity values associated with pollution and natural endowments will appear very small. This is partly because the underlying quantities do not change a lot from one year to the next. The total acreage designated as protected wilderness, for instance, or the number of species subject to protection against the risk of extinction, does not vary much each year. Even if high marginal values are assigned to such changes, the resulting changes in the value of environmental and natural capital will be small compared to changes in human capital.

11.4 Hartwick's Rule on Sustainable Consumption Paths*

An economic growth path is said to be 'optimal' if it corresponds to the solution of a maximization problem, as in equation (11.9). However, the path resulting from an optimization is not necessarily sustainable. The consumption path might go to zero at some time in the future, for instance. This is especially likely to be the case in an economy with an essential but non-renewable resource and a positive discount rate. From the perspective of time $t = 0$, if the future is discounted at a positive rate and production depends on the non-renewable resource, it is easy to derive cases in which the optimal path involves full depletion of the resource and a zero consumption level thereafter. As has been noted extensively in the natural resource economics literature, in order to avoid the zero-consumption outcome, technology must be sufficiently substitutable with the resource, the contribution of technology to production must grow fast enough, and the discount rate must be low enough. Once all these features are built into a growth model, however, it gets very difficult to solve.

A different approach to the problem was Hartwick's (1977) demonstration that investment of resource rents into renewable capital could yield an outcome in which per capita consumption does not decline. 'The Hartwick Rule,' as it came to be called, thus defines a sustainable path, but it is not an optimal path. It applies to the case in which the resource is optimally depleted, but the savings/consumption decision is not determined by the solution to (11.9).

The argument works as follows. Suppose there is a production function

$$y = f(K, R, L) \tag{11.17}$$

where y is the output, K is capital, R is a non-renewable resource and L is labour. For simplicity we assume $L = 1$, so all the analysis is in per-capita terms. Capital and the resource are both essential: if either is zero then so is output. The resource is taken from a non-renewable stock S, that is, $-R = \dot{S}$. The fixed extraction cost is a per unit, so the rents per unit from the flow of extraction are defined as

$$q \equiv (f_R - a).$$

The optimal extraction path follows Hotelling's Rule. The mine manager has, in effect, two assets: the resource in the ground and capital. The rate of return to capital is f_K. The rate of return to leaving the resource in the ground is $\dot{q} / q$. If the asset portfolio is optimally managed, both rates of return should be equal:

$$\dot{q} / q = f_K, \tag{11.18}$$

which implies

$$f_{RR}\dot{R} + f_{RK}\dot{K} = f_K q. \tag{11.19}$$

Note $\dot{L} = 0$ in the above. Also, (11.17) implies

$$\dot{y} = f_K \dot{K} + f_R \dot{R}. \tag{11.20}$$

If f is a Cobb-Douglas function

$$y = K^\alpha R^\beta L^\gamma$$

where $\alpha + \beta = 1$, then the following results are true:

$$f_K = \alpha y / K; \quad f_R = \beta y / R;$$

$$f_{RR} = \beta y (\beta - 1) / R^2 = f_R (\beta - 1) / R;$$

and $f_{RK} = \alpha \beta y / (RK) = f_K \beta / R.$

Using these, (11.19) becomes

$$\frac{\beta}{R} f_R \dot{R} - \frac{1}{R} f_R \dot{R} + \frac{\beta}{R} f_K \dot{K} = f_K q.$$

Rearrange this a bit to obtain

$$\beta(f_R \dot{R} + f_K \dot{K}) = f_R \dot{R} + R f_K q. \qquad (11.21)$$

Now suppose we apply the rule that investment in K just equals the resource rents:

$$\dot{K} = qR. \qquad (11.22)$$

Combining (11.21) and (11.22) yields

$$\beta(f_R \dot{R} + f_K \dot{K}) = f_R \dot{R} + f_K \dot{K}$$

which implies, using (11.20)

$$\beta \dot{y} = \dot{y}. \qquad (11.23)$$

But because $0 < \beta < 1$, (11.23) can only be true if

$$\dot{y} = 0.$$

Hence the economy is sustainable, in the sense that output is non-declining. Also, since consumption is a fixed fraction of output in this economy, consumption is likewise non-declining.

Equation (11.22) is known as 'Hartwick's Rule.' Hartwick's 1977 paper shows that as long as it holds, consumption is constant ($\dot{c} = 0$) even without assuming a Cobb-Douglas economy (although the assumption that capital does not depreciate is still necessary).

The optimization problem in equation (11.9) does not yield a solution path that corresponds with the constant-consumption path we derived by applying Hartwick's rule. Instead it yields a consumption path that typically rises for a while, peaks once, then falls to zero. If the discount rate is high enough, the consumption path simply falls continuously to zero. These outcomes obviously impoverish the generations born after the resource is gone, but they are 'optimal' from the perspective of time zero, since positive discounting means that the welfare of the far-future generations has a vanishingly small weight in the current decision calculus.

Optimality and sustainability can potentially be reconciled if there is technological growth, but the resulting models are very difficult to solve. Pezzey and Withagen (1998) presented a tractable, closed-form consumption path in a model with capital and resources which revealed a basic conflict between the optimal path and a sustainable path. In the steady state, if consumption is not decreasing the capital/resource ratio must be growing at a sufficient rate. If the capital/resource ratio is constant, consumption must be decreasing. The higher the discount rate, the faster the capital/resource ratio must be growing to maintain constant consumption.

Review Questions

1. What is the economic definition of sustainability? How does this compare to popular uses of the term?
2. Explain how the solution to the optimization problem (11.9) would compare to Hartwick's rule, in that $\dot{C} = 0$ forever, if (a) the utility function is of the form $U = \min\{C(0), C(1), \ldots, C(\infty)\}$, or (b) $r = 0$.
3. If we augment the national accounts with measures of natural capital and human capital, does this always imply that depletion of resource and environmental stocks will cause a reduction in 'green net national product'?
4. Why is it important to measure sustainability using the *values* of the various capital stocks, rather than simply the quantities?
5. What is the intuition behind the idea that currently available data (net national product) tells us something about the permanently sustainable consumption level? What are the main limitations of this interpretation?
6. Suppose we use an augmented definition of capital, so that we include both environmental and physical capital stocks. What does equation (11.11) imply will happen to the marginal value of environmental quality as consumption goes up over time?

References and Extra Reading

Cairns, Robert D. (2002). 'Green National Income and Expenditure.' *Canadian Journal of Economics* 35(1): 1–15.

Hamilton, Kirk (2001). 'Indicators of Sustainable Development.' World Bank mimeo, February.

Harwick, John M. (1977). 'Intergenerational Equity and the Investing of Rents from Exhaustible Resources.' *American Economic Review* 67(5): 972–4.

Hartwick, John (1978). 'Substitutability among Exhaustible Resources and Intergenerational Equity.' *Review of Economic Studies* 45(2): 347–53.

Hartwick, John (1993). 'National Wealth and NNP,' Queen's Economics Department Discussion Paper, May.

Hartwick, John (2000). *National Accounting and Capital.* Cheltenham: Edward Elgar.

Mulligan, Casey, and Xavier Sala-I-Martin (1995). 'A Labor-Income-Based Measure of the Value of Human Capital: An Application to the States of the United States.' National Bureau of Economic Research Working Paper No. 5018.

National Round Table on the Environment and the Economy (2001). 'A Proposed Framework for the Development of Environment and Sustainable Development Indicators Based on Capital.' Ottawa: Author mimeo, January.

Pezzey, John C.V., and Cees A. Withagen (1998). 'The Rise, Fall and Sustainability of Capital Resource Economics.' *Scandinavian Journal of Economics* 100(2): 513–27.

Solow, Robert (1991). 'Sustainability: An Economist's Perspective.' In *Economics of the Environment,* 3rd ed., Robert Dorfman and Nancy S. Dorfman, eds., 179–87. New York: Norton.

Usher, Dan (1994). 'Income and the Hamiltonian.' *Review of Income and Wealth* 40(2): 123–41.

Weitzman, Martin (1976). 'On the Welfare Significance of National Product in a Dynamic Economy.' *Quarterly Journal of Economics* 90: 156–62.

Weitzman, Martin, and Karl-Gustaf Löfgren (1997). 'On the Welfare Significance of Green Accounting as Taught by Parable.' *Journal of Environmental Economics and Management* 32(2): 139–53.

Wilcoxen, Peter J. 'Intertemporal Optimization in General Equilibrium: A Practical Introduction.' (1989). Impact Research Centre, University of Melbourne, Working Paper No. IP-45, December.

12 Policy Debates, Practice Exam, and Supplementary Questions

12.1 Policy Debates

Now it is time to put your skills at economic analysis to work. In this chapter I will describe some current environmental policy topics and invite you to think about how you would analyse it using the concepts and tools developed in this book.

12.1.1 Banning Incandescent Light Bulbs

Many western countries have enacted, or will soon enact, bans on incandescent light bulbs. They are urging households to switch to compact fluorescent lightbulbs (CFLs) instead. Similarly, some jurisdictions (California and the United Kingdom) have discussed banning plasma screen televisions, and a prominent British global warming expert named Sir Nicholas Stern was quoted on the front page of the *Times* of London on 23 October 2009 saying that mankind should give up eating meat in order to benefit the environment. All these policies have in common the desire to regulate specific aspects of consumer behaviour for the purpose of environmental protection. In Section 6.1 we discussed the principle of targeting: that regulations and taxes should be focused directly on the externality, not on related activities. We have seen this principle appear in a number of places, including in the general equilibrium model of Chapter 8.

If the principle of targeting is correct, then it cannot be a good idea to ban certain kinds of lightbulbs, televisions, or food. What the regulator is really interested in is emissions. Can you construct an argument showing that banning certain kinds of lightbulbs is an inefficient way of reducing emissions?

Here is one way to set it up. Suppose that there are N identical households. Suppose there are M goods denoted $x_1, ..., x_M$. The service s_j generated by good x_j arises from the quantity of x itself along with the electricity used to power it, denoted v_j. If a good needs no electricity then $v_j = 0$ and $s_j = x_j$, otherwise the relevant service is $s_j(x_j, v_j)$. Utility is

$$u(s_1, ..., s_M, Z)$$

where Z is the externality associated with emissions from electricity generation, defined as

$$Z = z(\Sigma v_j, A)$$

where A is the total abatement effort. The budget constraint is

$$\Sigma(p_j x_j + q v_j) + A = Y$$

where Y is income, q is the price of electricity and abatement is the numeraire. The first-order conditions are derived by maximizing utility subject to the budget constraint, that is, choose (x_j, v_j, A) to maximize $u(s_1, ..., s_M, Z)$ s.t. $\Sigma(p_j x_j + q v_j) + A = Y$. Now consider whether the first-order conditions imply $x_i = 0$ for a group of goods i. If not, consider what will happen to welfare if a regulation forces $x_i = 0$ while Z remains unchanged.

12.1.2 The Yucca Mountain Nuclear Waste Repository

For at least 30 years the U.S. government has been considering opening a nuclear waste repository at Yucca Mountain in Nevada. The idea is that a very deep vault in a geologically stable region would be the best place to put the nation's spent fuel rods from nuclear reactors. However, despite extensive construction work and research at the site, the facility has never opened. Currently nuclear waste is stored at reactors around the country. Developing the Yucca Mountain site would be very expensive, and there would be some hazards associated with transporting all the waste to it, rather than leaving it in reactors where it originates.

Look up some information on the Yucca Mountain project, and try to decide whether you think it is a good idea or not. How should the decision be made? What tools of cost-benefit analysis might be useful? Are there policy instruments, such as liability law or externality pricing, that could guide people to an efficient outcome in terms of development and use of such a facility?

12.1.3 Sewage Treatment in Coastal Cities

Some coastal cities, such as Victoria British Columbia, do not treat their sewage but instead pump it a long way out into the ocean and release it from a pipe on the sea bed. The argument in favour of doing so is that it is inexpensive and the sewage breaks down quickly in the ocean, long before currents can carry it to any other community. The argument against is that it may harm some marine ecosystems, there are occasional complaints from other communities that allege the sewage impinged on their shoreline anyway, and it is bad public relations for the City of Victoria. How should municipalities decide how much to spend on sewage treatment? If higher orders of government are worried that municipalities are not spending enough on sewage treatment, what kinds of remedies would be appropriate?

12.1.4 Greenhouse Gas Emissions and Development

As nations debate how to respond to the threat of global warming, some wealthy countries (especially in Europe) are keen to enact strict controls on greenhouse gas emissions, while less-developed countries are reluctant to do so. Countries like China and India have argued that the threat arises from the stock of emissions that built up during the twentieth century largely due to U.S. and European fossil fuel use, so developing countries should not have to bear the cost of reducing global greenhouse gas emissions. But many politicians in wealthy countries like the U.S. have warned that if they enact policies to restrict greenhouse gas emissions, and neither China nor India follow suit, their industries will simply migrate to the unregulated regions and emissions will not fall. Should the burden of greenhouse gas emissions reduction take into account historical emission rates? How might this be treated in an economic model of optimal emission controls when the externality is global rather than local? Also, if nations disagree about the position of the MD curve, are they thereby justified in choosing different internal abatement targets?

12.2 Practice Exam Questions

Points are given in brackets, indicating approximate number of minutes the question should take to answer.

Part A (70 points)

ANSWER EVERY QUESTION

1. **[10]** Suppose there are two firms with MACs given by
   $$MAC_1 = 200 - e_1 \text{ and } MAC_2 = 300 - 2e_2.$$

   The regulator tells each firm to reduce emissions to 70 units each. At the same time firms are told that if they go over 70 units they must pay a charge of $60 for each extra unit of emissions. Describe the resulting level of emissions of each firm and the total amount paid in emission fees.

   Now suppose the regulator gives each firm 100 permits, and instead of the charge for extra emissions, allows the firms to trade permits. What will each firm emit, and will the total level of emissions go up or down compared to the previous outcome?

2. **[10]** Suppose a regulator wants a firm to reduce its emissions by 20 per cent. The firm's emissions are a function of output and abatement. Explain (with a proof) whether the output-abatement combination selected by the firm would be the same if the regulator uses a tax on emissions rather than an emissions cap.

3. **[10]** Answer the following questions True or False.

   Other things being equal, in cases where the marginal damages are relatively flat it is likely better to use price instruments rather than quantity instruments.

   According to capital-theoretic models of sustainability, the value of wealth is determined by the utility stream it is expected to provide in the future.

A major challenge in reducing urban air pollution levels is that new cars today release, on average, about 2½ times as much particulate pollution per mile driven as did new cars in 1970.

By investing the rents from extracting non-renewable resources into reproducible capital, we can guarantee society will stay on an optimal consumption path, although not necessarily a sustainable one.

Although tradable permits and emission taxes both yield a cost-effective allocation of emission reductions, emission taxes are costlier to the economy because of tax interaction effects.

The factor endowment hypothesis predicts that trade liberalization will cause poor countries to become more pollution-intensive.

A regulator can eliminate the potential price distortion in a pollution permits market where a competitive fringe is dominated by a single large firm by not giving any permits to the dominant player.

If an emissions policy yields an outcome that is cost-effective it is, by necessity, also optimal.

In his study on the 'Race-to-the-Bottom,' David Wheeler found that Third World cities were attracting capital investment but air pollution was getting worse at the same time.

Firms are more likely to exaggerate their potential abatement costs if the proposed policy is an emissions standard, rather than a tax.

4. **[10]** The following diagram shows the iso-profit and iso-emission lines for a firm which has to pay for its own abatement a. The regulator is proposing to require all firms to reduce emissions to e_1 If the firm faces such a regulation its optimal output level will be y_1 as shown.

Figure 12.1 Output-abatement combination.

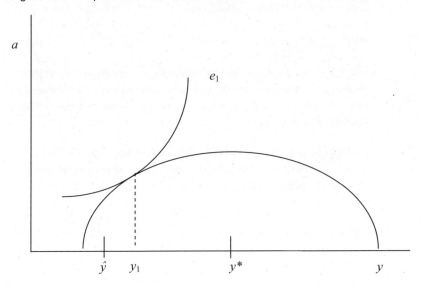

Suppose the firm makes the following argument to the regulator. 'From time to time, business grows and declines, and sometimes our output is much smaller. But the emission standard stays the same, which doesn't seem fair. Let's pick a level of output, say, $\hat{y}$ and make it a cut-off point, so that if our output falls to $\hat{y}$ or less, no emission standard is applied. Because our output is usually higher than $\hat{y}$, this will guarantee that our emissions are regulated most of the time.'

What effect, if any, will there be on the outcome if the regulator accepts this argument and establishes the cut-off $\hat{y}$ as shown, such that a firm whose output is equal to or less than that does not face an emission standard? Explain what will happen (if anything) to emissions, output, abatement effort, and profits.

5. **[10]** Copeland and Taylor derive the following expression to summarize the welfare change for a country moving from protection to free trade:

$$\frac{dV}{V} = -M\Delta p^d + (\tau - MD)dz$$

where V denotes national welfare, M denotes imports of the polluting good X, Δp^d denotes the change in the domestic relative price of X as a result of moving to open trade, τ denotes the domestic emissions charge on pollution emissions z, denotes the associated marginal damages and dz denotes the change in emissions.

Explain how this equation clarifies the debate over whether trade liberalization can actually make a country worse off by increasing pollution.

6. **[10]** Suppose a firm i can reduce the fraction of a damages award $D(E)$, where $E = \Sigma_i e_i$, it expects to pay by investing in legal representation L_i. Its success is measured using a contest success function $\rho(L_i, L_p)$ as defined in the course notes, where p denotes the plaintiff. Suppose also that the firm is one of multiple tortfeasors and the court applies an apportionment rule. Is a linear damage function sufficient to ensure that each firm's emissions are at the optimal level?

7. **[10]** The term 'Pigovian tax' refers to a tax on output in a situation where the production of a good generates a pollution externality. The idea is that if an externality exists, too much of the good will be produced. By putting a tax on the good, the regulator can force production down to the optimal level. Even though this is the standard presentation of the concept in most introductory textbooks, it would be unlikely to yield an efficient outcome. Using the iso-profits/iso-emissions diagram explain the circumstance in which a Pigovian tax would be efficient, and why in general it would not be the appropriate instrument to apply.

Part B (40 points)

ANSWER 1 OF THE FOLLOWING 2 QUESTIONS

B1 Suppose there is an externality that only occurs for two periods:

this year and next year. The damages this year, D_1, are caused by this year's emissions e_1, according to the damage function

$$D_1(e_1) = \beta e_1^2$$

where β is a known constant. The damages next year, D_2, are caused by next year's emissions e_2, as well as half of this year's emissions, which remain in the air. In other words the damage function for next year is

$$D_2(e_1, e_2) = \alpha(\tfrac{1}{2}e_1 + e_2)^2.$$

From the perspective of the first year, α is unknown. It could either have a high value (α^H) with probability q or a low value (α^L) with a probability $(1 - q)$. At the start of Period 2, the true value of α will be revealed.

The benefits of emissions each year are denoted $\pi(e_i)$, that is, the profits function is the same each period.

Work out a model that will allow you to characterize the answers to the following questions. I am mainly interested in whether you can model the problem so that a solution would clearly emerge, even if you do not derive the complete solution itself.

(i)   From the perspective of the start of Period 1, what is the optimal level of emissions in each period?
(ii) From the perspective of the start of Period 1, what is the optimal expected emissions tax for each period?
(iii) Assuming that the regulator adjusts the optimal tax at the start of Period 2 to take into account the revelation of the true value of α, would there be any value to the industry if it could find out the true value of α at the start of Period 1, rather than waiting until the start of Period 2?
(iv) How does the optimal emissions tax applied in Period 1 depend on q?

B2 Suppose there are two sectors. One produces output $f(L)$ using only labour (L) and sells it at price p. Its profits are given by $\pi_1 = pf(L) - w(1 + t)L$ where w is the wage rate and t is the tax rate on labour income. Another sector does not employ labour but generates emissions e during its production, which cause damages $D(e)$. Its profits are denoted $\pi_2(e) - \tau e$ where τ is the emissions charge. Government revenue $G = twL + \tau e$ is given to the household as a lump sum. The social welfare function is

$$W = \pi(e) - D(e) + pf(L) - wL.$$

(a) Why isn't G in the welfare function?

(b) Derive the optimal emissions tax and explain why we expect it to be less than the level at which marginal abatement costs equal marginal damages.

Part C (30 Points)

Suppose a government is considering making a commitment to reduce CO_2 emissions over the next 10 years. Explain, using specific models, how economic analysis can help answer THREE (**3**) of these questions. You must choose one from each pair: (a) or (b); (c) or (d); (e) or (f).

a) Whether the policy should involve controls on emission quantities or emission prices; or
b) How the presence of a dominant firm might distort a permits market.
c) How use of subsidies for emission reduction activity would differ in effects from emission charges; or
d) How using different forms of emission standards might change the costs of achieving a target.
e) Why the use of cap-and-trade rather than auctioned permits or an emissions tax increases the social cost of reaching the target; or
f) In what way the optimal level of an emissions tax is affected by the overall distortionary burden of the rest of the tax system.

12.3 Further Study Questions

1. Discuss two situations in which a regulator needs to pay attention to the incentives of firms to reveal private information, and explain the way the expected form of the policy can affect the willingness of firms to be truthful.

2. Suppose there are m firms. Firm 1 is a dominant player and the others are price-takers. Each firm is given Q_i^o permits and $\Sigma_{i=1}^m Q_i^o = L$. The market price for permits is denoted P. Each firm has a profit function $\pi^i(e_i)$ where e_i is emissions, and firms must hold one permit for each unit emitted. For price-taking firms note that permit demand is $Q_i = Q_i(P)$. The dominant firm chooses a market price for permits to maximize its profits.

   Prove that the higher the initial endowment of permits to Firm 1, the higher will be the equilibrium permit price.

3. The Sandmo model of optimal taxation in the presence of externalities yields the approximate solution

$$\theta_m = (1 - \mu)\left[-\frac{1}{\varepsilon_m}\right] + \mu\left[-n\frac{u_{m+1}}{u_m}\right].$$

   Explain the meaning of the parameter μ. If the deadweight loss of the overall tax system goes up, does that mean the environmental portion of the tax should rise or fall?

4. In a model of strict liability with apportionment, in which damages D are charged to multiple polluters in proportion to their share in total emissions (e_i / E), explain why we expect the resulting emissions level to equal the optimal emissions level if the total damages function $D(E)$ is linear.

5. Explain how trade liberalization can affect domestic pollution emissions through *scale, technique,* and *composition* effects.

6. Explain using a relative supply function model why trade liberalization could cause some types of pollution to increase in developed countries ('the North') and decrease in low-income countries ('the South').

   Now suppose the South imposes an import tariff on capital-intensive goods. Would we expect industry-generated pollution to rise or fall in the South? Explain.

7. Net national product is defined as current income minus capital depreciation. Explain how, in a simple dynamic economy, this reveals the maximum permanently sustainable consumption level.

8. What is the definition of 'wealth' in an economy with both consumption and savings?

9. In an economy with consumption and savings, provide a set of conditions in which the *optimal* consumption path would involve *constant consumption* over time.

10. In cost-benefit analysis, what are the three axes over which ben-

efits and costs are distributed and need to be collapsed to a single point? Explain each one carefully and discuss the techniques and uncertainties involved in the calculations.

11. Suppose that the ambient pollution level Z is a function of emissions, that is, $Z = Z(\Sigma_i e_i(y_i, a_i))$ where y denotes output and a denotes abatement. Suppose also that the emissions of individual firms cannot be observed. Would a charge t per unit of the ambient pollution concentration, that is, tZ, if assessed on each polluter, yield the same outcome as a tax per unit of emissions? Explain why or why not.

Index

A.H. Robins Co. *See* Dalkon Shield
Air pollution, historical, 10, 12–13,
    24–30
Antweiler, Werner, 216, 226
Arrow, Kenneth, 61, 71, 74
Audits, compliance, 144–50
Australia, 134, 153

Backstop price, 156–8, 165–6
Balanced budget requirement, 105,
    108
Banking permits, 157, 165–6
Barnett, Harold, 7
Baumol, William, 126, 183
Brazil, 14, 217–18
Brundtland Commission, 5–6

Cantor Fitzgerald, Inc., 155
Cap and trade, 153, 252. *See also* trad-
    able permits
Carbon dioxide emissions, 17–19,
    131, 135, 164, 177–9, 227
China, 14, 217–18, 246
Club of Rome, 6
Coase, Ronald; Coase theorem, 194–
    7, 209, 210–11
Command-and-control, 31, 97, 139

Common law; 34–6, 193*ff*
Competitive fringe model, 160–2
Composition effect, 215–17, 254
Conservation movement, 8–10
Contest success functions, 204–8, 250
Contingent valuation (CV), 60–3
Copeland, Brian, 215–19, 226, 249
Cost-effectiveness, 95, 97, 100, 153,
    161, 248
Cost-efficiency, 95
Credible commitment, 147–9
Cropper, Maureen, 126

Dalkon Shield, 204
Deadweight loss, 163, 171–2, 186,
    188, 254
Delicts, 35, 193
DES (Diethylstilbestrol), 199
Dingell, John, 164
Discounting, 40, 63–8, 74–7, 165, 166,
    229–35, 238–9, 241, 242
Double dividend, 172–4, 187
Dynamic efficiency, 110–12

Economic instruments, 97, 101,
    112–13, 156
Economic profits, 53–4

Ehrlich, Anne and Paul, 6–7 .
Enforcement, 142–50
Engels, Friedrich, 10
Environment Canada, 35
Environmental dumping, 214
Environmental Kuznets Curve, 37,
   39, 41–2, 44
Environmental Protection Agency
   (EPA), 35, 155–8, 168
Equimarginal principle, 95, 99, 117,
   153–4, 161, 169
European Union, 134, 153, 167,
   277
Externalities, 49–51, 135, 172, 179,
   188–9, 193–6, 254
Exxon Valdez, 61

First theorem of welfare economics,
   55

G.D. Searle Co., 204
Global warming, 17–24
Goulder, Lawrence, 178
Green Net National Product
   (GNNP), 236–9
Greenhouse gases, 18–23, 65, 153

Hahn, Robert, 160
Hartwick, John; Hartwick Rule, 229,
   235, 239–42
Hedonic valuation, 60
Helfand, Gloria, 136, 139
Hybrid instrument, 158–9

India, 218, 246
Inequality, 37, 56, 68–71, 74–6
Inspection and maintenance pro-
   grams, 133
Iso-emissions line, 80–5, 88, 90, 136–
   7, 150, 219–20, 250

Iso-profits line, 81–5, 88, 93–5, 219–
   20, 250

Jevons, Stanley, 10
Joint tortfeasors, 197–200, 211, 250

Kyoto Protocol, 35, 163

Liability law, 34, 97, 193*ff*, 246, 254

Malik, Arun, 144, 150
Marginal abatement cost function,
   derivation, 85–8
Marginal cost of public funds. *See*
   Deadweight loss
Marginal damages, derivation, 56–9
Marginal excess burden. *See* Dead-
   weight loss
Marginal external cost, 112–13
Market power, 99, 153, 160–2
Markey, Edward, 153
Mexico, 204, 217–18
Microwave Sounding Units, 21–4
Morse, Chandler, 7
Motor vehicles, and US emissions
   standards, 26, 28, 133

Negligence. *See* Liability law
Net National Product (NNP), 231–5.
   See also Green Net National
   Product
North American Free Trade Agree-
   ment (NAFTA), 214

Oates, Wallace, 104, 126, 183
Ohio, 141–2, 144
Ontario, 30, 32, 141
Ozone layer, 14–17

Pareto optimum, 55–6, 68, 70, 180–1

Parry, Ian, 174, 177
Pigovian tax, 34, 112–14, 119, 169, 250
Policy costs, 178–9
Polinski, A. Mitchell, 203, 206
Pollution haven hypothesis, 214, 217, 224, 227
Principle of targeting, 133–6, 182–3, 244

Quotas (non-auctioned permits), 164, 177–8

Ramsay, Frank, 68
Rents, resource, 235, 239–41; scarcity, 53, 163–4, 169, 177–8, 189
Revenue recycling, 172–9
Risk aversion, 71–7

Sandmo, Agnar; Sandmo model, 179–89, 208, 254
Scale effect, 215–17, 254
Segerson, Kathleen, 106, 108, 198, 204
Shavell, Steven, 200
Shogren, Jason, 205
Sierra Club, 3
Solow, Robert, 61, 229, 235
Standards, intensity, 87–8, 136–9, 150, 215–17, 220, 226, 227
Standards, level, 31, 87–8, 136–8, 150, 219
Standards, ratio, 31, 87, 136, 139–40
Stern, Sir Nicholas, 66, 68, 244
Strict liability. See Liability law
Subsidies, 99, 124–5, 182, 189–90, 252
Symmetry of price and quantity instruments, 126–7, 154, 169, 177, 223

Tariffs, 214, 227
Tax interaction effects, 172–9, 182–3, 248
Taylor, M. Scott, 215–19, 226, 249
Technique effect, 215–17, 254
Tertullian, 11–12
Tort law. See Liability law
Tradable permits, 34, 35, 97, 99–101, 116, 126, 132, 140, 153ff, 169, 177–8, 191, 197, 223, 248
Truth-telling incentives, 121–5, 141ff

Uncertainty, 68, 71–4, 108, 126–32, 143, 169, 206
UN Framework Convention on Climate Change, 91
United States: Acid Rain Allowances, 155–8, 162–3, 167; Clean Air Act Amendments of 1990, 91, 155; Clean Air Interstate Rule, 158; Environmental Protection Agency (EPA), 35, 155–8, 168

Victoria, British Columbia, 246

Waxman, Henry, 153
Weitzman, Martin, 126, 234, 236
Wheeler, David, 217–18, 248
Williams, Roberton, 177–8
World Bank, 28, 29, 30, 47, 215, 228
Worldwatch Institute, 4

Yucca Mountain, 245–6